Schöningh

TEACHERS' BOOK

Discover ...

TOPICS FOR ADVANCED LEARNERS

edited by Engelbert Thaler

The American Dream

Inventing a Nation

by Hannspeter Bauer

Sprachliche Betreuung: Elin Arbin

www.schoeningh-schulbuch.de
Schöningh Verlag, Jühenplatz 1–3, 33098 Paderborn

Druck 5 4 3 2 1 / Jahr 2015 14 13 12 11
Die letzte Zahl bezeichnet das Jahr dieses Druckes.

Umschlaggestaltung: Franz-Josef Domke, Hannover
Umschlagabbildung: © vario images/Tetra Images
Druck und Bindung: westermann druck GmbH, Braunschweig

ISBN 978-3-14-040087-9

Inhaltsverzeichnis

Die didaktische Konzeption

Die Themenheftreihe *Discover* ... richtet sich an Schülerinnen und Schüler der Sekundarstufe II und bereitet in Anlehnung an die Einheitlichen Prüfungsanforderungen in der Abiturprüfung (EPA) und die Rahmenrichtlinien der einzelnen Bundesländer interkulturell relevante, Jugendliche interessierende Themen methodisch-didaktisch auf.

Der Einstieg in das Thema, das in mehrere Kapitel untergliedert ist, erfolgt über eine Doppelseite „Getting started" mit Bildmaterial und einigen Einstiegsaufgaben. Die Texte weisen unterschiedliche Längen auf, sind aber insgesamt nicht zu lang und berücksichtigen verschiedene Textsorten. Reichlich Bildmaterial (Fotos, Zeichnungen, Cartoons, Grafiken, Tabellen, Karten etc.) ist funktional in die Texte und Aufgabenapparate integriert.

Der Aufbau der einzelnen Texte ermöglicht einen klar strukturierten Unterricht mit drei Phasen: *pre, while* und *post reading*. *Pre-reading*-Aufgaben führen zum Text hin, rufen das Vorwissen ab und bauen Erwartungshaltungen auf. Der eigentliche Leseprozess wird im Sinne eines *guided reading* durch gelegentliche Lesebeobachtungsaufgaben und (sparsame) Annotationen in den Fußnoten unterstützt. Im abschließenden Aufgabenapparat unter dem Titel „Activities" werden alle Fragen zu thematisch zusammengehörigen Blöcken mit einer kurzen inhaltlichen Überschrift in der Randspalte zusammengefasst. Diese Aufgaben lassen sich den drei maßgeblichen Bereichen zuordnen:

a) Inhalt (*comprehension*)
b) Struktur, Intention, Stil, Sprache (*analysis*)
c) Evaluation, eigene Meinungsäußerung, sprachproduktive kreative Aufgaben (*evaluation and creation*).

Wir wünschen Ihnen einen motivierenden und effektiven Unterricht.

Prof. Dr. Engelbert Thaler, Herausgeber

Discover ... The American Dream

Aufbau des Schülerheftes

Thema des Heftes ist der amerikanische Traum. Der Untertitel *„Inventing a Nation"* weist dabei auf eine erweiterte Perspektive. Der *„Dream"* soll als die philosophische, staatsbildende Konstante der Entwicklung der amerikanischen Nation gesehen werden. Das deutsche Verständnis von „Nation" ist nicht identisch mit dem amerikanischen. Während wir Deutschen uns im 19. Jahrhundert als Kulturnation „von der Etsch bis an die Memel" definierten, was dabei zunächst keine Gleichsetzung von Nation und Staat beinhaltete, ist im amerikanischen Verständnis die Nation immer auch zugleich der Staat im Sinne der Staatsphilosophen der Aufklärung. Die Selbstverständlichkeit, mit welcher ein bunt zusammengewürfelter Haufen von Männern unterschiedlichster nationaler Provenienz 1776 mit einem Federstrich eine Nation gründen, die nur ein Jahrhundert später zu den Weltmächten aufsteigen wird, lässt sich nur aus dem festen Glauben an die Möglichkeiten, diesen Traum konkret umzusetzen, verstehen. Der amerikanische Traum wird im Laufe der Jahrhunderte immer wieder neu erfunden, angepasst auf neue veränderte Situationen, erweitert um Elemente, die zunächst nur impliziert waren (*„all men are created equal"*). Die Faszination, die bis heute jährlich Tausende Menschen anspornt, die amerikanische Staatsbürgerschaft zu erwerben, steckt in dieser robusten Modernität des amerikanischen Traumes von der Nation.

Der Aufbau des Buches legt vier, sich z. T. überlappende, diachrone Schnitte durch die amerikanische Geschichte, welche insgesamt gesehen nur unterschiedliche Aspekte derselben Sache darstellen.

„Foundations of a Dream" beschäftigt sich mit einigen grundlegenden Texten aus der amerikanischen Geschichte, ohne deren Kenntnis für die Lernenden in Deutschland viele Reden bzw. ähnliche historische Quellen kaum zu verstehen sind. Martin Luther King, aber auch Barack Obama z. B., beziehen sich in vielen ihrer Reden und Interviews auf Inhalte und Aussagen der hier vorgelegten Texte. Die rhetorische Vernetzung wird nur auf der Basis der, bei Amerikanern vorauszusetzenden, Textkenntnis für die Lernenden erkennbar. *„Frontiers of a Dream"* analysiert die materiellen Voraussetzungen für die Entwicklung der amerikanischen Nation. Mit dem Abschluss der Erschließung des Kontinents am Ende des 19. Jahrhunderts, entwickelt sich das jetzt explizit so benannte Konzept des *„American Dream"*. Das dritte Kapitel *„In the Wake of a Dream"* legt den Fokus der Betrachtung auf die Entwicklung der Einwanderung und die sich verändernden Sichtweisen im Verständnis der Nation als *„E pluribus unum."* Das letzte Kapitel, *„A Dream Deferred"*, spiegelt die Konflikte bei der Konkretisierung der hohen ethischen Werte der Unabhängigkeitserklärung im Laufe der Jahrhunderte.

Das Heft hat einen klaren historischen Bezugsrahmen, will aber kein Geschichtsbuch sein. Wo allerdings historische Quellen analysiert werden, geschieht das unter Gesichtspunkten, welche auch im bilingualen Sachfachunterricht zugrunde liegen. Die Aufgabenstellungen orientieren sich an Konzepten des *task based learning* und bemühen sich, ein hohes Maß an Schülerorientierung in die Bearbeitung der Texte einzubringen. Dabei werden durchgehend die einheitlichen Anforderungsbereiche des gymnasialen Englischunterrichts berücksichtigt, sodass auch ein permanentes Üben der im Abitur relevanten Arbeits- und Analysetechniken möglich wird. Die zahlreichen Redetexte des vorliegenden Bandes ließen es zudem sinnvoll erscheinen, einen Ausbildungsschwerpunkt auf die Redeanalyse zu legen. Hierzu wurde dem Band ein Glossar der wichtigsten rhetorischen Mittel beigegeben.

Tabellarische Textübersicht

Foundations of a Dream

Autor, Text	Inhaltliche Schwerpunkte	Textsorte/ Medium	Wortzahl
The Declaration of Independence	– Erklärung der staatlichen Unabhängigkeit der 13 amerikanischen Kolonien – grundlegende Definition von Menschen- und Bürgerrechten	politische Erklärung; expositorischer Text	216
The Bill of Rights	– Darlegung grundsätzlicher Bürgerrechte	Gesetzestext; expositorischer Text	504
Samuel Francis Smith: America the Beautiful	– patriotische Hymne auf das Land und Gott	Gedicht	135
Francis Scott Key: The Star-Spangled Banner	– Kriegslied – Verherrlichung der Fahne und der Nation – Primat der amerikanischen Nation	Gedicht/Lied	330
Abraham Lincoln: The Gettysburg Address	– Kriegsrede zur Einweihung eines Soldatenfriedhofs – Beschwörung der Einheit der Nation – Heldengedenken	Rede; argumentativer/persuasiver Text	280
Bill Maher: Taking What's Best from the French	– Problematisierung des gespannten amerikanisch-französischen Verhältnisses – Vergleich der Gemeinsamkeiten und Unterschiede der beiden Nationen – Betonung der gemeinsamen historischen und philosophischen Grundlagen – Kritik an der xenophobischen Haltung der Bush-Administration und großer Kreise der Republikaner	Zeitschriftenkolumne; argumentativer/ persuasiver Text	947
Worksheet im Lehrerheft			
Worksheet 1, S. 32	Walt Whitman: I Hear America Singing		

Frontiers of a Dream

Autor, Text	Inhaltliche Schwerpunkte	Textsorte/ Medium	Wortzahl
John Gast: American Progress	– historisches Gemälde – westward movement – Stufen der Besiedlung des Kontinents – Vertreibung der Urbevölkerung – Idealisierung des Fortschritts	Gemälde	–
Frederick J. Turner: The Significance of the Frontier in American History	– Analyse demographischer Daten – historische Beschreibung des Siedlungsprozesses – Vergleich mit anderen historischen Besiedlungsprozessen	historischer Vortrag; expositorischer Text	818
Alexander Keyssar: The West	– Besiedlung des Kontinents westlich des Mississippi im 19. Jahrhundert – Eisenbahnbau nach dem Bürgerkrieg – der Homestead Act – die Warnungen Powells vor Dürreperioden	Sachtext; expositorischer Text	721
Mark Knopfler: Telegraph Road	– die Straße als Ausgangspunkt für Siedlungen – Aufstieg und Zerfall einer Siedlung – die Straße als Metapher für den Traum	Song	397

Autor, Text	Inhaltliche Schwerpunkte	Textsorte/ Medium	Wortzahl
John F. Kennedy: The "New" Frontier: Address at Rice University on the Nation's Space Effort	– die Zukunft der USA liegt in der Raumfahrt – Konzept eines Mondprogramms für die 1960er-Jahre – Motivation des Raumfahrtprogramms	Rede; argumentativer Text	1106
James Truslow Adams: The American Dream	– sozialgeschichtliche Bestandsaufnahme – Definition des Begriffs des American Dream – Erwartungen an die Zukunft	Sachtext; expositorischer Text	753
Janis Joplin: Mercedes Benz	– Wünsche nach materiellem Reichtum – satirische Aufnahme amerikanischer Konsumklischees	Song	159
Worksheet im Lehrerheft			
Worksheet 2, S. 58	Jeff Lynne, Wild West Hero (Song)		

In the Wake of a Dream

Autor, Text	Inhaltliche Schwerpunkte	Textsorte/ Medium	Wortzahl
US Census: Immigration from 1850 to 2000	– Daten zur Zuwanderung in den letzten 150 Jahren	statistische Grafik	–
Emma Lazarus: The New Colossus	– Loblied auf die Freiheitsstatue – Vergleich der alten und der neuen Welt – Einladung an die Welt zur Immigration in die USA	Gedicht	114
E Pluribus Unum	– Symbole des Staates	Siegel	–
Joseph Bruchac: Ellis Island	– Konflikt eines Menschen zwischen seinen beiden verschiedenen Identitäten – kontrastierende Betrachtung der USA	Gedicht	125
Amy Bloom: And Lost There, a Golden Feather in a Foreign, Foreign Land	– Ankunft einer Auswanderin auf Ellis Island – erste Eindrücke im fremden New York – Diskrepanz zwischen Traum und Realität	Romanauszug; narrativer Text	757
Arnold Schwarzenegger: Republican National Convention Address	– persönliche Lebensgeschichte – Gründe für die Übernahme der amerikanischen Staatsbürgerschaft – positive Bewertung der amerikanischen Nation als ein Volk von Einwanderern	Rede; argumentativer/persuasiver Text	1290
T. C. Boyle: The Tortilla Curtain	– zwei Männer argumentieren über den Nutzen bzw. die Gefahren unkontrollierter Einwanderung – Sollte die Einwanderung in die USA gestoppt werden?	Romanauszug; narrativer Text	884
Gregory Rodriguez: Migrate, then Integrate	– Veränderungen in den Zuwanderungsstatistiken – die Trennung und Entwicklung unterschiedlicher ethnischer Bevölkerungsgruppen – Tendenzen zunehmender Integration in der jüngeren Generation	Zeitungskommentar; expositorischer Text	807

Autor, Text	Inhaltliche Schwerpunkte	Textsorte/ Medium	Wortzahl
John McCain: Border Security and Immigration Reform	– Notwendigkeit von umfassenderen Grenzkontrollen – der Einfluss der Immigration für den Arbeitsmarkt – Amerika als das gelobte Land des 21. Jahrhunderts	Rede; argumentativer Text	304
Worksheet im Lehrerheft			
Worksheet 3, S. 86	How to Analyse Charts		

A Dream Deferred

Autor, Text	Inhaltliche Schwerpunkte	Textsorte/ Medium	Wortzahl
John Steinbeck: The Grapes of Wrath	– Veränderungen durch die Industrialisierung der Landwirtschaft – Landvertreibung und Armut während der Wirtschaftskrise der 1930er-Jahre	Romanauszug; narrativer Text	1256
Bruce Springsteen: The Ghost of Tom Joad	– Beschreibung von gesellschaftlichen Außenseitern – Anknüpfung an ein historisches Vorbild	Song	280
Daniel J. Kevles: A Divided Society	– Beschreibung der Entwicklung der Beziehung zwischen weißer und nicht weißer Bevölkerung in den 1960er- und 70er-Jahren – Analyse der neu entstandenen Problembereiche (städtische Armut)	Sachtext; expositorischer Text	598
Langston Hughes: Harlem	– das Scheitern der Teilnahme am amerikanischen Traum	Gedicht	53
Lorraine Hansberry: A Raisin in the Sun	– das Scheitern des persönlichen Traums vom Glück – Auswanderung nach Afrika als mögliche Lebensentscheidung	Dramenauszug	418
Martin Luther King: I Have Been to the Mountain Top	– Bewertung der historischen Entwicklung der Menschheit in den letzten Jahrtausenden – das Aufstreben von Bürgerrechtsbewegungen in den USA und in afrikanischen Staaten – die Hoffnung auf eine bessere Zukunft	Rede; argumentativer Text	1118
Robert F. Kennedy: Announcement of Martin Luther King's Death	– Mitteilung der Ermordung M. L. Kings – Würdigung seines Lebens – Aufruf zur Einheit und zum friedlichen Miteinander	Rede; argumentativer/persuasiver Text	611
Barack Obama: "A More Perfect Union"	– die Entwicklung der individuellen Rechte in den USA seit der Gründung – Bewertung der Bedeutung der verfassungsmäßigen Rechte – Darstellung der eigenen Biographie als Beispiel für den amerikanischen Traum	Rede; argumentativer Text	639
Robert Barnes/Michael D. Shear: Obama Makes History	– Obamas Sieg bei den Präsidentschaftswahlen – die historische Bedeutung der Wahl des ersten schwarzen Präsidenten	Zeitungsbericht; expositorischer Text	564

Worksheets und Klausuren im Lehrerheft	
Worksheet 4, S. 123	How to Analyse a Cartoon
Klausur 1, S. 127	Langston Hughes: "I Too Sing America"
Klausur 2, S. 130	Barack Obama: Victory Speech, Chicago, Nov 4, 2008

Weiterführende Hinweise

Die wesentlichen Informationsquellen zu den einzelnen Texten werden jeweils bei der Darstellung der Texte (Unterrichtsempfehlungen, bzw. *Author and Text*) gegeben.
Für alle Themen nützlich ist die Seite der *Library of Congress*: www.loc.gov
Ebenso umfangreich ist das Datenarchiv des Weißen Hauses: www.whitehouse.gov.
Für alle statistischen Recherchen bietet der US-Census extensives Datenmaterial: www.census.gov

Die im Lehrerhandbuch angesprochenen Methoden sind ausführlich in den beiden Methodentrainern von Grieser-Kindel et al., *Method Guide*, Schöningh 2006 und 2009 dargestellt und erläutert.

Getting started

Die Bilder im Schülerbuch zeigen zwei Seiten desselben Landes; während der berühmte Schriftzug und die Freiheitsstatue sofort positive Assoziationen hervorrufen, werden die anderen beiden Bilder zunächst erst einmal in einem Heft zum *American Dream* befremdlich wirken. Die Schülerinnen und Schüler sollten daher zunächst einmal für sich ihre möglichen Assoziationen auf einem Blatt aufschreiben. Anschließend können die Ergebnisse, u. U. unter einer Kopie des Bildes, auf einer Folie gesammelt und gemeinsam besprochen und ggf. problematisiert werden.
Die interessanteste Frage knüpft sich danach an die „*Green Card*“: warum wollen so viele Menschen aus der ganzen Welt jedes Jahr eine Einreiseerlaubnis bekommen? Was spricht für den/die Einzelne/n eigentlich dafür oder dagegen?
Die Frage kann durch eine sogenannte SWOT-Analyse, die bei strategischen Planungen, z. B. auch der eigenen Lebensplanung verwendet wird, beantwortet werden:

Strengths: attributes of the person that are helpful to achieving the objective.	
Weaknesses: attributes of the person that may hinder achieving the objective.	
Opportunities: *external* conditions that are helpful to achieving the objective.	
Threats: *external* conditions which could hinder achieving the objective.	

Hiermit können alle Lernenden für sich selbst überprüfen, ob eine „Green Card“ für sie erstrebenswert wäre, oder nicht.

Solutions

Activities p. 4

The United States has been a land of many dreams. What is behind these dreams? Do they still come true, or have they ever come true at all?
Have a look at these pictures. What ideas or associations come to your mind? Complete the mind map.

Picture 1: “Hollywood” – movies – stars – dream world – success – glamour – money	**Picture 3: “Beggar”** – poverty – on the street – no shelter – trash – hunger – left out
Picture 2: “Statue of Liberty” – New York – freedom – new world – dream – independence – welcome – hope	**Picture 4: “Hut”** – outsider – poverty – isolation – dirt – no future – left out

The Declaration of Independence (Painting)

John Trumbull

Painter and work

John Trumbull, born in 1756 in Connecticut, first studied law at Harvard University before becoming a painter. Serving in the Connecticut Militia he came to the attention of General George Washington when he drew a detailed plan of the enemy's fortifications in Boston. He served as an adjutant until 1777. In 1780 he sailed to England to study the art of painting. He was incarcerated and nearly hanged the same year. He was released on the condition that he leave the country. Shortly afterwards Thomas Jefferson and John Adams asked him to paint a series of historical paintings about the Revolutionary War.
"The painting of Declaration of Independence" began in 1786 with the consulting help of Jefferson in Jefferson's house in France. Trumbull first left out the heads and only added them later (John Adams was added in London in 1787 and Jefferson in Paris the same year). The background of the painting was finished in 1789 from sketches made on location in Philadelphia. In the following years he painted many miniature portraits of persons who assembled in Congress in New York. Lacking financial support he left the painting unfinished and began to work as a secretary, staying for many years in England again. He returned to America in 1815 and only took up work in 1816, when both houses of Parliament – now seated in Washington – hired him to copy and enlarge four of his major historical paintings for the Capitol. The big canvas painted from 1817 to 1819 is on display in the rotunda of the Capitol in Washington, the much smaller original painting can be seen at Yale university. You will also find the painting on the reverse side of the $2 bill.

Unterrichtsempfehlungen

Das Bild von John Trumbull sollte nicht nur als Einstimmung in einer Einstiegsphase verwendet werden, sondern als eigenständiger visueller Text bearbeitet werden. Hierzu kann zunächst auf Folie ein Pressefoto eines aktuellen Ereignisses (G8 Gipfel, Vertragsunterzeichnung etc.) gezeigt werden. Das Bild sollte den Lernenden bekannte Personen der Zeitgeschichte bei einem förmlichen Moment zeigen. Die Beschreibung des Fotos kann bereits zur Vorentlastung bzw. Semantisierung des notwendigen Besprechungsvokabulars dienen. Auch solche Fotos sind gestellt und zeigen symbolische Situationen (z. B. langes Händeschütteln für die Fotografen).
Die Unterschiede zwischen dem Pressefoto und dem historischen Gemälde werden an der Tafel in zwei kontrastierenden Spalten festgehalten, die im Laufe der Erarbeitung sukzessive ergänzt werden.
Bei der Beschreibung des historischen Gemäldes sollte darauf geachtet werden, dass nicht vorschnell interpretiert wird, sondern zunächst eine sachlich neutrale Beschreibung des Sichtbaren erfolgt. Hierbei ist es methodisch sicher hilfreich, wenn das Bild als Farbfolie vorliegt, sodass eine gemeinsame Erarbeitung im Unterrichtsgespräch erfolgen kann. Da einige der historischen Informationen den Schülerinnen und Schülern nicht vorliegen, muss hier in kurzen Lehrerinformationen (s. u.) im Laufe der Besprechung (Aufgaben 1 bis 3) weitergeholfen werden (der Hinweis auf das Entstehungsdatum kann z. B. ein nützlicher Impuls sein).
Rückgreifend auf das zu Beginn verwendete Pressefoto kommt die Lerngruppe mithilfe

der Gegenüberstellung im Tafelanschrieb zu dem Schluss, dass es sich bei dem Bild um eine symbolische Aufbereitung eines historischen Ereignisses handelt, welche keine realistische Abbildung beansprucht und von den Zeitgenossen auch nicht als solche verstanden wurde.

Solutions

Describing a historical painting, p. 6

1. **Give a description of the painting (room, decorations, persons, etc).**
   The room seems to be a very big hall or assembly room. There are chairs for the members of the assembly and a table and a chair for the person presiding over the gathering. On the wall are a number of flags; the flag of the American colonies and the Royal Flag of England can clearly be distinguished. Many people (more than forty) are gathered in this room. Most of them are sitting and watching while six men are standing at a table covered with documents. Five of them seem to be addressing the person sitting at the table. The role of the sixth man (on the right) seems to be that of an assistant to the man sitting and presiding over the meeting. It is obvious that their session must have come to a decisive moment, as everybody is looking at the group gathered around the table.

2. **Which group is the most prominent in the picture?**
   The five men in the centre of the painting are the focus of attention. Nevertheless the man sitting at the table must be important, too, as they are presenting their document to him.

3. **How has this been emphasized by the painter?**
   Historical paintings of the 18th century do not try to show the situation at an exact moment in history, but have to be seen as a subjective rendering of the situation and the people involved, and this is also the case with John Trumbull's painting. The members of congress did not sign the Declaration of Independence on July 4; some of the persons shown in the picture were not even there and did not sign the document at all.
   The painter set the five main authors of the Declaration of Independence in the middle of the painting, thus emphasizing their prominent role. Furthermore he shows them in a determined way (see position of the hands of John Adams). Thomas Jefferson as the driving force of the group is holding the parchment with both his hands; he is the tallest person of the whole painting, standing in the exact middle of the picture, framed by his conjurers.

The Declaration of Independence (Text)

Authors and text

On June 11, 1776, after more than a year of fighting in the American Revolutionary War, the thirteen American colonies, represented by their delegates (two to seven per state) at the Second Continental Congress in Philadelphia, appointed a committee of five men (John Adams, Roger Sherman, Robert R. Livingston, Thomas Jefferson and Benjamin Franklin) to draft a "Declaration of Independence." The document was meant to explain the reasons why the thirteen states wanted to become independent from the British Crown. After some general aspects had been discussed, the task of writing a first draft was left to Thomas Jefferson, who finished his work in only 17 days. The first draft was discussed and modified by the whole group and a first fair copy was presented to Congress on July 2. After further work on the exact wording, that for some went too far, for others not far enough, the document was adopted on July 4, 1776. The original text was destroyed, while the "official version" which is on display at the National Archives in Washington, DC was the version that was finished and signed. The exact date of the signing is still disputed, but it seems that the engrossed parchment was signed by most members of Congress on August, 2.

Unterrichtsempfehlungen

Zur weitergehenden Vorbereitung des Textes der *Declaration* ist folgender Aufsatz sehr hilfreich: www.archives.gov/exhibits/charters/declaration_style.html
Es wurde im Rahmen dieses Bandes nur der kurze staatsphilosophisch wichtige Eingangsteil der *Declaration* gewählt. Zur Veranschaulichung des Gesamttextes ist es sicherlich sinnvoll, eine Folie mit der Abbildung des Dokuments zu verwenden (findet sich z. B. bei Wikipedia); noch schöner ist eine Faksimile Reproduktion (z. B. erhältlich über http://store.ushistory.org
Die *pre-reading activities* knüpfen an die Bildanalyse an und dienen der inhaltlichen Vorentlastung. Sie sollten als Hausaufgabe bzw. zur Bearbeitung im Selbstlernzentrum gegeben werden. Zur Einstimmung auf die gesamte Reihe kann man an dieser Stelle auch Plakate anfertigen lassen, die in späteren Phasen immer wieder im Unterrichtsraum den Bezug zu diesem Moment der amerikanischen Geschichte ermöglichen. Allgemein didaktisch ist eine kontinuierliche Sammlung von Ergebnissen, aber auch biografischen Abrissen und Landkarten im Unterrichtsraum lern- und behaltensfördernd und ermöglicht den Rückbezug und eine Vernetzung mit bereits Gelerntem. Die textvorbereitenden Aufgaben helfen den Schülerinnen und Schülern, bei der späteren Textarbeit den historischen Bezug herzustellen. Durch die Beschäftigung mit den Biografien der sechs Hauptakteure wird zudem Spannung und Interesse geweckt (deshalb der Quizcharakter der Fragestellungen), indem die auf dem Gemälde Dargestellten nun konkreter Gestalt annehmen. Die Ergebnissicherung schließt diesen Teil der Vorentlastung ab.
Der Text ist sprachlich und inhaltlich sehr anspruchsvoll und sollte gemeinsam erarbeitet werden. Nach einer ersten Lektüre, in welcher ggf. noch sprachliche Unklarheiten geklärt werden können, erstellen die Lernenden eine „Übersetzung" in modernes Englisch. Die nachfolgende Gruppenarbeit (Aufgabe 2) dient zur weiteren Klärung von inhaltlichen Schwierigkeiten und zur Korrektur. Die unterschiedlichen Versionen können ausgehängt und miteinander verglichen werden (*gallery walk* – Museumsrundgang), sodass letztendlich in der Diskussion eine Verständigung über die Hauptaussagen des Textes für alle Lernenden möglich wird.
Aufgabe 3 dient der inhaltlichen Reorganisation des Textes. Einzelne philosophische Gedanken und Grundannahmen des Textes werden jetzt, stark verkürzend, in ihren philosophisch historischen Zusammenhang eingeordnet. Dies ist sicherlich sehr anspruchsvoll und kann eine Kooperation mit den gesellschaftswissenschaftlichen Fächern Philosophie und Geschichte sinnvoll machen. Das staatsphilosophische Konzept des *„social contract"* als grundlegende Basis für das Selbstverständnis des amerikanischen Staatsbürgers ist hierbei für die weitere Erarbeitung des *„American Dream"* unerlässlich (siehe oben Erläuterungen in „Aufbau").
Die effizienteste Erarbeitung von Aufgabe 4 bietet das *„group puzzle and group pyramid"*, da hierdurch die Konzentration auf eine überschaubare Anzahl von Begriffen (besonders Oberbegriffen) erreicht werden kann und gleichzeitig eine größtmögliche Schülerbeteiligung erzielt wird.

Solutions

Before you read p. 6

Use the Internet to find out more about the five persons standing in the middle of the painting.

– **Give a brief abstract of their lives.**
http://en.wikipedia.org/wiki/Committee_of_Five
a very interesting interactive website designed for educational purposes can be found at: www.archives.gov/exhibits/charters/declaration.html

– **Why are they so prominent in this scene (historical background)?**
The "Committee of Five" was asked by the Continental Congress in June 1776 to draft a resolution that might be adopted by the assembly, which was in disagreement regarding many questions at that time. Thus five men from different colonies were nominated to establish a first concept of a resolution. The five finally presented a document to Congress, which was discussed (July 2 through July 4) and finally agreed on (by twelve of the thirteen colonies, for formal reasons the state of New York abstained from voting, but agreed a week later). The five men can be seen as the "authors" of the Declaration; therefore they are prominently set in the middle of the painting.

– **One of them hasn't signed the *Declaration of Independence*. Who is it and why?**
Robert R. Livingston did not sign the Declaration of Independence. Though he was one of the five drafters, appointed by the Continental Congress in June 1776, he was recalled by his state (New York) before July 4, where he soon became Chancellor, which is the highest judicial officer of the state.

– **John Hancock's signature is the first and most flamboyant under the *Declaration*. What was his role at this time? Sketch a short history of the man.**
John Hancock is known by most Americans for his signature and far less for his historical role. He was born on January 12, 1737 in Massachusetts and was schooled at Harvard University. He inherited a huge fortune from his uncle and was one of the wealthiest men in the country. In the early 1760s he resided in England for several years and was considered loyal to the English crown at the beginning of his career. In the mid-1760s, now living as a merchant in Boston, he became a friend of Samuel Adams (and his brother John Adams) and thus came in contact with revolutionary ideas. He soon played an important political role in his state. For the British officials he was considered a "smuggler" (for not paying taxes) and a traitor, and was threatened with capital punishment. Using his huge fortune he supported the further development of the revolutionary militia of the "Minutemen." In the late 1760s he took part in several violent incidents with British officials in Boston and also had some (though obscure) part in the famous Boston Tea Party in December 1773 that later (1775) led to the Revolutionary War. Consorting with Samuel Adams, Hancock became very popular in his hometown and was elected delegate to the Continental Congress in 1774 and became the President of the Second Continental Congress in Philadelphia in May 1775. He was an ardent supporter of independence from Britain and played a leading role uniting the Congress towards a final decision. As President of the Congress he was the first to sign the final document. Using the still-free space he signed the document with a bold stroke that still stands out from those of the other signers. Until his death in October 1793 he remained a highly respected politician in his state, where he was elected to the governorship nine times in his life.

Activities p. 7

1. **Write down the message of the *Declaration* in your own words.**
We, the people of the English Colonies of America, have decided to separate from our homeland. We think we are entitled to declare our separation, as the Laws of Nature and of Nature's God give us the right to do so.

Our firm political belief is that all human beings are created equal and that they all possess some inalienable rights, i.e. life, liberty and the pursuit of happiness. We believe that governments should protect and guarantee these rights and if a government is not willing to do that, the people have got the right to establish their own government that will respect the rights mentioned above.

2. **In groups of four or five agree on one final draft.**
   Individual answer

3. **Thomas Jefferson wrote the first draft of the *Declaration* combining philosophical ideas of Hobbes, Locke and the later philosophers of the Enlightenment, like Rousseau. Research (→ e.g. *Wikipedia*) these philosophers and their theories and draw a poster of the main ideas/concepts.**
   This task could be done in separate group work and should produce comparable results. A common frame might support a more organized presentation of the findings. The poster might look like this (probably giving more details):

	"Natural" condition		Act of Transition		Social Contract – State
Hobbes	humans are asocial self interest individual rights	→	cede their individual rights to higher authority	→	absolute government that creates binding rules
Locke	state of nature in fear of each other	→	cede their individual rights to form a group "neutral judge"	→	government is legitimate if it protects the common good natural rights, i.e. life, liberty and property
Rousseau	state of nature humans behave in a selfish way	→	cede their individual rights to a popular sovereignty freely chosen by themselves	→	general will → civil society rules the behaviour of the citizens

4. **In the second chapter of his *Second Treatise of Civil Government* (1690) John Locke states: "[...] no one ought to harm another in his life, health, liberty, or possessions."**
   Jefferson reduced this to the three aspects of "life, liberty and the pursuit of happiness." Whereas "life" and "liberty" are clear concepts, "the pursuit of happiness" is a very broad and unspecified idea. Draw a mind map of what it consists of in your opinion.
   Individual answers; some ideas might be drawn from John Locke's original wording. Permit as many qualified answers as possible to show the extensiveness of this idea.

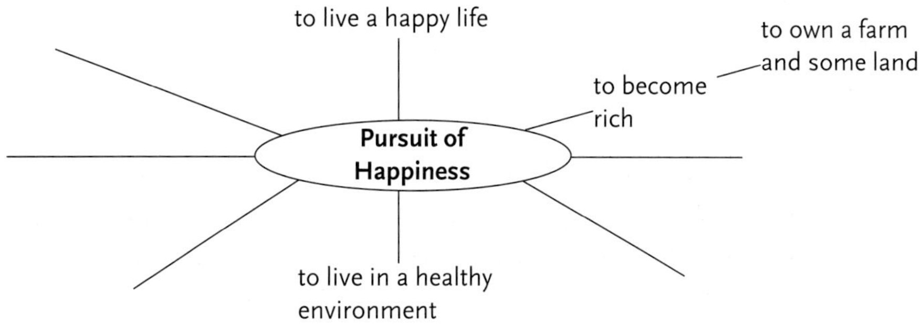

The Bill of Rights (1791)

Author and text

The Bill of Rights is a detailed list of civil rights that were granted to the citizens of the newly founded United States. The bill was advocated by a strong group of Anti-Federalists (among them Samuel Adams, John Hancock and others) who feared a too powerful central government, introduced by the Constitution. As no civil rights were included in the Constitution they urged the Congress to pass a Bill of Rights, coined after the Virginia Declaration of Rights from June 1776, drafted by George Mason, that had already influenced Thomas Jefferson in his conception of the Declaration of Independence.
The young Virginian delegate James Madison (born 1751), representing the Anti-Federalist group in the Congress, drafted twelve amendments to the Constitution (1789) that would allow the Anti-Federalists to accept it (Thomas Jefferson in a letter to James Madison: "Half a loaf is better than no bread"). Ten of the twelve amendments were ratified by the Congress (one of the two that were excluded was ratified in its original wording in 1992). The process of ratification by the thirteen states began in November 1789, New Jersey being the first state to sign the document, now entitled "Bill of Rights"; the last (of ten) to sign after a long discussion between the author Madison and his opponents was Virginia (December 1791). Three states never signed the Bill of Rights (Georgia, Massachusetts, and Connecticut) until forced to do so in 1939.

Unterrichtsempfehlungen

Der *„Bill of Rights"* ist eine frühe Erklärung der Bürgerrechte und spielt bis heute im Bewusstsein der Amerikaner eine große Rolle. Im Schülerbuch stehen nur die ersten 10 Artikel, welche nach einem zweijährigen Ratifizierungsverfahren 1791 erlassen wurden, weitere wesentliche Ergänzungen folgten 1865 (XIII: Abschaffung der Sklaverei), 1870 (XV: Wahlrecht für Wahlberechtigte aller Rassen), 1920 (XIX: Frauenwahlrecht), 1971 (XXVI: Senkung des Wahlalters auf 18 Jahre). Das 27. und bisher letzte *Amendment* (Entschädigung für Senatoren und Kongressabgeordnete) wurde 1992 ratifiziert, lag aber bereits seit 1789 zur Ratifizierung vor.
Ausführliche Informationen bieten zahlreiche Internetseiten; neben der Wikipedia sei verwiesen auf:
www.archives.gov/exhibits/charters/bill_of_rights.html
www.loc.gov/rr/program/bib/ourdocs/billofrights.html
Der Text ist sprachlich schwierig und sollte als Hausaufgabe vorbereitet werden. Hierbei kann als erste inhaltliche Erschließung bereits Aufgabe 1 gestellt werden. Die Ergebnisse können in einer Pyramidendiskussion in Gruppen (etwa 4 bis 5 Schülerinnen und Schüler) gesammelt werden und dann präsentiert und diskutiert werden. Ggf. kann die Sammlung aber auch im lehrergeleiteten Unterrichtsgespräch geleistet werden.
Die zweite Aufgabe verknüpft den historischen Text mit der Lebenswirklichkeit der Schülerinnen und Schüler. Die Richtlinien und Schulgesetze aller Bundesländer fordern die inhaltliche Auseinandersetzung und Kenntnis dieser fundamentalen Rechte unserer Verfassung. Im Englischunterricht bietet sich hier eine gute Möglichkeit diese Forderung umzusetzen. Eine geeignete Ergebnissicherung könnte an Tafel/OHP in Form einer Gegenüberstellung (s. u.) erfolgen. Eine Diskussion der Bedeutung dieser Grundrechte kann sich anschließen.
Aufgabe 3 dient der Vernetzung der bisher bearbeiteten Texte. Die Summe der Aussagen stellte für die *„founding fathers"* ihr staatsphilosophisches Konzept dar. Diese Kernaussagen ziehen sich durch alle politischen Dokumente der amerikanischen Geschichte und sind für das Verständnis unerlässlich. Die vierte Aufgabe soll die geschichtliche

Situation klären und lässt sich auch sehr gut zur häuslichen Bearbeitung (Geschichtsbuch; Internet) stellen.
Das *Second Amendment* ist nicht erst seit dem Film von Michael Moore auch als Problem im Bewusstsein der deutschen Schülerinnen und Schüler angekommen. Auch in Deutschland ist in den letzten Jahren die Diskussion über den Waffenbesitz schärfer geworden und jeder neue Amoklauf führt zu lebhaften Debatten. Hier bietet sich, nach gründlicher Vorbereitung in den jeweiligen Gruppen, eine Debatte des Themas an. Diese sollte von den Lernenden selbst gehalten und moderiert werden.
Die letzte Aufgabe bezieht sich wiederum nur in der ersten Texterschließung auf inneramerikanische Probleme. Auch in Europa hat sich nach dem 11. September vieles verändert, sind Grundrechte eingeschränkt worden. Der erste Cartoon ist inhaltlich wegen seiner zahlreichen administrativen Bezüge (NSA/FISA etc.) bei der ersten Rezeption schwieriger, in seiner Kernaussage (tradierte Freiheitsrechte vs. aktuelle Sicherheitsregelungen) dann allerdings recht einfach. Das Franklin-Zitat im zweiten Cartoon könnte in leistungsstarken Klassen auf der Basis des jetzt erarbeiteten Vorwissens zu einem schriftlichen „*Comment*" genutzt werden. Die Lösung der letzten Aufgaben (Cartoons) ist in Form einer kriterialen Musterlösung (Abitur etc.) gehalten.

Solutions

Activities p. 9

1. The 10 Amendments can be divided up into three groups of amendments, corresponding to the specific rights they aim to protect. Make a list and try to find appropriate headings for each of the amendments.

Group 1: I to IV – Rights and liberties of the individual citizen I: Freedom of religion/freedom of speech/freedom of press/freedom of assembly/right to petition II: Right to militia in sovereign states/right to bear arms III: Protection from quartering troops IV: Protection of individuals from unreasonable search
Group 2: V to VIII – Legal rights of individuals facing legal prosecution or controversy V: Due process of law/interdiction of double jeopardy/interdiction of self incrimination/protection of private property VI: Trial by impartial jury/rights of the accused VII: Civil trial by jury VIII: Prohibition of excessive bail and cruel punishment
Group 3: IX & X – rights not retained by the constitution or attributed to the federal government IX: Protection of rights not named in the Constitution and retained by the people X: Powers of sovereign states and people

2. The German *Grundgesetz* also protects individual rights. Correlate the rights stated in the First Amendment with the corresponding articles of the German *Grundgesetz.*

Bill of Rights USA	Grundgesetz für die Bundesrepublik Deutschland I. Die Grundrechte
First Amendment Congress shall make no law – respecting an establishment of religion, or prohibiting the free exercise thereof	Artikel 4 (1) Die Freiheit des Glaubens, des Gewissens und die Freiheit des religiösen und weltanschaulichen Bekenntnisses sind unverletzlich. (2) Die ungestörte Religionsausübung wird gewährleistet.

Bill of Rights USA	Grundgesetz für die Bundesrepublik Deutschland I. Die Grundrechte
– abridging the freedom of speech, or of the press	Artikel 5 (1) Jeder hat das Recht, seine Meinung in Wort, Schrift und Bild frei zu äußern und zu verbreiten und sich aus allgemein zugänglichen Quellen ungehindert zu unterrichten. Die Pressefreiheit und die Freiheit der Berichterstattung durch Rundfunk und Film werden gewährleistet. Eine Zensur findet nicht statt.
– [abridging] the right of the people peaceably to assemble	Artikel 8 (1) Alle Deutschen haben das Recht, sich ohne Anmeldung oder Erlaubnis friedlich und ohne Waffen zu versammeln.
– [abridging the right of the people] to petition the Government for a redress of grievances	Artikel 17 Jedermann hat das Recht, sich einzeln oder in Gemeinschaft mit anderen schriftlich mit Bitten oder Beschwerden an die zuständigen Stellen und an die Volksvertretung zu wenden.

Activities p. 10

3. In groups collect and write down passages from the Amendments that reflect the basic ideas of the *Declaration of Independence* (e.g. "all men are created equal" and the "unalienable rights, [...] life, liberty and the pursuit of happiness").

All men are created equal	Applies to amendments I to VIII
Life	Amendment V and VIII
Liberty	Amendments I to VIII
Pursuit of Happiness	(due to the complex idea it cannot be attached to a specific amendment – but the sum of all amendments contribute to this idea)

4. Some passages are closely related to the historical situation at that time. Find these and explain the historical background.

Amendments II and III in particular reflect the historical situation of the Revolutionary War. The armed rebellion (see "Minutemen" above) made the revolution against the British government possible. The British forces were often quartered in people's houses (see list of injuries in the Declaration of Independence). The right to petition had been violated by George III, but students probably won't know this fact, stated at the end of the list of injuries in the Declaration of Independence ("We have Petitioned for Redress in the most humble terms: Our repeated Petitions have been answered only by repeated injury.")

5. The Second Amendment is the most controversial today. The NRA (National Rifle Association) maintains that the right of every American to keep firearms should not be limited, whereas many Americans would prefer more limitations and controls.

- **In groups discuss the Second Amendment and design a pro or contra poster.**
- **Stage a debate about the topic.**

Students should draw information from various sources (pro and contra) → Internet.

The debate should include the two sides and a chairperson (or two) leading the discussion. (For details see "Mace Debate," Wikipedia). After a first exchange of positions the audience may give individual statements or ask questions. A final statement from both sides closes the debate. At the end a vote should be cast.

6. After September 11, 2001 the Bush administration restricted numerous liberties with the aim of ensuring higher security. Have a look at the two cartoons.

- **In groups choose the one cartoon you think expresses the objection to the restrictions best. Give reasons.**

– **Write a letter to the editor commenting on the cartoon in view of the *Bill of Rights*.**

Note: to analyse the two cartoons you should use **Worksheet 4** (p. 123).

The student	
uses the adequate style of a letter to the editor	AFB III
states which cartoon he/she refers to (Jeff Parker, *Florida Today*/Margulies, *The Record*)	AFB II
comments on the message of the cartoon: the secret spying of people's houses and flats by the NSA.	AFB III
points out that the Fourth Amendment guarantees the "right of the people to be secure ..."	AFB III
comments on the infringement of this amendment by the Bush administration	AFB III

America (The Beautiful) (1832)

Samuel Francis Smith

Author and text

The song is a well-known hymn about the beauty of the American continent, which also includes references to political ideas and praises God. It was written by Samuel Francis Smith, who was a Baptist clergyman born in 1808 in Boston. Smith attended Harvard University and Andover Theological Seminary. He entered the Baptist ministry in 1832. Asked by his friend Lowell Mason to translate a German patriotic song, he used what he thought was a German tune and wrote five verses within just thirty minutes. Revising the draft he crossed out one verse (originally the third of five) that he considered too aggressive for what was intended to be a peaceful hymn. The song soon became famous all over the country after it was performed by a choir at Boston Park Smith Church on July 4, 1832. The use of an "English tune" later became subject to controversial discussion, but did not stop its popularity. Smith wrote hundreds of songs and hymns in his lifetime. He died in Boston in 1895.

Unterrichtsempfehlungen

Der Text ist ein Lied und sollte daher, wenn möglich, zunächst als solches rezipiert werden. Es gibt eine Reihe von leicht zugänglichen Aufführungen, u.a. Yolanda Adams (von 2004) und ebenso leicht findbar (YouTube) der Vortrag von Aretha Franklin bei der Amtseinführung von Barack Obama am 20. Januar 2009. Schon dies allein unterstreicht die Aktualität, welche dieses Lied noch heute im amerikanischen Bewusstsein genießt.

Die Erarbeitung sollte eine systematische Texterschließung sein, so wie sie auch für die Abiturprüfungen vorgesehen ist, wobei Aufgabe 1 zur „Comprehension" gehört, Aufgaben 2 bis 4 führen zu einer strukturierten „Analysis", mit Aufgabe 5 wird der Teil „Comment" abgedeckt. Die Ergebnisse der Abiturprüfungen in mehreren Bundesländern der letzten Jahre belegen, dass besonders der Aufgabenbereich „Analysis" immer noch unzureichend gelöst wird. Im vorliegenden Band werden daher für eine Vielzahl von Texten hierfür ausführliche Analyseaufgaben gestellt, aus welchen die Unterrichtenden nach Notwendigkeit auswählen können. Zur Erleichterung der ersten formalen Analyse (Aufgabe 3) wurde zudem dem Schülerbuch ein ausführliches Glossar (S. 71 f.) beigegeben, welches die notwendige Begrifflichkeit illustrierend vermittelt. Zum anderen stehen Aufgaben, welche die systematische Textarbeit methodisch unterstützen (hier

Aufgabe 2). Die Erarbeitung des Liedes ist an dieser Stelle bewusst kleinschrittig angelegt, im Abitur würden die Ergebnisse der Aufgaben 2 bis 4 durch den Arbeitsauftrag „analyse the poem" eingefordert. Ein Lied ist ein mehrfach kodierter Text. Eine explizite Aufgabe zur Besprechung der „music" wird hier dennoch nicht gestellt, es ist aber trotzdem sinnvoll, diese Ebene nach einer möglichen Vorführung (Audio/Video) anzusprechen.
Die ersten drei Aufgaben eignen sich zur häuslichen Vorbereitung; sollte der Kurs aber noch wenig Übung haben, können sie auch im Klassenverband im Unterricht bearbeitet werden, wobei Aufgabe 1 eine Gruppenarbeit mit anschließender Sammlung auf einer Folie nahe legt. Die zweite Aufgabe sollte sinnvoller Weise in Einzelarbeit gelöst werden (→ Glossary). Aufgabe 3 kann wiederum in Gruppenarbeit gestellt werden (mit kurzer begründender Präsentation). Die vierte Aufgabe lässt sich am besten im Unterrichtsgespräch bearbeiten, wobei eine gut lesbare Folie mit den in Aufgabe 2 und 3 eingebrachten Markierungen hilfreich ist. Die letzte Aufgabe eignet sich als Hausaufgabe.

Solutions

Activities p. 12

1. **Find and name stylistic devices (see list p. 71 f.). What is their function in the text?**
First the rhyme scheme should be mentioned: aabcccb/aadeeed/ffghhhg/aabcccb. The students may not find the apostrophes (the word and explanation is not in the glossary) at the beginning of stanzas one, two and four.
The poem has a simple, repetitive structure (rhyme scheme/anaphora/repetition) that is typical of folk songs.

Anaphora	Land where ... Land of ... (4 f.) Let music ... (15) Let mortal tongues Let all that breathe ... Let rocks their (18 ff.)
Alliteration	**r**ocks and **r**ills (11) **G**reat **G**od (28)
Apostrophe	My country (1) My native country (8) Our father's God (22)
Assonance	Sw**ee**t fr**ee**dom (17)
Enumeration	thy rocks and rills,/thy woods and templed hills (11 f.)
Including 'we'	Our father's God (22) To Thee we sing (24) our land (25) protect us (27) our King (28)
Metaphor	templed hills (12)
Personification	let rocks their silence break (20) author of liberty (23)
Simile	my heart with rapture thrills/like that above (13 f.)

2. **Using different colours mark all personal pronouns in the poem. Name the differences between stanzas 1, 2, 3 and 4.**
Students should mark the first person singular, used in stanzas one and two, as well as the first person plural, used in the last stanza. There are no personal pronouns in stanza three. The old form of the second person singular (thee/thy) is

used in the first two stanzas, as well as in the last stanza, now spelled with a capital 'T'.

3. **The poem can be divided into three parts. One stanza clearly stands out as different from the rest of the text. Find a heading for this stanza. In some printed versions of the song this stanza is even left out. How do you judge the importance of this stanza?**
It should have become clear by now that stanza three stands out from the rest of the poem. The first two lines do not have the rhyme 'a' pattern, there are no personal pronouns and the apostrophe is also missing. An important feature of this stanza is the word field sound (music; ring; song; ... sound). The situation sketched in this stanza is that of the resurrection. In a song it may be understood as a sort of "bridge" before the final and most important stanza. It nevertheless is very important because it underlines the profound Christian intention and message of the song, highlighted in the last stanza.

4. **Using your findings from task 1 to 3 compare the first and the last stanza. Describe the main differences and changes in topic. Also consider the title of the poem.**
The first and the last stanza have identical rhyme schemes. In both stanzas "liberty" is mentioned, but in stanza four "God" is the author of liberty. The first stanza is still, like the title of the song, addressed to the "country", whereas the last stanza only deals with religious belief in the might of God. In the first stanza a speaker ("I") is addressing "America".

5. **Throughout the 19th century the song was used as a national anthem (though not officially named as such). Comment whether you think it appropriately conveys the ideas of the American ideals.**
The students should name
– the fervent patriotism of the whole poem, reflected in the appraisal of the natural grandeur of the North American continent.
– the concept of "liberty" (or freedom), named five times in the text.
– the idea of the "God given country" which is the main topic in the last stanza, certainly fits with the general ideas of the 19th century.

The Star-Spangled Banner

Francis Scott Key

Author and text

The American National Anthem glorifies the American flag. It is a fervent declaration of patriotic values. The song was written by Francis Scott Key, a lawyer from Georgetown (born 1779; died 1843). He wrote the text on September 14, 1814, after he witnessed a night of terrible bombing near Fort McHenry. F. S. Key spent that night in British quarters, after negotiating with British officers the release of an American prisoner. The British soldiers did not allow him to return to his home, as he had seen the disposition of the British forces preparing to attack Baltimore. The text was published six days later in *The Patriot* under the title "The Defence of Fort McHenry", using an old English air titled "Anacreon in Heaven", written by John Stafford Smith some time between 1770 and 1775. Francis Scott Key continued a successful career as a lawyer.

Unterrichtsempfehlungen

Das Lied sollte allen Schülerinnen und Schülern bekannt sein. Die Aufgaben geben wieder eine systematische Texterarbeitung vor.

Die *Pre-reading*-Aufgabe ist angesichts des besonderen Umgangs mit unserer eigenen Nationalhymne notwendig. Historische, aber auch inhaltliche Gründe verbieten es, heute noch die erste Strophe des „Deutschlandliedes" zu singen. Die französische Marseillaise ist ein revolutionäres Kampflied (englische Übersetzung unter: www.fordham.edu/halsall/mod/marseill.html), das vor allem den Freiheitswillen der neuen jungen Republik ausdrückt. Interessant sind die Parallelen zu einigen Aussagen des *„Star-Spangled Banner"* (die gegnerischen Soldaten sind „Söldner", und damit „slaves"). Wesentlich ist die Bewusstmachung der hohen symbolischen Bedeutung von Nationalhymnen für das Selbstverständnis von Nationen.

Etwas abweichend von dem in den Aufgaben vorgegeben Erarbeitungsgang besteht allerdings an dieser Stelle auch die Möglichkeit, eine etwas weiter ausholende zusätzliche Erschließung anzusetzen.

Die Lerngruppe bekommt die Textvorbereitung als Hausaufgabe. Zu Beginn der Stunde spielt der/die Unterrichtende dann eine möglichst „klassische" Version des Liedes (das Internet/YouTube bieten zahllose Quellen). Um die Konzentration auf das Lied zu bewahren, sollte allerdings besser nur eine Audio- und keine zu stark ablenkende Videofassung verwendet werden. Nach einer ersten Spontanphase, in welcher auf dem rechten Tafelflügel (siehe unten) erste Eindrücke zur Musik gesammelt werden, erfolgt die Bearbeitung der Aufgabe 1. Wie auch in „America (The Beautiful)" ist in diesem Lied das semantische Feld /nature/ (grün markieren lassen) in allen Strophen dominant. Daneben steht ebenso breit verteilt das Feld /war/ (rot markieren). Als letztes Feld kommt in der letzten Strophe das semantische Feld /religion/ (blau) hinzu. Auch hier ist eine Parallele zu Samuel Francis Smiths Lied erkennbar. In einer ausführlicher als durch die Aufgaben vorgegebenen Erarbeitung können jetzt die wichtigsten Aussagen der „Lyrics" an der Tafel gesammelt werden. Der Tafelanschrieb könnte etwa so aussehen:

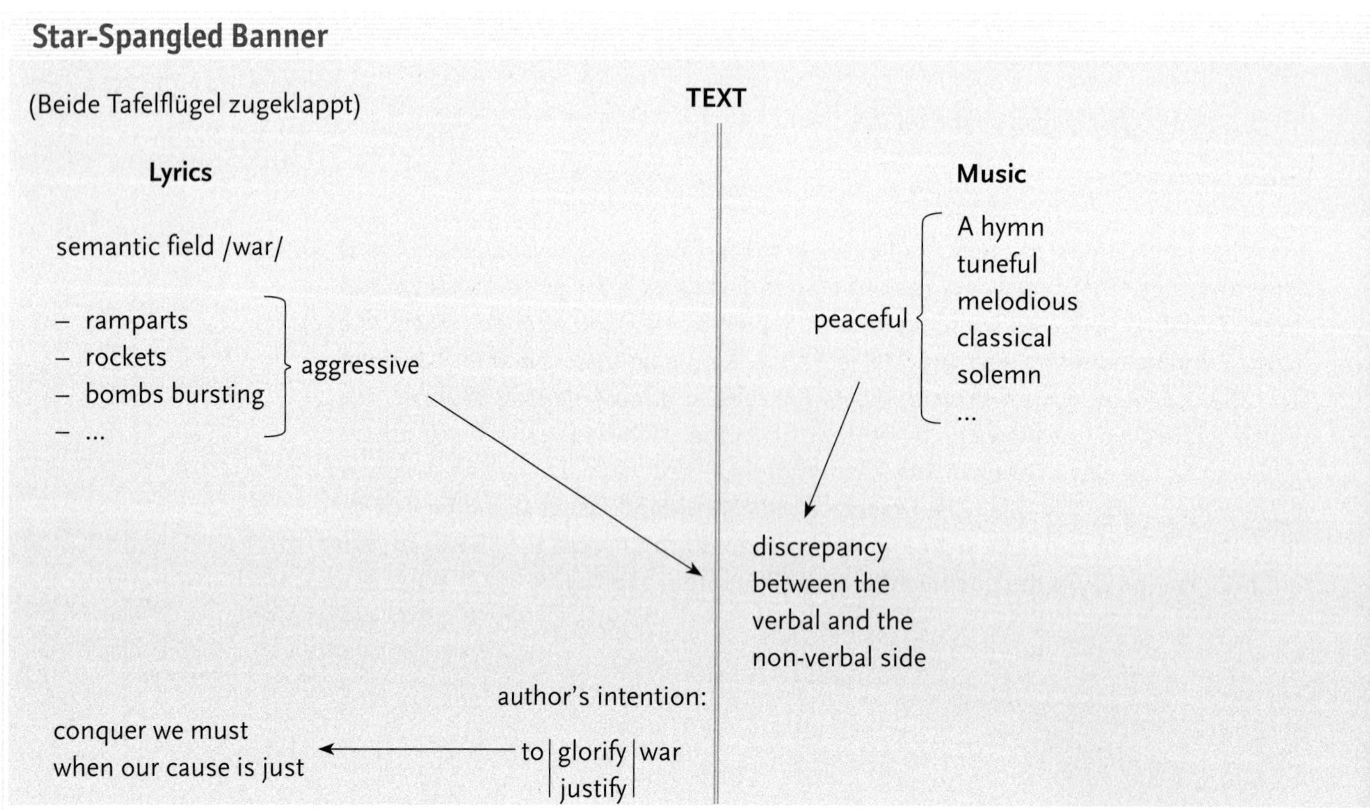

Die Gegenüberstellung macht die Diskrepanz der beiden Textebenen recht deutlich. Bevor mit den anderen Aufgaben weitergearbeitet wird, präsentiert der/die Unterrichtende eine andere Fassung des „Star-Spangled Banner". Jimi Hendrix hat sie beim Woodstockfestival live dargeboten und die Stones haben ihre nachfolgenden Livekonzerte hiermit als „offizielle" Hymne begonnen. Ein Fassung gibt es auf der *Woodstock* DVD, sowie an verschiedensten Orten im Internet. Es sollte auf keinen Fall das Video verwendet werden, weil Hendrix' Gitarrenspiel extrem ablenkend wirkt. Diese Version ist den wenigsten Schülerinnen und Schülern heute noch bekannt und entspricht auch nicht ihrem Musikgeschmack. Das Faszinierende an dieser Instrumentalfassung ist, dass man aufgrund der extremen Verfremdung doch jederzeit weiß, an welcher Stelle des Textes man sich befindet (die „bombs bursting in air" explodieren auch mit unerbittlicher Härte aus den Lautsprechern). Der rechte Tafelflügel wird jetzt aufgeklappt und die Lernenden ergänzen in einer Spontanphase bereits die wesentlichen Merkmale:

Star-Spangled Banner

(Flügel zugeklappt) **TEXT** (Flügel aufgeklappt ➔)

Lyrics	**Music** (Hendrix)
semantic field /war/	aggressive: – discordant; – parts of the original are recognizable; – odd; – squeaking; – shrill; – piercing; he tries to evoke the bombing / destruction
– ramparts; – rockets; – bombs bursting; – … } aggressive ➔	verbal and non-verbal side match
conquer we must when our cause is just ⟵	author's intention: to evoke / anathematize / condemn the destruction caused by war

Diese Fassung der Hymne spiegelte sicherlich 1968 die Gefühlslage der jungen Generation. Es bietet sich jetzt an, die Textsorte der *Parody* zu erarbeiten, da alle wesentlichen Elemente bereits angesprochen wurden. Auf einem gesonderten Tafelflügel (rechts aufgeklappt z. B.) werden die wichtigsten Merkmale zusammengetragen:

(rechter Flügel aufgeklappt ➔)

a parody
- imitating sth/sb (A ➔ A')
- exaggerating
- distorts
- ridicules
- mocks
- derides

(distorts / ridicules / mocks / derides: aspects of sth, traits of sb)

Die Bearbeitung kann jetzt als Gruppenarbeit mit Aufgabe 3 fortgeführt werden. Das Gespräch kann dabei angeregt werden, indem die ursprüngliche dritte, von Smith aber schnell als zu gewalttätig wieder gestrichene Strophe als zusätzlicher Denkanstoß eingegeben wird (auf Folie):

No more shall tyrants here
With haughty steps appear
And soldier bands
No more shall tyrants dread
Above the patriot dead
No more our blood be shed
By alien hands.

Die letzte Aufgabe führt zur allgemeinen Diskussion (möglicher weise als „debate" → Vorbereitung in Gruppen, Hilfsmittel Geschichtsbücher) der amerikanischen Außenpolitik bis zum heutigen Tage.

Solutions

Before you read p. 12

Find out more about the origin, history and usage of some other national anthems, like the German *Einigkeit und Recht und Freiheit* or the French *Marseillaise*.

The *Song of the Germans* (*Lied der Deutschen*) was written by Hoffman von Fallersleben in 1841 reflecting the hopes of the German "Vormärz" to reach the goal of a whole, unified Germany, governed along modern democratic principles and no longer by the will of princes and kings. Along with the new "black, red and golden" flag it stood for the idea of a republican nation, and was adopted by the 1848 convention in Frankfurt, but became a "revolutionary" song after the failure of the March revolution. After the First World War it was made the national anthem of the newly founded democratic German state in 1922. Nazi propaganda changed, or misrepresented, the message of the first stanza, so that the song was forbidden after the war. In 1952 Adenauer used the third stanza as a new national anthem.

The *Marseillaise* is a revolutionary song, written as *War Song for the Army of the Rhine* by Claude Joseph Rouget de Lisle in 1792, that soon became popular among soldiers (especially volunteers from Marseille). It reflects the Prussian and Austrian invasion at the beginning of the revolution. It became the national anthem in 1795, but was banned by Napoleon and was only restored as the French nation's anthem in 1879.

Activities p. 13

1. **Find the three dominant semantic fields and mark them in different colours. You will find at least two of them in most patriotic songs or speeches. What is their function?**

   The most prominent semantic field that can be found throughout the song is /war/(mark in red). Examples are: perilous fight (3), ramparts (4), rockets' red glare (5), bombs bursting in air (5), foe's haughty host (10), band (17), havoc of war (18), battle's confusion (18), blood (20), refuge (21), hireling (21), slave (21), terror of flight (22), gloom of the grave (22), war's desolation (26), victory (27), conquer (29).

   The second one, sharply contrasting the first, is /nature/(mark in green). Examples are: dawn's early light (1), twilight's last gleaming (1), on the shore (9), towering steep (11), the gleam of the morning's first beams (13), shines on the stream (14). There are no examples in stanzas three and four. The third semantic field is only present in the last stanza: /religion/(mark in blue). Examples are: blest (27), heaven-rescued land (27), the Pow'r (28), In God is our trust (30).

Nature reflects the often-praised beauty of the American continent, acclaimed in many patriotic songs (see Smith). This is usually combined with "religion" to underline that America is God's own country. The dominance of the semantic field /war/ stresses that this song is a war song, hailing the flag as the nation's symbol.

2. **Text grammars distinguish between two different types of *we:* the "receiver including *we*" and the "receiver excluding *we*." Which one is used in this text, and what is the intended effect?**
   The "receiver including *we*" is used in this text. It stresses the importance of a group against others outside this group.

   IT
   (the others)
   ↕
   I → WE ← YOU

3. ***The Star-Spangled Banner* was only adopted by Congress as the national anthem in 1931. At that time it had become quite common to sing it at the opening of official celebrations and sports events.**
   Compare *America* and *The Star-Spangled Banner*. Make a list of what they have in common and where they differ. Which one do you think is the better national anthem?

America	Star-Spangled Banner
– beauty of nature, land	– beauty of nature, land
– untainted nature	
– God reigns the country	– God reigns the country
	– the people are prepared to fight for their country

   – individual answers to be discussed

4. **Line 29 reads: "Then conquer we must, when our cause is just." Discuss whether this is an adequate motto for American foreign policy.**
   History books will tell you that it is an adequate motto, since the USA has, from its beginnings, tried to gain larger parts of the continent (see SB p. 21). Some of these acquisitions were settled by treaties (i.e. Louisiana purchase, 1803; Oregon Territory, 1846, Alaska, 1867), but other were taken by war (i.e. Texas and most of the south-west). Theodore Roosevelt's foreign policy in Asia (China) and in the Caribbean was based on military strength and is similar to the European imperialistic idea of the white man ruling the world. After the Second World War Korea, Vietnam and many struggles in South America underline the continuation of that policy. You could even add the "space race" of the Cold War to that list. Many conflicts in today's world were caused by US interference and military aggression.

The Gettysburg Address (1863)

Abraham Lincoln

Author and text

This short but poignant speech is one of the cornerstones of American rhetoric. In just 270 words President Lincoln tries to persuade his audience that the Civil War must come to an end and the Union re-established. His speech is dedicated to all American soldiers, Unionist and Federalist, and underlines the common political heritage of the nation.

Abraham Lincoln was the 16th President of the United States (1861–1865). He was born on February 12, 1809, the son of poor farmers in rural Kentucky. He led a hard childhood life in the wilderness, helping with farm work and with barely any time for education. As he remembered in his 1860 memoirs: "[...] when I came of age I did not know much. Still somehow, I could read, write, and cipher ... but that was all." He struggled hard to get an education, became a soldier in the Black Hawk War (1832) and became a captain. Then he worked as a lawyer for the Illinois legislature, travelling the country constantly for eight years. Due to his impressive debating skills, he won the Republican Party's nomination for President in 1860. His strict anti-slavery policy caused the secession of eleven southern states, led by Jefferson Davies. Fighting began in April 1861 and lasted until 1865. It was the deadliest war in American history, causing more than 620,000 soldier deaths and a never-specified number of civilian casualties. From July 1–3, 1863 more than 150,000 soldiers fought at Gettysburg in one of the bloodiest battles of the war. This battle was a turning point and as Lincoln delivered his speech in November, General Ulysses Grant was driving General Lee's armies southward.

President Lincoln wasn't the main orator at Gettysburg, but had only been asked to give a short dedication. Facing an audience of about 15,000 people his speech took just two minutes. The impact of this short address was nevertheless nonpareil. A stenographic version appeared in the *New York Times* the next day and five more versions, some handwritten and signed by the President himself, still exist today.

Lincoln was re-elected President in 1864. He was shot and killed by an actor on April 14, 1865 while attending a theatre performance in Washington only five days after General Lee surrendered. Lincoln's violent death finally settled the war and in December 1865 the 13th Amendment abolished slavery in the United States.

Unterrichtsempfehlungen

Es gibt zahlreiche Quellen zu Lincolns Rede und zum amerikanischen Bürgerkrieg im Allgemeinen. Der einfachste Zugang ist über die offizielle Seite des Weißen Hauses:
www.whitehouse.gov/about/presidents/AbrahamLincoln/
Detaillierte Ausführungen zu den Ereignissen in Gettysburg finden sich unter:
www.gettysburgfoundation.org/lincoln-address.htm
und bei der Library of Congress:
www.loc.gov/exhibits/gadd/
Eine Kopie der Originalseite der New York Times von 20. November 1863 mit der Rede Lincolns steht in der Wikipedia:
http://en.wikipedia.org/wiki/File:Gettysburg_Address,_New_York_Times.jpg
Dem Bedürfnis eine Rede nicht nur zu lesen, sondern zu hören, kommen mehrere Veröffentlichungen nach. Neben der vertonten Darbietung von Johnny Cash kann man bei YouTube diverse nachinszenierte Fassungen hören.

Die erste Aufgabe zielt auf eine Grundstrukturierung des Textes und kann mit der gesamten Lerngruppe schnell erarbeitet werden. Um die Systematisierung für alle zu gewährleisten, ist eine Sammlung dieser und der folgenden Ergebnisse im Tafelanschrieb sinnvoll. Für die weitere Erarbeitung wäre es günstig, wenn der Redetext als Folie vorläge, damit die Lerngruppe die Vernetzung der einzelnen Textelemente sehen kann. Die zweite Aufgabe zielt darauf, die textinhärenten Vernetzungen herauszustellen. Besonders gesprochene Texte bedürfen einer starken Vernetzung der Hauptgedanken, damit die Zuhörerschaft dem Redner folgen kann. Zur besseren Bearbeitung in Gruppen, kann eine Kopie des Textes verwendet werden, sodass der Text farbig markiert werden kann und die einzelnen Verweisstränge deutlich herausgearbeitet werden können (auf Folie markieren).

Wenn danach die allgemeine Textaussage klar geworden ist, werden in Einzelarbeit die rhetorischen Mittel gesammelt und in ihrer Funktion anschließend bewertet werden. Die Lösung der letzten Aufgabe findet sich im Prinzip in der Ausgabe der *New York Times* vom 20. November 1863 wieder. Die Aufgabe kann als Hausaufgabe gestellt werden und sollte in einer Präsentation der schriftlichen Produkte enden, bei denen die Lerngruppe entscheidet, welche/r Reporter/in am besten die Aussagen des Präsidenten wiedergibt.

Fourscore and seven years ago our fathers brought forth on this continent a new nation, conceived in liberty, and dedicated to the proposition that all men are created equal.
Now we are engaged in a great civil war, testing whether that nation, or any nation so conceived and so dedicated, can long endure. We are met on a great battlefield of that war. We have come to dedicate a portion of that field as a final resting place for those who here gave their lives that the nation might live. It is altogether fitting and proper that we should do this.
But, in a larger sense we cannot dedicate – we cannot consecrate – we cannot hallow – this ground. The brave men, living and dead, who struggled here, have consecrated it far above our poor power to add or detract. The world will little note nor long remember what we say here, but it can never forget what they did here. It is for us, the living, rather, to be dedicated here to the unfinished work which they who fought here have thus far so nobly advanced. It is rather for us to be here dedicated to the great task remaining before us – that from these honored dead we take increased devotion to that cause for which they gave the last full measure of devotion; that we here highly resolve that these dead shall not have died in vain; that this nation, under God, shall have a new birth of freedom; and that government of the people, by the people, for the people, shall not perish from earth.

Solutions

1. **The speech is clearly subdivided into three parts that refer to three different periods of time. Begin a table for your analysis by giving the three parts an appropriate time label.** Activities p. 15

Past	Present	Future
Fourscore and seven years ago (1)	Now (4)	will little note (12) unfinished work (16 f.) task remaining before us (20 f.) shall (26 ff.)

2. **Lincoln expresses several recurrent ideas, underlining them by the repetition of specific words; one of these is the concept of a "nation", another one is "liberty"/ "freedom". Find other significant repetitions of words.**

nation (2)	nation (4) (5) (7)	nation (28)
dedicate (2)	dedicate (5) (6)	dedicate (9) (16) (20)
liberty (2)	–	freedom (29)
–	live/life (7) (8)	live/life (10) (15)
–	–	dead/die (10) (22) (26) (27)

3. **Use the list of stylistic devices (p. 71 f.) and analyse which rhetorical devices Lincoln uses. Discuss the intended effect upon the listeners.**

Alliteration	**p**oor **p**ower (11)
Antithesis	living and dead (10) add or detract (11)
Including 'we'	(passim, 14 times) our (1); we (4) ...
Parallelism	that from these honored dead ...; that we here ... that these dead ...; that this nation ...; and that government ... (21–30) of the people, by the people, for the people (30 f.)
Quotation	"that all men are created equal" (2 f.)
Repetition	we cannot dedicate – we cannot consecrate – we cannot hallow (9 f.)
Synonyms	fitting and proper (8)

4. **You are a reporter working for *The Yankee Gazette* (a "northern" paper of that time). Write a report about the commemorations at Gettysburg. Your readers will be most interested to learn what the President said. Remember that you did not have a tape recorder nor was there any printed text of the speech. So you have to report from memory.**
Individual answer; the text should at least contain a paraphrase of the main thoughts:
At the beginning of his very short speech Lincoln referred to the nation's forefathers, quoting "that all men are created equal." He thinks that this long civil war was a test whether our nation could survive. Concerning the dedication of the new graveyard he added that we could not dedicate the place, because the brave men who fought in the war could only be honoured by those still living continuing the work of building the nation. He told the audience that he thought that the world would hardly notice this historical moment. The President told the audience to dedicate themselves to the unfinished work so that the task could be finished. At the end he added that he hoped for a new birth of freedom so that the "government of the people, by the people, for the people should not perish from earth."

Taking What's Best from the French

Bill Maher

Author and text

Bill Maher (pronounced [ma:r]) was born in 1956. He holds a BA in English and History. He is one of the most popular stand-up comedians in the USA, looking back on a career that now spans more than three decades. He is considered a political libertarian, supporting ideas that promote individual freedom. Maher is not affiliated with any of the parties, but in recent elections has supported the democratic candidate. Maher has gained some prominence in Europe since his satirical documentary film *Religulous* was released in 2008.
The text, published as a comment in *Newsweek*, is full of irony and questions conservative opinions by comparing and juxtaposing them with original concepts of the founders of the American nation. He reminds the readers that the basic ideas of American independence were brought to the new continent from France, founding a nation on the philosophical concepts of the Enlightenment. He especially criticizes the xenophobic and more specifically francophobic attitude of many conservatives in the USA, outlining that many ideas and views from France are still valuable today.

Unterrichtsempfehlungen

Der sehr lange Text sollte in die häusliche Vorbereitung gegeben werden. Hierbei kann bereits Aufgabe 1 zur inhaltlichen Erschließung gestellt werden. Bevor in der Unterrichtsstunde in Gruppen die Ergebnisse zusammengetragen werden, müsste sichergestellt werden, ob der Text durchgehend erschlossen wurde (*vocabulary questions*). Wenn alle Fragen geklärt sind, wird in Gruppenarbeit die kontrastierende Tabelle erstellt. Dies stellt sicher, dass ein größtmöglicher Teil der Vergleiche herausgearbeitet wird. Die Ergebnisse werden von den Gruppen auf Folie gesammelt, wobei nicht die Präsentation aller Folien notwendig sein wird, sondern nur einer (ausführlichen), die dann um das Fehlende ergänzt wird. Auf dieser Master-Folie werden anschließend die „*Main topics*" farbig markiert und die erarbeiteten Themen noch einmal gesondert auf der Tafel festgehalten.
Aufgabe 2 findet sinnvoller Weise zunächst einmal in Einzelarbeit (Hausaufgabe) statt, da hier zum ersten Male der typische Aufgabenbereich 2 erarbeitet werden soll. Die Sicherheit in der stilistischen Analyse können Schülerinnen und Schüler nur durch häufiges eigenes Üben erlangen.
Der letzte Schritt evaluiert nicht nur den Artikel von Maher, sondern reflektiert die in dieser Einheit erworbenen Kenntnisse über die amerikanische Verfassungsgeschichte und die fundamentalen Werte der Nation. Die Fishbowl-Diskussion sollte zunächst in Gruppen Pro und Contra (möglichst freiwilliger Zuordnung) vorbereitet werden. Es ist wichtig, dass die Schülerinnen und Schüler lernen, dass Argumente begründet werden müssen und dass man auch auf Gegenargumente der anderen Seite reagieren muss.
An einem Tisch mit zweimal fünf Stühlen nehmen dann jeweils vier Vertreter einer Seite und eine „Chairperson" Platz. Diese Person soll nur auf den korrekten Ablauf der Diskussion achten. Die restliche Lerngruppe sitzt hinter der jeweiligen Seite. Dabei besteht die Möglichkeit, dass Schülerinnen und Schüler aus dem Publikum für eine Zeit am Tisch Platz nehmen, um neue Argumente einzubringen.

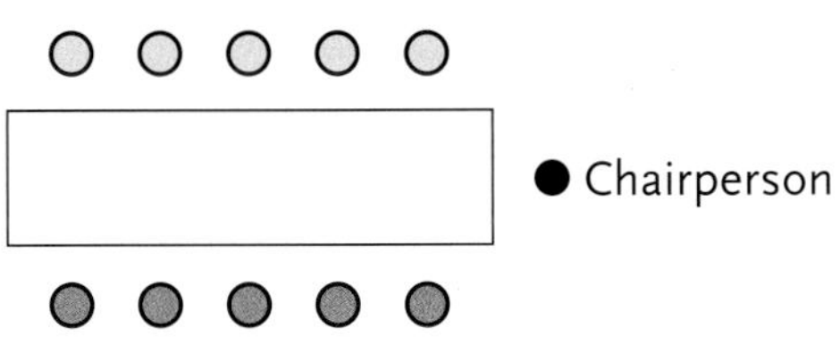

Im Anschluss kehren die Schülerinnen und Schüler in ihre jeweiligen Gruppen zurück und bekommen die Aufgabe, das bzw. die besten Argumente der Gegenseite herauszustellen. Dies erfordert eine zusätzliche Konzentration auf das Gesagte und stellt implizit auch noch eine positive gegenseitige Verstärkung da.
Abschließend kann der/die Unterrichtende die These noch einmal zur Abstimmung stellen. Das beschriebene Verfahren fördert die Mündlichkeit und stärkt das argumentative Kommunikationsverhalten auch im Hinblick auf mündliche Prüfungen und spätere berufliche Anwendungen.

Solutions

1. **In groups make a list of what Bill Maher says a) about France and b) about the USA. Compare the two lists. What are the main topics?** Activities p. 17

France	USA
- health care system that covers everybody - did not participate in war against Iraq - Enlightenment - mature - people vote (85 % turnout) - candidates are well-read - do not care about candidate's private life - nude beaches - privacy - high unemployment - immigrant problem - lowest poverty rate - lowest income-inequality rate - greenest country - lowest carbon dumping - lowest electricity bill - 20,000 miles of railroads that work - intellectuals - sex during the day - *menage à trois* - lingerie - the tongue (French kiss)	- first in military might - snotty billionaires - ranked 37th in health care - xenophobic - candidates are asked about evolution, prayer in school, abortion, stem cell research, gay marriage (i. e. controversial issues which are not particularly important) - a nation of 6-year-olds - dependent on Mideast oil - trolley at the mall (i. e. Americans are lazy) - bullets (weapons)

The comparison is mainly based on (a) political issues, (b) technology & the environment, (c) sex

2. **The text is written as an argumentative text giving arguments pro and contra an issue. On the other hand Maher uses a number of images and rhetorical devices that rather classify the article as a persuasive text. Begin by considering the following, then find more:**

Simile:	an ill-read xenophobic bumpkin like George W. Bush (l. 36 f.)
Hyperbole:	In France, everyone has a mistress. (l. 64) Costa Rica and Slovenia, which are both year away from discovering dentistry. (l. 16 f.)
Including 'we':	We are not first (l. 12) we think they're rude (l. 44)
Irony:	our wonderfully conceived and brilliantly executed war in Iraq (l. 5 f.) Noted military genius Donald Rumsfeld (l. 42)
Metaphor:	children of the French Enlightenment (l. 30) turned it into a musical called *the* Constitution (l. 30 f.)
Metonymy:	don't tell Alabama. (l. 39) Pierre Six-pack (l. 53) We have bullets. (l. 74) the tongue (l. 76)
Parallelism:	the lowest poverty rate ... the lowest income-inequality ... the greenest ... the lowest carbon dumping ... the lowest electricity bill (l. 69-72) France has ... We have ... It has ... We have ... France has ... We have ... (l. 72 ff.)
Quotation:	Voltaire wrote "men are born equal" (l. 40)
Rhetorical question:	You want a health care system that covers everybody and costs half as much? (l. 3 f.) You know who else did that? (l. 27 f.) What's the word I'm looking for? (l. 43)

What is the intended effect of these rhetorical devices?

The use of irony, the rhetorical questions and the change from first person singular to first person plural (including 'we') clearly shows the persuasive intention of the author. There are numerous direct addresses to the reader, trying to get him/her involved and to share the author's arguments, which are emphasized by metaphors and metonymies.

3. **In a fishbowl discussion (four in favour, four against) discuss the statement: "[...] it has been said that it [the Constitution] was written by geniuses so it [the country] could be run by idiots." (l. 32 f.)**

Pro	Con
- some of the Presidents were not qualified for the job, example: George W. Bush - for more than 200 years the Constitution has not been changed - 13 insignificant colonies developed into the leading nation of the world	- the Constitution had to be amended several times - the founders left many questions (i. e. slavery) open for later generations to solve - some regulations reflect the spirit of the time and are no longer fitting for today's world (i. e. Second Amendment)

Worksheet 1

Das Gedicht „I Hear America Singing" von Walt Whitman kann an verschiedenen Stellen der Reihe eingesetzt werden. Es ergänzt die patriotische Lyrik von Smith, Key, aber auch Emma Lazarus. Es fügt sich ebenso in die Erarbeitung des Konzepts des "American Dream" (nach James Truslow Adams in Chapter 2) ein.
Der Stil des Gedichts ist sehr einfach, wenngleich auch hier einige stilistische Elemente herausgearbeitet werden können. Aufgabe 1 zielt darauf hin, die übergreifende Metapher des gesamten Gedichts zu verbildlichen, indem die 13 genannten Personen- bzw. Berufsgruppen in die Amerikakarte eingesetzt werden: Sie alle repräsentieren „*e pluribus unum*" die Nation. Sie alle arbeiten und sind stolz auf die Früchte ihrer Arbeit. Bemerkenswert bei der Auswahl ist, dass es sich ausschließlich um manuelle Tätigkeiten handelt.
Die zweite Aufgabe kontrastiert die beiden doch sehr unterschiedlichen Gedichte von Smith und Whitman. Während Smith ein Loblied auf das Land, die Natur und selbstverständlich auch auf Gott singt, zeigt uns Whitman in Momentaufnahmen das arbeitende Volk als Repräsentanten der Nation.
Die dritte Aufgabe zielt auf eine Visualisierung des Textes. Die Kommentatorin vergleicht das Gedicht recht despektierlich mit einer Pepsi-Werbung; auch in Deutschland sind den Schülerinnen und Schülern sicherlich Kampagnen wie „Morgens halb zehn in Deutschland" (Knoppers) bekannt, zu denen es im Internet zahlreiche Parodien gibt. Ähnlich könnte der Videoclip entwickelt werden, wobei es hier dem Unterrichtenden freigestellt bleiben muss, den theoretischen Entwurf (*Storyboard*) konkret umzusetzen (hoher Zeitaufwand!).

Worksheet 1

I Hear America Singing

Walt Whitman (1860)

I hear America singing, the varied carols[1] I hear,
Those of mechanics, each one singing his as it should be blithe[2] and strong
The carpenter singing his as he measures his plank or beam,[3]
The mason[4] singing his as he makes ready for work, or leaves off work,
The boatman singing what belongs to him in his boat, the deckhand singing on the steamboat deck
The shoemaker singing as he sits on his bench, the hatter[5] singing as he stands,
The wood-cutter's song, the ploughboy's on his way in the morning, or at noon intermission or at sundown,
The delicious singing of the mother, or of the young wife at work, or of the girl sewing or washing,
Each singing what belongs to him or her and to none else,
The day what belongs to the day – at night the party of young fellows, robust, friendly
Singing with open mouth their strong melodious songs.

[1] **carol** a joyful song
[2] **blithe** happy, free from care
[3] **beam** a large, heavy piece of wood
[4] **mason** a worker who builds or works with stone
[5] **hatter** one that makes hats

Activities

1. Fill in the professions or groups the speaker names in the poem.

"I Hear America Singing"

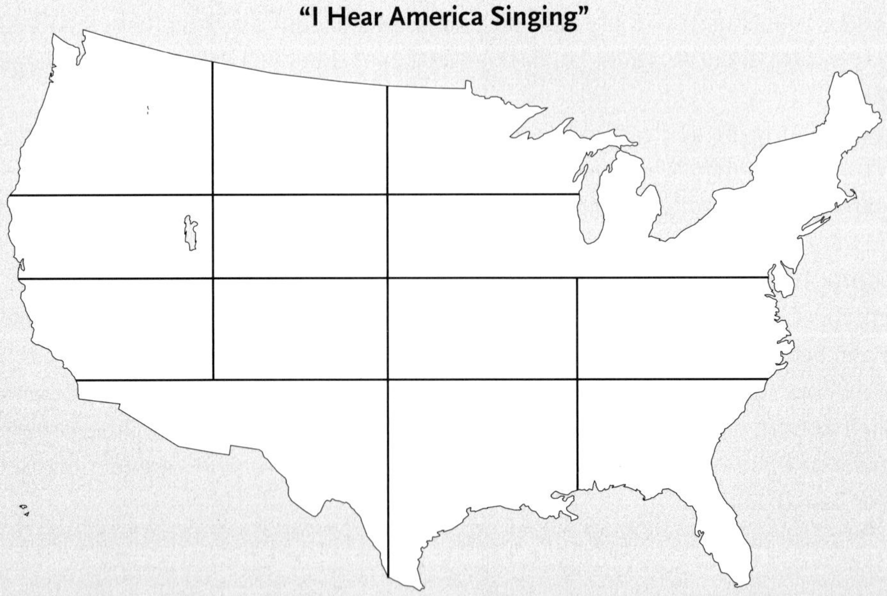

2. Compare Whitman's poem to Smith's *"America (The Beautiful)."* Name the main differences between the two poems.

Worksheet 1

3. In her literary blog Loren Webster states:
"I Hear America Singing" is one of those deceptively simple poems that still manages to manifest Whitman's poetic power. Of course, if it were written today people would probably merely consider it a Pepsi commercial cliché, it's that good.
(www.lorenwebster.net/In_a_Dark_Time/2002/07/25/i-hear-america-singing/)
Imagine you want to produce a video clip of the poem for YouTube. In groups sketch a storyboard of the visual rendering of this poem.
Would you add music? If yes, which song would you choose?

1	2	3	4
5	6	7	8
9	10	11	12
13	14	15	16

Worksheet 1 Solution

1. **Fill in the professions or groups the speaker names in the poem.**
   mechanics, carpenter, mason, boatman, deckhand, shoemaker, hatter, woodcutter, ploughboy, mother, young wife, girl, young fellows

2. **Compare Whitman's poem to Smith's "America (The Beautiful)." Name the main differences between the two poems.**
   The comparison should not be too formal. The most apparent difference is the lack of stylistic devices like rhyme, rhythm or metre. The lines are run-on lines, often too long to be printed in just one line. A contrast can also be found in the content. Referring to the tasks of the Smith poem it will become evident that Smith focuses on a description of the natural beauty of the country (→ semantic fields), whereas Whitman describes manual workers doing their daily jobs. Both poems have a common aspect in the notion of "singing", omnipresent in both texts, with the only difference that in Smith's text the speaker is the singer, and in Whitman's text the speaker listens to the labourers singing.

3. **Imagine you want to produce a video clip of the poem of YouTube. In Groups sketch a storyboard of the visual rendering of this poem. Would you add music? If yes, which song would you choose?**
   Individual answers; the storyboard has been limited to 16 frames so that all 13 groups plus three additional frames can be presented.

American Progress (Painting)

John Gast

Painter and work

John Gast's success as a painter is largely based on this one painting. Its nationwide public success was due to a publication by George Crofutt, who printed an engraving of the oil canvas together with a short interpretation, linking the painting to the doctrine of "Manifest Destiny."

Unterrichtsempfehlungen

Das Gemälde von John Gast findet sich in zahllosen Schulbüchern sowohl für das Fach Geschichte, als auch Pädagogik und natürlich Englisch. Die grundlegende Einfachheit der allegorischen Darstellung drängt eine Besprechung im Unterricht auf. Das Bild ist allerdings nur auf den ersten Blick selbsterklärend. Die komplexe Komposition mehrerer metaphorischer Einzelelemente macht eine genaue Betrachtung notwendig. Ein häufiger im bilingualen Sachfachunterricht verwendetes Verfahren der Zerlegung in einzelne, in sich bedeutungstragende Teile, bietet sich für die gründliche, schülerorientierte Erarbeitung an.
Hierfür sollte eine gute Farbfolienkopie des Gemäldes in sechs Teile zerschnitten werden (s. u.), welche von fünf Schülergruppen selbständig bearbeitet werden. Der Mittelteil des Bildes mit der Darstellung der *„Colombia"* bleibt zunächst ausgespart.
Die Schülerinnen und Schüler bekommen die Aufgabe, ihren Bildausschnitt genau zu beschreiben (nicht zu interpretieren). Dabei sollten auch Details gewürdigt werden (zur Analyse s. u. Activity 1). Es kann dabei sinnvoll sein, den jeweiligen Gruppen ein *„support system"* mit Vokabular (*buffalo, wagon, plough, stage coach* etc.) und zweisprachige Wörterbücher zur Verfügung zu stellen. Die nachfolgenden Präsentationen erfüllen Aufgabe 1. Eine sinnvolle Systematisierung könnte durch folgendes Tafelbild gewährleistet werden:

Group 1	Group 2	Group 3	Group 4	Group 5
Indians	Settlers	Hunters	Farmers	Townspeople

Wenn alle Elemente (bis auf die *„Columbia"*) abschließend geklärt sind (schwierig ist zum Beispiel die Beschreibung des Gewässers im fünften Ausschnitt, welches den Mississippi darstellen soll), wird die schwebende Columbia aufgelegt und in jetzt mehr lehrergeleitetem Unterrichtsgespräch analysiert. Die poetische Symbolgestalt des amerikanischen Kontinents, die ihren Namen vom Entdecker Christopher Columbus („Land entdeckt von …") abgeleitet bekommen hat, erscheint seit der Mitte des 18. Jahrhunderts in zahllosen Darstellungen (immer weiblich), Ortsnamen, Schiffsnamen etc. Ein Brainstorming bzw. eine kurze Internetrecherche wird eine Vielzahl von Referenzen zu Tage fördern (z. B. hieß die Astronautenkapsel bei der ersten Mondlandung Columbia, ein Spaceshuttle trägt den Namen, CBS ist Columbia Broadcasting System, Columbia Pictures hat die bildlicher Darstellung noch im Filmlogo usw.). Den Schülerinnen und Schülern könnte die Bezeichnung *Washington D.C.* geläufig sein, die je-

nen „*district*" bezeichnet, der dem *Federal Government* nach Artikel 1 der Verfassung zugestanden wurde. Dieses Gebiet wurde 1791 nach George Washington benannt und bekam den Zusatz „*District of Columbia*". Diese Hintergrundinformationen sind für deutsche Lernende sicherlich notwendig, um die weiße, schwebende Frauengestalt mit dem symbolischen Stern auf der Stirn nicht als „*angel*" zu missdeuten.
Erst jetzt kann das ganze Bild (am besten mit dem Schülerbuch) in seiner Komposition gedeutet werden. Es dominiert die Bewegung von rechts nach links, oder genauer, von Osten nach Westen. Auf der Gesamtdarstellung wird auch der halbrunde Horizont erkennbar, der den Kontinent wie eine eigene, in sich geschlossene Weltkugel erscheinen lässt. Ebenso wird die hell/dunkel-Teilung gut erkennbar.
Als Weiterführung der Interpretation wäre eine Internetrecherche zum Thema „*Manifest Destiny*" sinnvoll. Neben den vertrauten Webadressen (Wikipedia), ist der kurze Artikel von John L. O'Sullivan, der den Begriff prägte, lesenswert (www.mtholyoke.edu/acad/intrel/osulliva.htm). Interessant sind aber auch einige Beiträge auf der offiziellen Seite der amerikanischen Regierung, z. B. der Link:
http://history.state.gov
Eine vertiefende Beschäftigung (z. B. als Projektarbeit) könnte sich mit den verjagten Menschen auf der linken Bildseite beschäftigen (*Manifest Destiny and its impact on the Native American*).

Solutions

Activities p. 18

1. Have a look at the painting. Describe what you see (from left to right).

Indians running/taking flight
Horse pulling two women
Buffalo running
Open land, prairie
Dark clouds
Snow-capped mountains
A coastline

A prairie
A wagon pulled by oxen
A rider (Pony Express?)
A tribal dance
A wagon train
Snow-capped mountains
Dark clouds

Four men (hunters); one of them on a horse; the first and the second (behind the horse) carrying guns, the fourth a shovel and a pickaxe
Bushes
A stream/creek
On the left a bear; on the right a deer.

Two men (farmers) working in a field
A plough pulled by two oxen
A farmhouse; a fence
Trees and bushes

A wide plain
A river junction
Many ships on the water
A city and a bridge across the eastern part of the river
Three railroad trains running west
A telegraph line
A stage coach
The sky is a light grey colour
The sun is rising in the east

Columbia, carrying a schoolbook and pulling a telegraph wire, moving west

2. **Look up the word "progress" in a dictionary. Which meaning is illustrated by this picture?**
   1 the process of getting better at doing something, or getting closer to finishing or achieving something [...]
   2 to make progress [...]
   3 change towards a better society because of developments in science and fairer methods of social organization

   (*Longman Dictionary of Contemporary English*, 3rd Edition 1995)

   The third definition is illustrated by this painting.

3. **Imagine you had this picture on an overhead transparency and you didn't know which side was the top. How could you tell by the composition of the picture?**
   The painting clearly depicts the movement towards "The West", so the overall movement in the picture should be from the right side (east) to the left (west).

The Significance of the Frontier in American History

Frederick J. Turner (1893)

Author and text

Frederick J. Turner was born in Portage, Wisconsin in 1861. At that time the small town of Portage was a typical frontier town, the streets filled with woodcutters, trappers and Indians. He graduated from Wisconsin State University in 1884. Six years later he received his Ph. D. from Johns Hopkins University in Baltimore. In 1892 he was made full professor of History at his alma mater in Wisconsin. He held this position until 1910, when he was appointed to Harvard University. Professor Turner retired in 1922, leaving numerous disciples all over the American continent and thus influencing the interpretation of American history and democracy. He died ten years later in 1932.
The text has been taken from his most influential work. It was first given as a speech at a meeting of American historians and first printed in the proceedings of that annual meeting. It soon became extremely influential among intellectuals as well as politicians because it offered an explanation for the uniqueness of the American nation, its institutions and its history.

Unterrichtsempfehlungen

Turners Text ist für Schülerinnen und Schüler recht schwierig zu verstehen, da es sich hierbei um einen wissenschaftlichen Vortrag handelt, welcher ursprünglich nur für einen sehr kleinen, historisch gebildeten Kreis von Zuhörern geschrieben war. Der Text sollte zu Hause vorbereitet werden, ebenfalls ist es sicherlich sinnvoll, die historische Entwicklung (siehe Karte im Schülerbuch S. 21) zu besprechen, da Turner die Kenntnis über die territoriale Entwicklung bei seinen Adressaten voraussetzt. Karten sind als hochgradig verschlüsselte, nicht-lineare Texte nur selten Element des Sprachenunterrichts. Für bilinguale Kurse dürfte die Karte keine Schwierigkeiten bieten, für die anderen Kurse (und dies dürfte die Mehrheit sein), muss sie schrittweise rezipiert und besprochen werden.

An dieser Stelle wäre es sinnvoll, Referate zu den verschiedenen Territorien zu vergeben und sukzessive im Unterricht, am Besten vor der Behandlung des Textes, einzuholen. Es ist wichtig für die Schülerinnen und Schüler zu wissen, dass der Kontinent bei der Staatsgründung 1776 nicht vollständig „amerikanisch" war, ja dass nur ein kleiner Teil (der Osten in hellbraun) den neuen Staat bildete. Der Rest des Kontinents wurde auf sehr unterschiedliche Weise erworben, bzw. erobert. Die Begrifflichkeit (➔ *purchase, cession* bzw. *annexion*) der Karte hilft hierbei die amerikanische Westbewegung zu beschreiben und zu deuten.

Als erstes erfolgt der *„Louisiana Purchase"* (1803). Napoleon betreibt europäische Kontinentalpolitik und hat nur wenig Interesse an überseeischen Gebieten, da er seine Soldaten in Europa benötigt. Deshalb verkauft er zur Stärkung seiner europäischen Interessen ein Landgebiet, das fast dieselbe Größe hat wie die ursprünglichen Gründerstaaten. Nach Napoleons Niederlage bei Waterloo und dem Wiener Kongress bereinigen Großbritannien und die Vereinigten Staaten ihre Grenzen und Interessensgebiete im Norden (*„British Cession"*, 1818). Ebenso trennen sich die Spanier 1819 von kleineren Gebieten, welche sie militärisch gegen die neu entstehenden Nationalstaaten in Lateinamerika nicht mehr sichern können (in Louisiana und Colorado). Ebenso trennte sich Spanien gegen eine Geldzahlung von den bereits durch amerikanische Truppen besetzten Gebieten in Florida (*West Florida – East Florida Cession*, 1819). Die Amerikaner profitierten dabei von den noch instabilen Strukturen nach der napoleonischen Herrschaft in Europa. Zum Ende des amerikanischen Bürgerkrieges wird die ursprünglich spanische, nach einem Unabhängigkeitskrieg (➔ Film: *Fort Alamo*) jedoch inzwischen (seit 1835) eigenständige Republik Texas gegen schärfste Proteste, aber mit Zustimmung der Mehrheit der Bevölkerung annektiert.

Das *Oregon Territory* war ursprünglich von Spanien vereinnahmt worden. Im 18. Jahrhundert hatten sich aber rein anglophone (britische als auch amerikanische) Gemeinschaften herausgebildet. 1846 regelte der amerikanische Kongress vertraglich mit Großbritannien die Aufnahme dieses Siedlungsgebietes in die Vereinigten Staaten. Die Vereinigten Staaten führten seit der Übernahme der Republik Texas Krieg gegen Mexiko (1846–1848). Der *„Gold Rush"* von 1848 und die ständige Bewegung zur Pazifikküste hatten zu einer amerikanischen (anglophonen) Besiedlung des Gebietes geführt, sodass Mexiko zunehmend die Kontrolle über diese Gebiete verlor. Mexiko gab den Kampf verloren und trat das Gebiet an die Vereinigten Staaten ab. Die letzte größere Landerwerbung (*Gadsden Purchase*, 1853) war bereits durch das Konzept des transkontinentalen Eisenbahnnetzes bedingt. Der amerikanische Botschafter in Mexiko (James Gadsden) kaufte Mexiko Gebiete im südlichen Arizona und New Mexiko ab, um die südlichste transkontinentale Eisenbahnlinie bauen zu können. Der *Alaska Purchase* kam 1846 auf Betreiben der russischen Regierung zustande, welche sich in finanziellen Schwierigkeiten befand und die Begehrlichkeiten Großbritanniens auf den Westteil des Kontinents militärisch nicht zu parieren wusste. Man trat daher die Flucht nach vorne an und bot der amerikanischen Regierung das Gebiet zum Kauf an. Für 7,2 Millionen Dollar wurde der riesige Nordwestteil des Kontinents 1846 amerikanisch, ein Deal, der vom Kreml im 20. Jahrhundert bestimmt hundertfach verflucht wurde.

Während der Imperialismus der europäischen Großmächte fester Bestandteil des Geschichtscurriculums ist, bleibt der amerikanische Imperialismus zumeist undiskutiert.

Hawaii und seine Nachbarinseln waren von James Cook 1779 entdeckt worden. Hawaii ließ sich aber nicht durch die Engländer beherrschen, sondern wurde unabhängiges Königreich. Dabei nahm es aus strategischen Gründen mit den ungefährlich eingeschätzten Vereinigten Staaten bevorzugte Handelsbeziehungen auf und ermöglichte der amerikanischen Flotte auch die Stationierung von Kriegsschiffen in Pearl Harbor. Hawaii entwickelte sich in der Mitte des 19. Jahrhunderts zu einem wichtigen Handelspunkt im Pazifik. 1894 waren die Beziehungen der Bevölkerung zum amerikanischen Staat so weit entwickelt, dass die inzwischen mehrheitlich aus Einwandererfamilien bestehende Bevölkerung sich zur Republik erklärte, die aber schon vier Jahre später durch einen Beschluss des amerikanischen Kongresses, der die militärische Bedeutung der Inselgruppe (im spanisch-amerikanischen Krieg) völkerrechtlichen Fragen opferte, amerikanisches Territorium wurde. Diese Kenntnisse (mit Ausnahme von Hawaii) der amerikanischen Territorialentwicklung setzt Turner bei seinen Zuhörern selbstverständlich voraus.

Trotz dieser Schwierigkeiten bei der Rezeption sollte der Text nicht ausgelassen werden, da er einen wesentlichen Bestandteil des Konzepts des *„American Dream“* darstellt, indem er erstmalig die Besonderheiten der Entwicklung der USA von denen der europäischen Völker und Institutionen abgrenzt und daher bis heute Grundlage in der amerikanischen Geschichtsinterpretation geblieben ist. Theodore Roosevelt als auch John F. Kennedy (siehe Text Schülerbuch S. 26 ff.) rekurrieren bei ihren Konzepten auf genau diese Theorien.

Die Erarbeitung sollte mit einer ersten Strukturierung des vorliegenden Textes beginnen. Folgende Gliederung erscheint möglich:

Line	Headline	Function
1 – 11	The end of the frontier line	Opening his essay with a quote, stating a recent development
12 – 42	The development of American civilization and institutions	Establishing the historical basis for his thesis
43 – 55	The "Frontier Thesis"	Definition of the term "frontier"
56 – 68	The importance of the frontier for the development of America	Conclusion of his argument, leading to further speculation

Für fortgeschrittene Schülerinnen und Schüler bietet der Text zudem in sprachlicher Hinsicht ein hervorragendes Modell zum Abfassen eines argumentativen wissenschaftlichen Textes.

Die Aufgaben fokussieren auf jeweils einen der vier Teile, wobei der erste ausgespart wurde. Aufgabe 1 könnte in Gruppenarbeit als *Placemat* bearbeitet werden, wobei die Schülerinnen und Schüler zunächst ihr eigenes Verständnis niederschreiben und dann im Austausch mit den anderen zu einer gemeinsamen Deutung gelangen. Am besten legt man (s. u.) in die Mitte des *Placemat* eine Folie, sodass das Ergebnis für alle präsentiert werden kann.

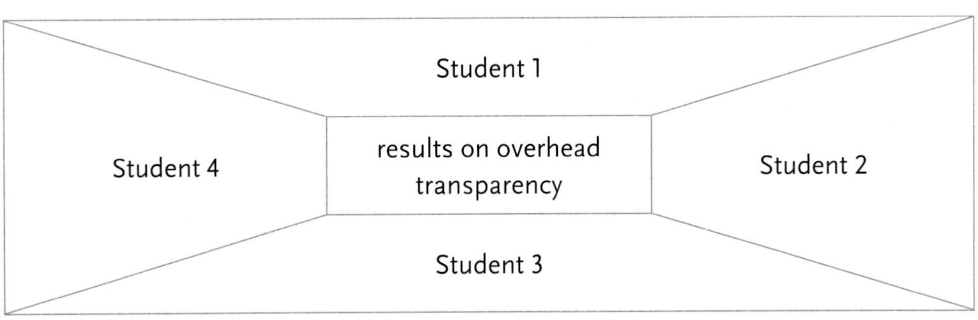

Der Kern von Aufgabe 2 liegt im dritten Teil des Textes. Dort greift Turner auf die offizielle Definition des *„Frontier“*-begriffs zurück (Z. 51 f.). Diese vorderste Linie der Zivili-

sation (demographisch definiert) hat er allerdings im vorhergehenden Text bereits als nur erste Stufe einer weitergehenden gesellschaftlichen Entwicklung beschrieben. Diese historische Entwicklung könnte im Tafelanschrieb wie in der Lösung zu Aufgabe 2 skizziert systematisiert werden:
Aufgabe 3 rekurriert auf historische Kenntnisse der Sekundarstufe I bzw. des Geschichtsunterrichts in der Einführungsphase der S. II (Jgst. 10 Gymnasium bzw. 11 Gesamtschule). Die griechische Kolonisation des gesamten Mittelmeer- (und z.T. auch Schwarzmeer-) Raumes fand ihren Höhepunkt zwischen 750 und 550 v. Chr. In dieser Zeit entwickelten sich, aus genau den Gründen, die Turner im Text nennt (Z. 59–62), Kolonien (immer als Polis) rund um das Mittelmeer. Den Schülerinnen und Schülern könnte zumindest Marseille, Nizza, Neapel, Tarent oder Tripolis als griechische Gründung bekannt sein. Die Aufgabe eignet sich weniger zur ausführlichen Erarbeitung in der Schule, sondern sollte als Hausaufgabe (Internetrecherche) gegeben werden.
Dasselbe gilt für Aufgabe 4, deren Inhalt zumeist Bestandteil des Geschichtskurses im ersten Jahr der Qualifikationsphase ist (Stichwort „Imperialismus"). Hier sollte gezielt Material zur amerikanischen Expansion des ausgehenden 19. und beginnenden 20. Jahrhunderts gesichtet werden. Die Karte im Schülerbuch (S. 21 *„U.S. Territorial Acquisitions"*) kann dabei Ausgangspunkt der Fragestellung sein. Wichtig ist es, den Lernenden zu verdeutlichen, dass das Erreichen des Pazifiks nicht das Ende der amerikanischen Landnahme bedeutete.

Solutions

Before you read p. 19

Describe the map. What do you notice about the settlement of the continent? Compare your findings with what you said about the painting above.

The settlement of the continent developed from the north-east coast towards the west. Until 1830 the Mississippi had been the "natural frontier" between the settlements in the east and the open prairies in the west. After 1830 steamboat commerce spread settlements on both banks of the river. The first bridge was built in 1856, the first railroad crossing a year later. This opened the land west of the Mississippi for settlers, who began moving westward.
All these elements (boats, bridge, cities, railroads, settlers etc.) are also depicted in the painting, thus telling the story of the westward movement.

Activities p. 21

1. **Turner writes: "The peculiarity of American institutions is the fact that they have been compelled to adapt themselves to the changes of an expanding people," (ll. 14ff.). Explain in your own words what he wants to express with this description.**

   In contrast to the established institutions in Europe, the American institutions underwent a rapid change from first a primitive organization in a new settlement (on the frontier line) with basic democratic features (electing a "responsible" leader) to a more complex organization in a growing town (as soon as it became part of the interior country) to the complex development of a state government (last step, becoming part of the Union). What Turner wants to express is that the Americans learned to develop their institutions in accordance with the growing population.

2. **The "frontier" had so far only been a mere demographical term. What are the reasons that this text changes it into a "historical concept"?**

Demographic	Sociological	Political/Historical
density of two or more (inhabitants) to the square mile (l. 52)		meeting point between savagery and civilization (l. 43 f.)
	primitive industrial society, without division of labor (l. 29 f.)	rise of representative government (l. 27 f.)
	manufacturing civilization (l. 30)	differentiation of simple colonial government into complex organs (l. 28 f.)

3. **Turner compares the American colonization to the colonization of the Mediterranean Sea by the Greeks. From your historical knowledge explain why he has chosen the Greeks and not the Romans.** Activities p. 22
The Greek settlements on the Mediterranean coasts all adopted the same political structures as their mother cities, thus exporting and establishing the early democratic system of the "polis" whereas the Romans conquered the land and kept the colonies in political dependence with Rome.

4. **Turner was right when he stated that "the first period of American history" had been closed. The 1890s mark the turning point for the United States towards a world power. Search information for important historical events concerning the USA in that decade.**
During the 1890s, the United States began to establish itself as one of the leading global powers, getting involved in conflicts and acquiring territories outside the North American continent. The Monroe Doctrine had already established the pan-American dominance of the US. It was once again strengthened by Theodore Roosevelt's foreign policy in Latin America. Beginning in the nineties the US confronted Spain over several issues, especially the rule of Cuba and Puerto Rico. Besides this war the Americans annexed Hawaii (1898) and began to seize the Philippine Islands, 7,000 miles west of the American continent but of high strategic importance with regard to China ("Open Door Policy").

The West

Alexander Keyssar

Author and text

The text has been taken from a popular American history book (*Inventing America*), written and edited by four leading American historians. Alexander Keyssar, co-author of this book, is the Matthew W. Stirling Jr. Professor of History and Social Policy and has received several distinguished nominations. He was also a finalist for the Pulitzer prize, the winner of the Los Angeles Times Book Award and the prize for Best Book by the American Historical Association (2000).

Unterrichtsempfehlungen

Der expositorische Text wurde wegen seiner konzisen Darstellung der Besiedlung des amerikanischen Westens gewählt. Der Text ist sprachlich ausreichend entlastet und sollte zur häuslichen Vorbereitung gegeben werden. Die wesentlichen Aussagen des Textes werden danach in der schulischen Arbeit durch das *Think* (HA) – *Pair* – *Share* Verfahren herausgearbeitet. Hierbei bietet sich eine gemeinsame Sammlung z. B. auf

einer Folie (s. u.) an, allerdings kann auch eine Aufbereitung durch die Schülerinnen und Schüler auf Postern (Museumsrundgang) sinnvoll sein, da eine Reihe von Fakten zum Verständnis nachfolgender Texte wichtig sind und eine Präsenz der Resultate im Klassenraum hilfreich wäre, um später leicht den Rückbezug zu leisten.
Die Lösung zu Aufgabe 1 reorganisiert den Text anhand von W-Fragen. Aufgabe 2 sollte durch eine (häusliche) Internetrecherche ausgearbeitet werden (ggf. auch Schülerreferate). Ein guter Einstieg ist dabei die Website der Library of Congress http://memory.loc.gov/learn//features/timeline/riseind/railroad/rail.html.
Die Theorien des *„popular wisdom"* sind breit dokumentiert und existierten in allen Kulturen. Besonders europäische Auswanderer brachten solche aber auch auf völlig unbekannte Kontinente (Amerika, Australien, Afrika) mit und erlitten damit häufig Schiffbruch. Eine individuelle Sammlung kann zu einer breiten Diskussion solcher vereinfachenden Theorien genutzt werden.
Die letzte Aufgabe verlangt einen Perspektivenwechsel und ist evaluativ angelegt (Anforderungsbereich III).

Solutions

Activities p. 24

1. Make a list of the most important facts given in the text. Discuss your findings with your neighbour and prepare a presentation for the whole class (think – pair – share).

When did the movement take place?
- after the Civil War (1864) and the completion of the railway lines (1869) (l. 1 f.)
- the population of the Pacific and Mountain States almost doubled in the 1870s and again in the 1880s (l. 6 ff.)
- in 1910 more than 25 million people were living west of the Mississippi (l. 9 f.)
- by 1900 all territories (except Oklahoma, New Mexico and Arizona) had been admitted to the Union as states

Who moved West?
- migrants west of the Mississippi were Scandinavians, Germans, Irish, Canadians (l. 15 ff.)
- migrants in the Southwest came from Mexico (l. 17)
- many migrants in California were Chinese (l. 18)
- African-Americans from the south fled, many to Kansas (l. 19)
- the majority were native born Americans (l. 21 f.)

How did they travel?
- settlers moved in family units along the same latitude (l. 23 f.)
- railroads made the movement easier (l. 24)

Why did they move West?
- they wanted land (l. 28)
  - claimed free land under the Homestead Act (l. 29 f.)
  - bought land from railway companies (l. 30 f.)

What happened after the first movement?
- they ignored the risks of the West (→ aridity) (l. 48)
- first farming was successful (l. 58 ff.)
- beginning in 1889, rains subsided, results were devastating (l. 63 ff.)
- many farmers (sometimes half of the population) left the region (l. 67)

2. Find out more about the railroads and their importance in the second half of the 19th century.

- 1862 Pacific Railway Act passed by Congress
- May 10, 1869 first transcontinental railroad finished
- railroad companies received millions of acres of public land from the government to sell and finance the construction

- railroad construction brought money and commerce into yet unsettled areas and stimulated the development of towns and cities - by 1900 four transcontinental railroads were built and the railroad system was completed

3. **"Rain follows the plow." Do you think the farmers were just stupid to believe in these "rules" or do ideas like that still exist today?**
   Considering the limited knowledge of meteorology and the strong religious beliefs of that time, such an idea doesn't seem naïve, especially since the farmers were proved right at first. Students might make a list of similar errors. A good start for research is: http://en.wikipedia.org/wiki/Obsolete_scientific_theory

4. **In a comment in *Newsweek* ("Democracy: If You Want to Free Your Country, First Liberate Its Land", Sept. 20, 2008) Fareek Zakaria argues that "The 1862 Homestead Act, which gave away 10 percent of the land in the United States, [converted] a backward peasant society into a modern capitalist one, which then creates the basis for civil society and democracy." Compare this thesis to the opinion given in the text.**
   The text clearly contradicts Zakaria's very positive opinion, as it states that "the typical westward migrant [...] bought land from a public land office" (l. 30). Keyssar even adds, with regard to the impoverished industrial workers, that "the Homestead Act never did offer a realistic escape" (l. 42f.). In Keyssar's opinion it therefore did not "free the country", as Zakaria states. Nevertheless nearly 2 million people claimed land under the Homestead Act, so it might still be seen as an incentive for the westward movement.

5. **Imagine you live in 1870 and you are an immigrant from Ireland. You have settled in Oklahoma and filed for land under the Homestead Act. Write to your cousin Patrick and tell him about your life trying to persuade him to come to America with his family.**
   Individual answer should include:

Student uses the form of a private letter
points out the facts to his cousin: - Free land - Easy to clear - Railroads facilitate travel - Many Irish settlers - ...

Telegraph Road

Mark Knopfler

Author and text

Mark Knopfler is a British musician, born in Glasgow August 12, 1949. With his brother he co-founded the band Dire Straits and wrote most of their songs. The song was composed in 1982 and first published on the album *Love over Gold*.

Unterrichtsempfehlungen

Ein Song sollte wie im täglichen Kontext üblich zunächst immer als Hörverstehenstext rezipiert werden. Dieser sehr lange Song (14:12 min) nimmt natürlich sehr viel Unterrichtszeit in Anspruch. Dennoch sollte es in den meisten Lerngruppen möglich sein, mit

wenigen Vorentlastungen (z. B. den Informationen aus Aufgabe 4) sowie der *pre-reading activity* (SB S. 24) den Song als reinen Hörverstehenstext zu dekodieren; es besteht im Unterricht allerdings die Möglichkeit, das lange Intro (2 min) auszublenden und den Song nach 9:38 min. anzuhalten, da die restlichen 5 Minuten rein instrumental sind.
Aufgabe 1 zielt auf diese erste Textverständnissicherung, die z. B. stichwortartig im Plenum an der Tafel erfolgen kann oder zunächst in schriftlicher Fixierung in Partnerarbeit. Danach sollte mit dem Songtext (Schülerbuch) weitergearbeitet werden. Aufgabe 2 ist nicht sehr umfangreich und kann in einer kurzen *think (write) – pair – share* Phase bearbeitet werden. Die Lernenden sollen erkennen, dass der Aufbruch (nach Westen) auch immer eine Flucht aus einer unbefriedigenden Situation sein kann. Abschließend wird der Text analytisch auf die wichtigsten stilistischen Elemente untersucht. Diese Aufgabe sollte keine zu große Unterrichtszeit beanspruchen und in die häusliche Bearbeitung gegeben werden, da es sich hierbei auch um eine individuelle Lernleistung handelt.
Die weiteren Aufgaben führen im Sinne des *task-based-learning* zu einer Erarbeitung der „*Road*"-Metapher, die ein wesentliches Element einer Vielzahl von Texten zum *American Dream* ist.

Solutions

Activities p. 25

1. Retell the history/story of "Telegraph Road" in your own words.

History of Telegraph Road
A long time ago – A man comes walking along a track – He makes a home in the wilderness, choosing what he thinks is the best place – He builds a cabin and he gathers/hunts so he can stay there through the winter – He begins farming
Later – Other travellers come down the track and settle there, too
The following years/decade(s) – A community is established, including • Churches • Schools • Lawyers and laws (rules) – The infrastructure develops • Railroads are built • Streets are constructed • The road is given a name
Time passes (hard times/a war) – Mining begins to exploit the ore found – The road is widened
Today – The road is busy (→ lots of people live there) – Factories are closed (→ unemployment) – People long to get away from this place to be free again

2. The singer (narrator) of the song offers a possibility how to end the misery. Do you think his suggestion is realistic?

The singer suggests that one can get away from the place by moving further on. He states that "[the birds] can always fly away from this rain and this cold" (l. 27). The movement westward stands for the hope of a better life. Nevertheless this is a doubtful dream today, as the West no longer fulfils all the hopes of those driving into the sunset.

3. Make a list of the most important stylistic devices used in the song. What effect do they create?

Activities p. 26

Alliteration	**S**ang a **s**ong (15) **R**olling **r**iver (17) **S**ome **s**eed that's been **s**owed (25) **S**igns **s**aying **s**orry (41)
Anaphora	From out of this darkness ... From these rivers ... From the anger ... (35 ff.)
Antithesis	I'd sooner forget but I remember those nights (30)
Assonance	Pl**ou**ghed up the gr**ou**nd (6) c**o**ld lake sh**o**re (6)
Interior rhyme	Sack on his back (2) Reap from some seed (25)
Metaphor	We're gonna have to reap from some seed that's been sowed (25) Life was just a bet on a race between the lights (31) Rivers of headlights (36) I've run every red light on memory lane (38)
Metonymy	The churches [...] the schools (9) The mines [...] the ore (13)
Parallelism	They never went further, they never went back (8) These rivers of headlights these rivers of rain (36) You had your head an my shoulder you had your hand in my hair (32)
Personification	Telegraph sang a song (15) My radio says (18)
Repetition	Then came the churches, then came the schools, Then came the lawyers, then came the rules Then came the trains (l. 9 ff.) Then came the mines, then came the ore Then there was a hard time, then there was a war (l. 13 f.)
Simile	So deep and so wide/Like a rolling river (16 f.)

Additionally the students' attention might be focused on the rhyme scheme, mainly pair rhymes, but with cross rhymes at the end of the song (l. 36–39). The symbolism of the "birds" (l. 26) could also be pointed out.
The apparent effect of some of the devices, especially the repetition, is to speed up the song, which is also enhanced by the music. The lack of rhyme at the end of the bridge (l. 20 f.), on the other hand, slows it down before the guitar solo.

4. Mark Knopfler wrote the song travelling along Highway 24 in Michigan. He tried to imagine the history of the road and the settlements from the early times until today. In a project work gather all the information you can find about "Telegraph Road". You may illustrate your poster with photos. Use the lyrics of the song as guidance.
The best starting point for this project is probably the Internet; Wikipedia has two special entries for "Telegraph Road" (one for the road, one for the song). The task is intended to build up the visual imagination of the students.

5. "Telegraph Road" is one of the longest songs (14:12 min) in pop history. Therefore it is not often played on the radio. A local radio station has asked for propositions for a special Fourth of July programme. Write an e-mail giving your reasons why this song should be played.
Dear DJ XY,
I heard your request for the special Fourth of July programme and I want to propose "Telegraph Road" by Dire Straits. I know the song is very long, but it tells the his-

tory of our country from the first settlers until today. It tells about the development of our communal structures, how our country was built. Although the song is not totally optimistic, I think we should face these problems and find a solution, even if it is just longing for new horizons, new frontiers. Besides the music is just fantastic; and the guitar solo is one of the most famous in pop history and the long instrumental ending underlines the dream of a better future.
Thank you in advance for playing the song,
Happy July 4th, yours
XYZ

6. **On its western end Telegraph Road is continued by the even more famous Route 66. Draw a mind map noting ideas as to why roads play such an important role in American popular culture.**
The mind map may start as follows, the students will add further ideas on their own:

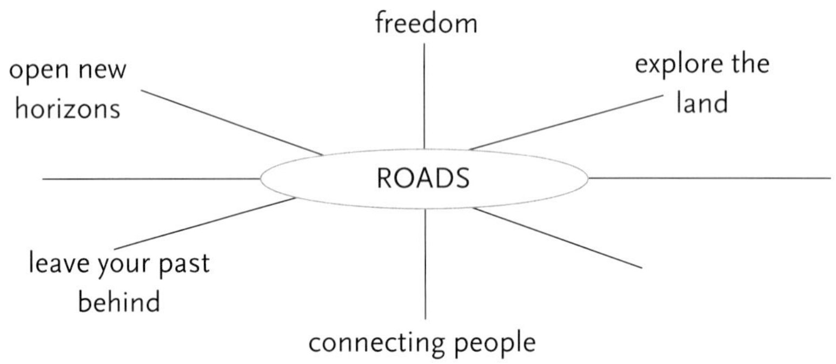

The "New" Frontier: Address at Rice University on the Nation's Space Effort

John F. Kennedy

Author and text John Fitzgerald Kennedy, 35th President of the United States, was born on May 29, 1917 in Massachusetts and was assassinated in office on November 22, 1963. JFK is one of the most brilliant, but also controversial, persons in 20th century history. On one hand his outstanding leadership in foreign and interior policy (Cuban Missile Crisis, Berlin Wall, Space Race, Nuclear Test Ban Treaty, Civil Rights, End of Racial Discrimination) come to mind; on the other hand he was responsible for the Bay of Pigs Invasion in Cuba and engaged the US in the Vietnam War. He started his political career in 1947, when he became a member in the House of Representatives; later in 1953 he was elected Senator of Massachusetts. In 1960 he ran for President and won against Richard Nixon and became the 35th President in January 1961. In his nomination speech (July 15, 1960) he had already sketched a wide spectrum of new ideas, coining the term of the "New Frontier". In his speech at Rice university in Houston, Texas, given on September 12, 1962 he further developed the concept of the New Frontier to include the "Space Race". At this moment the US was technically behind the USSR in their effort towards manned spaceflight. The Russians had launched the satellite Sputnik in 1957, an event that caused public shock about the lack of technical knowledge in the USA. In a speech given in a joint session of the two Houses in Congress on May 25, 1961 Kennedy had declared: "I believe that this nation should commit itself to achieving the goal, before this decade is out, of landing a man on the moon and returning him back safely to the earth." The speech at Rice University, near the new Houston Space Center, was intended to explain the details of the project, which most of his fellow Americans still considered impossible to fulfill.

Unterrichtsempfehlungen

Das Thema „Raumfahrt“ hat bis heute nichts von seiner Anziehungskraft verloren, wenngleich wir dem Ganzen heute etwas nüchterner gegenüberstehen. Die Ankündigung, innerhalb von weniger als 10 Jahren einen Menschen auf den Mond und sicher zurückzubringen, war 1961 reine Utopie, Science Fiction, die der Realität weit voraus war. In der Retroperspektive ist das Programm, das Kennedy in Gang gesetzt hat, aufgrund seines Erfolges richtig gewesen. Für die Zeitgenossen und Zuhörer im Auditorium in der Rice University war es das aber sicher nicht in jeder Beziehung. Den heutigen Schülerinnen und Schülern werden der Zugang zur Rede und die Bedingungen der Situation zunächst nur schwer zu vermitteln sein. Die Textanalyse des Aufgabenapparats beschränkt sich daher größtenteils auf die Möglichkeiten im Rahmen dieses Lehrwerks. Eine tiefere Erschließung bietet sich z. B. über den Film *„The Right Stuff“* an, nach dem gleichnamigen Roman von Tom Wolfe, der aber mit mehr als vier Stunden Spielzeit auch sicherlich nicht in den Rahmen eines Englischkurses passt. Es wäre allerdings denkbar, kurze Ausschnitte zur Einbettung zu verwenden. Ebenso vermittelt der Film *„Apollo 13“*, der den Lernenden vielleicht bekannt ist, einen guten Eindruck von den Problemen der jungen Raumfahrt. Eine weitere Möglichkeit bestünde in einem (längerfristig initiierten) Projekt, in dem eine kleinere Schülergruppe referieren könnte.
Das *„New Frontier“* Konzept von Kennedy umfasste primär soziale und innenpolitische Reformen; die Raumfahrt war nicht das dringendste, jedoch das symbolträchtigste Element in diesem Konstrukt der Erneuerung der amerikanischen Gesellschaft. Aufgabe 1 zielt in diesem Kontext auf eine Reorganisation des bisher zum *„Frontier“*-Begriff Erlernten. Dieser erste Zugang zum Text kann in häuslicher Erarbeitung, auch mit Rückgriff auf die bisherigen Texte, geleistet werden. Die zweite Aufgabe abstrahiert die Gründe für den Flug zum Mond.
Die Reden der beiden Kennedy-Brüder zeichnen sich durch eine rhetorische Brillanz aus, die bis zum ersten Auftreten von Barack Obama im öffentlichen Diskurs der Vereinigten Staaten verloren zu sein schien. Die dritte Aufgabe stellt sich allein aus diesem Grunde; zugleich bietet sich hier die Gelegenheit, das gesamte Analyserepertoire auszuschöpfen, da eine Vielzahl von rhetorischen Mitteln in diesem persuasiv angelegten Text vorhanden sind.
Die vierte Aufgabe benötigt eine umfängliche Vorbereitung und kann bei Zeitmangel weggelassen werden. Es ist auf jeden Fall zur Bearbeitung notwendig, die soziale und innenpolitische Situation sowie die außenpolitischen Bedingungen zu recherchieren. Kennedys Rede liegt ein Jahr nach dem Bau der Berliner Mauer und nur einen Monat vor der Kuba Krise (die zum Redezeitpunkt allerdings noch nicht zu erahnen war). Dahinter verbirgt sich auch die Frage, ob die bemannte Raumfahrt eher einer zivilen Organisation (NASA), oder der zu diesem Zeitpunkt technologisch gleichwertigen Air Force übertragen werden sollte. Vieles sprach für diesen zweiten, von der Sowjetunion beschrittenen Weg. Alle diese Fragen haben einen hohen Stellenwert, sind allerdings nicht beiläufig zu erarbeiten, sodass hier eine gründliche Vorplanung notwendig erscheint. Die *Hot Seat*-Diskussion (siehe auch Grieser-Kindel/Henseler/Klein, *Method Guide*, S. 102 f., sowie Schallhorn/Peschel, *Method Guide*, S. 67 f.) sollte in Gruppen (= Interessengruppen, z. B. „social/economical“, „educational“, „civil rights“ etc.) vorbereitet werden. Der Vertreter auf dem *Hot Seat* braucht sicherlich ein oder zwei *„shadows“*, um ihn/sie zu unterstützen. Insgesamt sollte die Gesprächsrunde auf 15 Minuten konzipiert sein, u. U. unter der Leitung eines Moderators.

Aufgabe 5 stellt es den Schülerinnen und Schülern nach einer genauen Reproduktion der Argumente frei, diese positiv befürwortend oder negativ ablehnend zu bewerten.

Solutions

Activities p. 28

1. **Contrast the old frontier to this new frontier: what do they have in common, what is different?**

The Old Frontier (F. J. Tuner)	The New Frontier (J. F. Kennedy)
The existence of an area of free land, its continuous recession, and the advance of American settlement westward explain the American development. (l. 9 f.)	Man in his conquest for knowledge and progress, is determined and cannot be deterred. (l. 4 f.)
A continually advancing frontier line, and a new development for that area (l. 33 f.) The frontier is the outer edge of the wave. (l. 43)	The exploration of space will go ahead, whether we join in or not. (l. 6)
	Space can be explored and mastered without feeding the fires of war. (l. 33 f.)
Each frontier did indeed furnish a new field of opportunity, a gate of escape from the bondage of the past. (l. 58 ff.)	New knowledge to be gained, and new rights to be won (l. 25 f.) Frontier of science and space (l. 58 f.) New hope for knowledge and peace (l. 82)

It should be pointed out that Kennedy repeatedly uses the word "progress" in his speech, using it exactly in the same sense discussed for the Gast painting (s. a.). Kennedy's frontier is less tangible, less concrete than Turner's clearly defined line. The repetition of "knowledge" as one aspect of the concept should be outlined. Kennedy at least points to the dangers of war, which Turner completely failed to mention, though the conquest of the West did not always advance peacefully.

2. **Draw a mind map collecting and organising all reasons Kennedy gives for space travel:**

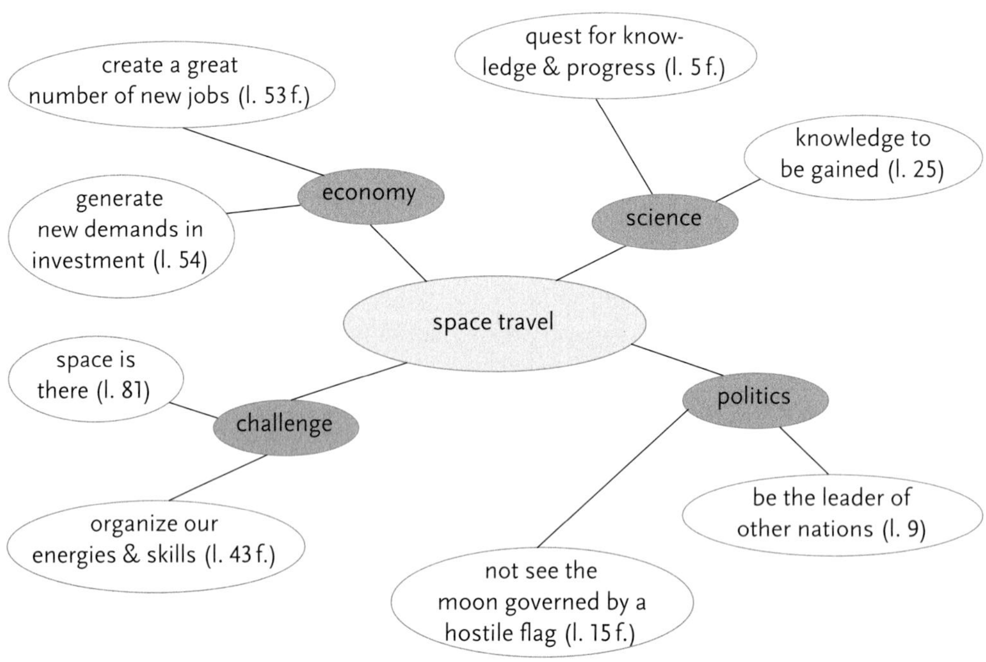

3. Examine the rhetorical devices Kennedy employs to convince the audience.
The speech is filled with rhetorical devices. The following list gives the most important but is far from being complete:

Alliteration	**f**eeding the **f**ires (l. 34) its **h**azards are **h**ostile (l. 37)
Anaphora	We choose to go to the moon. We choose to go to the moon ... (l. 41)
Antithesis	by a hostile flag of conquest, but by a banner of freedom (l. 16 f.) we shall not see space filled with weapons of mass destruction, but with instruments of knowledge and understanding (l. 17 f.) force for good or ill (l. 28) I do not say that ..., but I do say that (l. 31 ff.) one that we are willing to accept, one we are unwilling to postpone (l. 44 f.) not because they are easy, but because they are hard (l. 42 f.)
Assonance	the r**a**ce for sp**a**ce (l. 9)
Enumeration	There is no strife, no prejudice, no national conflict (l. 36) there is new knowledge to be gained and new rights to be won (l. 25 f.) and this city and this Sate, and this region (l. 56)
Including 'we'	history of our progress teaches us (l. 5) whether we join it or not (l. 7) [we, our & us are used more than 40 times throughout the speech]
Inversion	can we help decide (l. 30)
Litotes	a staggering sum, though somewhat less than we pay for cigarettes and cigars every year. (l. 65)
Metaphor	We set sail on this new sea (l. 25) this new ocean will be a sea of peace or a new terrifying theater of war (l. 30 f.) feeding the fires of war (l. 34) the heart of a large scientific and engineering community (l. 60 f.) As we set sail ... on the most hazardous and dangerous and greatest adventure on which man has ever embarked. (l. 83 ff.)
Metonymy	the eyes of the world now look into space (l. 14)
Parallelism	our leadership in science ..., our hopes for peace ..., our obligations to ourselves (l. 20 f.) to make this effort, to solve ..., to solve them ... and to become ... (l. 22 f.) without feeding ..., without repeating (l. 34) There is no strife, no prejudice, no national conflict (l. 36) furthest outpost on the old frontier of the West will be the furthest outpost on the new frontier of science and space (l. 57 ff.)
Personification	this country rode the first waves ... (l. 10 f.) the space effort itself, while still in its infancy (l. 53)
Quotation	"all great and honorable actions ..." (l. 2 f.) "Because it is there." (l. 79 f.)
Repetition	the first waves of ..., the first waves of ..., the first wave of ... (l. 10 ff.) we mean to be a part of it, we mean to lead it (l. 13 f.) we have vowed that we shall not see it ... We have vowed that we shall not see space filled ... (l. 15 ff.) not because they ..., but because they are ..., because that goal ..., because that challenge (l. 42 ff.) we're going to do it ... we ought to do the job ... this will be done ... It will be done during ... But it will be done. And it will be done before (l. 72–76)
Rhetorical Question	Why climb the highest mountain? Why, 35 years ago, fly the Atlantic? (l. 40)

4. In 1962 there were other problems that required a great deal of money. In a hot seat discussion question Kennedy on the space programme.
Some ideas could be

- Use of the space programme in general - Money could be used to solve social problems - Use of scientific findings uncertain; money should be used for universities and better education - Success of the programme is doubtful (see recent failures) - Risk of a Cold War in space - Military aspects - Risks - Costs will have to be paid by everyone (higher taxes?) - Will there be black astronauts? - Where will the new industries settle? (Texas and Florida only?)

5. As a journalist you have attended the meeting where Kennedy gave this speech. Under the heading "President Kennedy wants every American to spend 50 cents a week for space travel" write an article outlining the main arguments given in the text.
This is a combined task that (1) requires the reproduction of facts given in the text (AFB I) and (2) the evaluation and statement of a personal opinion (AFB III) blended in a re-creation-of-text exercise.

The student:	
names the most important arguments in favour of the space programme - Exploration of space will go ahead and America must be the leader - US wants prevent space from being filled with weapons of mass destruction - US have to become the world's leading space-faring nation - There is new knowledge to be gained and new rights to be won - Space industry creates a great number of new companies - Space industry generates new demands in investment and skilled personnel	AFB I
gives the fundamental financial aspects - Space budget stands at $5,400 million a year (1962) - Will rise by 20 % (from 40 cents per person per week to 50 cents per person per week)	AFB I & II
evaluates the risks and advantages - US lagging behind USSR - Unknown risks and hazards - Failure of the space programme - New jobs for qualified personnel - Creation of new industries - High stimulus for research/universities - Assuring a peaceful development of space	AFB III
states his/her personal opinion and gives reasons for his/her decision	AFB III

The American Dream

James Truslow Adams

Author and text

James Truslow Adams was an American historian. He was born in 1878 in New York and died in 1947 in Southport, Connecticut. After his studies at Brooklyn University and Yale he became an investment banker in 1900, working at the New York stock exchange. In 1912 he began a career in government institutions, serving the military intelligence service and representing the USA at the Paris Peace Conference after the First World War. Soon after that he took up writing and began his academic career, publishing several books on American and European history. His book *The Founding of New England* earned him the Pulitzer Prize in History in 1922. His most influential work is *The Epic of America* (1931), which has been translated into many languages, in which he coined the term "American Dream", understood as an ethical doctrine during the years of economic crisis, as opposed to the simpler meaning which is used today (see text below). His strong dislike of any communist theory is matched in his work by a complete rejection of consumerism. The book was an instant success and topped the bestseller lists in 1932. In the thirties Adams spent many years in London and published several bulky reference books on American History.

Unterrichtsempfehlungen

Der Text von Adams ist im Rahmen der Reihe unverzichtbar, zumal seine Aussagen die Stereotypen des „amerikanischen Traumes" von Reichtum und Wohlstand konterkarieren und ein wesentlich mehr der Aufklärung und damit den *„Founding Fathers"* verhaftetes Bild vermitteln. Eine gründliche Texterarbeitung ist absolut notwendig, um klischeehafte Antworten und Einschätzungen in Schülerarbeiten zu vermeiden und zu einer grundsätzlicheren Beurteilung des *„American Dream"* zu kommen. Dies ist auch der Grund für die persönliche Stellungnahme zu den von Adams vorgebrachten Konzepten („Betrifft mich ...").
Aufgabe 1 sollte als Hausaufgabe vorbereitet werden und dann im Unterricht in einer angemessen langen Partnerarbeit z. B. auf Folien gesichert werden. Vollständigkeit ist hierbei im Hinblick auf die nachfolgenden Aufgaben, die alle auf 1 basieren, unabdingbar. Daher sind auch Adams negative Definitionen („ ... is not ...") aufgenommen worden. Das Ergebnis der Lerngruppe sollte in einen „Mastertext" (Folie, oder besser noch Plakat) überführt werden, der im weiteren Verlauf als Rückbezug zur Verfügung stehen sollte.
Aufgabe 2 zieht prinzipiell noch einmal die Quintessenz aus den in Aufgabe 1 gewonnenen Erkenntnissen und ist am besten in Gruppenarbeit auf einer *Placemat* zu lösen, welche dann präsentiert und diskutiert werden kann. Die dritte Aufgabe ist nicht nur landeskundlicher Natur, sondern kann auch in Beziehung zu der eigenen deutschen Geschichte gesetzt werden. Das Thema steht in allen Geschichtsbüchern. Darüber hinaus sind einige mögliche Adressen für die Internetrecherche:

- Die wirtschaftswissenschaftliche Abhandlung von Professor Brad DeLong der University of California in Berkeley, die zahlreiche informative Diagramme anbietet und verschiedene wirtschaftswissenschaftliche Erklärungen für die Krise anbietet: www.j-bradford-delong.net/tceh/Slouch_Crash14.html
- Ein detaillierter Abriss des US Historikers Frank Smitha: www.fsmitha.com/h2/ch15wd.html
- sowie: http://en.wikipedia.org/wiki/Causes_of_the_Great_Depression

Die vierte Aufgabe führt in den Anforderungsbereich III und verlangt eine eigene Stellungnahme. Mögliche Einstiege in die Diskussion sind Beiträge deutscher Austauschstudenten in amerikanischen Zeitschriften, welche, besonders zur Zeit der Präsidentschaft Bushs, sehr kritisch Stellung zum *„Dream"* nehmen (*Nightmare*). Ein Beispiel findet sich unter: www.ndsmcobserver.com/2.2756/is-the-american-dream-becoming-a-nightmare-1.271222
Aufgabe 5 greift ein Element der *„Getting Started"*-Seite (Schülerbuch S. 4) auf. Wenn es dort bereits wie vorgeschlagen bearbeitet wurde, kann es hier wegfallen, ansonsten finden sich die Hinweise an angegebener Stelle oben.
Die letzte Aufgabe überträgt die erarbeiteten Konzepte auf Deutschland und verlangt eine

persönliche Auseinandersetzung mit den vermittelten Werten. Hier werden sicherlich auch Ergänzungen/Erweiterungen notwendig werden, da wir in Deutschland wesentlich sozialstaatlicher denken als dies in Amerika der Fall ist (siehe Diskussion über Präsident Obamas Vorschlag einer Krankenversicherung in den USA 2009). Die hier geforderte persönliche Stellungnahme sollte auch unter dem Aspekt der Förderung der Mündlichkeit gewertet werden und damit z. B. auf Teile der mündlichen Prüfung vorbereiten.

Solutions

Activities p. 30

1. With your partner make a list of the major elements of the "Dream", as Adams defined them.

The American dream	Not the dream
The dream of a land in which life should be better and richer and fuller for every man, with opportunity for each according to his ability or achievement (l. 3 ff.)	
	not a dream of motor cars and high wages (l. 7 f.)
a dream of social order in which each man and each woman shall be able to attain the fullest stature of which they are innately capable. (l. 8 ff.)	
be recognized by others for what they are, regardless of the fortuitous circumstances of birth position (l. 10 f.)	
	not ... dream of merely material plenty (l. 13)
a dream of being able to grow to fullest development as man and woman, unhampered by the barriers which had slowly been erected in older civilizations (l. 15 ff.)	
if the American dream is to be reality, our communal spiritual and intellectual life must be distinctly higher than elsewhere (l. 22 f.)	classes and groups have their separate interests, habits, markets, arts, and lives. (l. 24 f.)
	become stark realists, become once more class-conscious, and struggle as individuals or classes against one another (l. 26 f.)
those on top, financially, intellectually, or otherwise, have got to devote themselves to the "Great Society" (l. 28 f.)	
those who are below in the scale have got to strive to rise, not merely economically, but culturally (l. 29 f.)	
The very foundation of the American Dream of a better and richer life for all is that all, in varying degrees, shall be capable of wanting to share in it. (l. 32 ff.)	[not] "keeping up with the Joneses" (l. 35 f.)
	There is nothing in a fortune merely in itself or in a man merely in himself (l. 36 f.)
	no longer to build bigger (l. 42 f.)
to build better (l. 43)	
a genuine individual search and striving for the abiding values of life. (l. 45 f.)	

2. **"If we are to make the dream come true we must all work together, no longer to build bigger, but to build better." (l. 42 f.). Outline the main idea behind this challenge.**
   The main idea outlined in the findings (task 1) clearly opposes "material plenty" (bigger) to higher "moral values" (better). This means that every citizen is asked to share in the building of America, so that the society as a whole is set on a higher level. It is important that students point out that the American Dream is not focused on materialistic values; the rise from "dishwasher to millionaire" is only a success in view of the American Dream if the individual has succeeded in rising to a higher intellectual or moral life, serving the common interest of the "Great Society."

3. **Gather facts about the economic situation in the USA in 1931. Why would someone write a treatise about "The American Dream" at that time?**
   One of the reasons for the breakdown of the stock markets in 1929 was the overestimation of share values ("stock market bubble"). During 1931 world trade collapsed; in contrast to the latest crisis (2008) the US government did not use bailouts to help bankrupt banks and individuals, as most economists of the time advised inaction during the downslide. As a consequence manufacturing went down to 44% in 1931 (compared to pre-Depression in 1929) and a considerable percentage of the working population lost their jobs. President Hoover tried to restart the economy with some major projects, one being the "Boulder Dam" (today named "Hoover Dam") near Las Vegas, the biggest dam project ever undertaken at that time. But it was Franklin D. Roosevelt, winning the presidency over Hoover in 1932, pledging a "New Deal" in the distribution of the national wealth, who succeeded to redress the American economy.
   As the economy nosedived and the material losses touched all parts of the population, a new concept of the "Pursuit of Happiness", which was not based on material but on moral values, seemed necessary, calling everybody to collective efforts for a great society. The striving for material gains had led to the crash, so Adams based his new concept on deeper inspirations.

4. **Prepare and stage a debate about the question whether or not America is closer to the attainment of the "Dream".**
   Individual answer; the list (positive and negative) of task 1 could serve as a starting point for the discussion.

5. **There is a lottery for Green Cards every year. This proves that the "Dream" is still attractive for many people outside the USA. Are you tempted to emigrate to the USA or not? Give reasons.**
   The answers here can only be individual, as many factors have to be taken into consideration.

6. **Which components of Adams' concept would you adopt as guidelines for a "German Dream"? In groups make a poster and explain your choices.**
   Once again the list (task 1) will be used as a guide. The elements might be continued with aspects like

- integration,
- religious freedom
- elements of our social/welfare state
  - health insurance
  - pensions/social security

Mercedes Benz

Janis Joplin

Author and text

Janis Joplin was born on January 19, 1943 in Port Arthur, Texas. Growing up she was considered a social outcast at school. After graduation she began studies at the University of Texas in Austin, but never finished. She left Texas and found a new home in Haight-Ashbury in San Francisco. In 1964 she began recording songs with a local guitarist. At this time she became addicted to heroin, an addiction that would end her short career only six years later. Her San Franciscan friends tried to help her and sent her home to Texas, where, for a short period, she led a normal life, performing as a folk singer in local clubs and even enrolling to study sociology at Lamar University in Beaumont, Texas. In 1966 she moved back to San Francisco, becoming a notorious member of the newly forming Haight-Ashbury hippie community. She was discovered by the promoter of a psychedelic blues group named Big Brother and the Holding Company and she began touring the US with them. Their first album was released in 1967. The band had some very successful appearances at renowned concerts, such as Monterey (1967) and in 1968 the Wake for Martin Luther King in New York, joining stars like Paul Butterfield and Jimi Hendrix on stage. Joplin's powerful voice and her impact on the audience led to a kind of fame which the fragile person could not handle. Drugs and alcohol became her constant needs, so that her unfortunate appearance on stage at Woodstock (1969) had to be cut from the film. With her new band The Kozmic Blues she toured America and Europe. Despite their success the band broke up the same year and Joplin tried (for the last time) to get clean, taking a long vacation trip to South America. After returning in 1970 she went on tour with a newly created band called The Tilt Boogie Band. After some live appearances the band began recording the album *Pearl* in September 1970. "Mercedes Benz" is her last recording, done without the band as an a cappella piece in just one take. She was found dead in her hotel three days later. The album *Pearl* released posthumously in 1971, became her biggest success with her only number one hit single "Me and Bobby McGee". The song "Mercedes Benz" has been covered by numerous singers and bands, including Elton John, Taj Mahal and Guns N'Roses.

Unterrichtsempfehlungen

Der Song von Janis Joplin hat trotz seines schlichten Arrangements absolute Ohrwurmqualität. Jeder, der ihn einmal gehört hat, erinnert sich daran. Dies könnte, trotz der zeitlichen Distanz, auch bei unseren heutigen Schülerinnen und Schülern noch der Fall sein. Die Simplizität des Textes mit seinen Redundanzen macht diesen Song zu einer idealen Hörverstehensübung. Aufgabe 1 ist als Textverstehensaufgabe nur so zu verstehen, mit Textvorlage wäre sie eine völlige Unterforderung für jeden Oberstufenkurs. Der Song sollte mit dieser Aufgabenstellung (und geschlossenen Büchern) einmal vorgespielt werden. Nach der Sammlung der Ergebnisse (s. u.) an der Tafel kann ein weiteres Mal vorgespielt werden und die letzten Verständnisschwierigkeiten (z. B. „*Dialing for Dollars*") geklärt werden. Auch Aufgabe 2 sollte noch in rein auf dem Hörverstehen basierender Rezeption bearbeitet werden. Erst danach kann auf den Text im Schülerbuch zurückgegriffen werden. Eine weitere kreative Übung bietet sich an dieser Stelle an, indem man die Lerngruppe auffordert, weitere eigene Strophen zu schreiben, in welchen sie ihre eigenen Wünsche in dieser Form äußern, also:

- Oh Lord, won't you buy me a trip to LA ...
- Oh Lord, won't you buy me a smart cell phone ...
- Oh Lord, won't you buy me a ...

Diese kreative Übung ermöglicht den Lernenden sich in die Rolle der Sprecherin/Sängerin hineinzuversetzen.
Aufgabe 3 kann als kurze Kartenabfrage oder als *Placemat*-Diskussion bearbeitet werden.
In Aufgabe 4 wird ein weiteres Mal auf die wichtigen Aspekte des Adams-Textes zurückgegriffen, die hier noch einmal mit den Klischees vom *American Dream* kontrastiert werden. An dieser Stelle bekommt die zweite Spalte des oben erarbeiteten Textes besondere Bedeutung, weil eben genau diese Faktoren, die Adams so vehement ablehnt, als erstrebenswert genannt werden. Für die gesamte Reihe ist es essentiell, dass die Schülerinnen und Schüler verstehen, dass es im *American Dream* nicht um materiellen Gewinn geht, sondern dass andere Dinge wesentlich wichtiger sind.
Die letzte Aufgabe beinhaltet einen Widerspruch: der Song persifliert in sarkastischer Weise die Klischees des *Dream*. Ein Einsatz dieses Songs widerspräche also der Werbeintention („*buy a Mercedes Benz*"). Genau dies hat aber Mercedes 1995 getan, als sie den Song in das Zentrum einer Werbekampagne gestellt haben. Das Commercial ist heute noch leicht im Internet zu finden, z. B. unter: www.youtube.com/watch?v=AjTuRDW2NHY
Viele namhafte Musiker haben sich vehement gegen die Kommerzialisierung des nach 25 Jahren nur noch unzureichend copyright-geschützten Songs gewendet und argumentiert, Janis Joplin hätte dieser Verwendung niemals zugestimmt (siehe hierzu z. B.: www.pophistorydig.com/?tag=janis-joplin-mercedes-ad).
Der Commercial hat die Verkaufszahlen von Mercedes in den USA allerdings signifikant in die Höhe schnellen lassen, was belegt, wie professionell Marketingstrategen alte Reminiszenzen und Sympathien umlenken können, sodass die Generation der Baby Boomers ihre Ideen der ausgehenden Sixties nun auf positive Gefühle für das „un-amerikanische" Auto übertragen konnten, und die eigentliche Textaussage ganz einfach ignorierten. Die Vertiefung dieses Aspekts im Unterrichtsgespräch hätte deutlich positiv erziehenden und bewusst medienkritischen Charakter, denn dasselbe gilt für jede Generation und den Missbrauch ihrer Idole.
Auch in Deutschland wurde der Song in der Werbung eingesetzt, allerdings zuerst durch den Mitbewerber BMW bei der Vorstellung des Z3 Roadster: www.youtube.com/watch?v=-D3a49yjevA
2010 folgte dann bei der Einführung des neuen Mercedes-Sportwagens eine Plakat-/Anzeigenkampagne, in welcher nur der neue Flügeltürer und das Textfragment „*Oh Lord ...*" erschienen.
Die Diskussion der relevanten Aspekte dient an dieser Stelle zum einen der Umwälzung der elementaren Konzepte und Thesen des *American Dream*, zum anderen ermöglicht sie allen Lernenden einen Impuls zur eigenen Stellungnahme und Reflexion. Die Zeit für diese mündliche Sprachförderung sollte angesichts der fachdidaktischen Diskussion nicht zu knapp bemessen werden, da hier Begründung eigener Meinung und Reaktion auf kontroverse Aussagen geübt werden können.

Solutions

1. List what the singer asks for in each stanza.

Activities p. 31

1st stanza – a Mercedes Benz
2nd stanza – a color TV
3rd stanza – a night on the town
4th stanza = 1st stanza

2. **What type of text does the speaker use to ask for the fulfilment of her demands? Do you think this is adequate?**
The speaker uses the form of a prayer, addressing her demands to God. It is probable that many people do such things, though in Christian belief you should not ask for worldly things in your prayer.

3. **What do you think is the intended message of this song?**
The message is an ironic one, portraying American society as pursuing material happiness. Coming from the South Janis Joplin had certainly heard prayers said at the table before meals, and some of these may have included very earthly demands, like a pay rise or the success of a football team. So she plays on America's common Christian attitudes as well as greed for materialistic gain. Her song derides the consumerism inherent in American society.

4. **With a partner discuss whether the message of this song is in accordance with Adams' theory of the American Dream.**
The song, in its literal sense, is not in accordance with Adams' theory, because it contradicts what he says:
– not a dream of motor cars and higher wages
– not a dream of merely material plenty
– [not] "keeping up with the Joneses"
There are no moral values ("communal spiritual and intellectual life must be distinctly higher") mentioned in the text. On the other hand, Janis Joplin mocks these stereotypes and gives all these demands an ironic twist. So the intended message of Joplin's sarcastic song is well in accordance with Adams'.

5. **Being responsible for Mercedes Benz advertising in the USA, would you use the song for a radio/TV spot? Discuss with a partner and present and justify your decision in class.**
Students may find out that the answer to this question has been given by the German automakers themselves: in 1995 they used the song to promote a new Mercedes car in the USA and came out with a very successful campaign.
The question still has to be discussed, because the sarcastic prayer for material happiness might well backfire and hamper the campaign. Critical buyers might be disturbed by the use of this song, clearly rooted in the hippie movement of the sixties. On the other hand one could argue that today's audiences know nothing about the background of the song and are attracted by the catchy tune. One could even point out that some former hippies are well-established today and might drive a Mercedes. For maximum effect, one would only use the first stanza.

Worksheet 2

Der Song „Wild West Hero“ von Jeff Lynne ist eine unkritische Paraphrasierung uramerikanischer Klischees und gehört in seiner Aussage in die Trivialitäten des Pops. Seine Darstellung des *„American Dream,“* der Ritt in den Sonnenuntergang (nach Westen) und die damit assoziierte Freiheit sind Bestandteil unzähliger Filme (Western) und von Werbung (Marlboro). Die ersten Zeilen des Songs beschreiben ein Wunschdenken, einen Eskapismus aus einer nicht zufriedenstellenden Welt, das Bedürfnis, aus dem Alltagstrott in das Leben eines Helden zu schlüpfen, der mit seiner Umwelt („ride the range,“ „I'd ride the desert sands and through the prairie lands“) und anderen („the Indians' friend“) in Harmonie lebt und dort sein Glück („my western girl“) und existentielle Befriedigung („we need you here“) findet.

Die Erarbeitung setzt daher auch bei den Stereotypen ein und fragt in den ersten beiden Aufgaben die Sicht der Lernenden ab.
Die dritte Aufgabe bietet eine kreative und produktive Beschäftigung mit dem Songtitel als *pre-listening activity*. Es ist unwahrscheinlich, dass die Schülerinnen und Schüler den Song kennen, da er nicht mehr im Radio gespielt wird (außer auf Country-Sendern für Trucker).
Der Song ist leicht zu verstehen, nur *„range“* müsste vorentlastet werden (könnte mit *„Ranch“* verwechselt werden). Deshalb sollte er zunächst als reine Hörverstehensübung genutzt werden. Die Lernenden sollen hierdurch dazu angehalten werden, etwas genauer hinzuhören, was die Aussage eines Liedes ist, und damit auch im privaten Musikkonsum zu einer kritischeren Haltung erzogen werden (*media literacy*).
Die fünfte Aufgabe fasst noch einmal wesentliche Elemente des zweiten Kapitels des Schülerbuchs zusammen und fordert zu einer kritischen Reorganisation (AFB II) und Stellungnahme (AFB III) auf. Die Präsentation sollte in Gruppen vorbereitet werden und als Gegenüberstellung auf Postern erfolgen.
Die letzte Aufgabe ist sehr umfänglich und daher als Projekt konzipiert. Hier bleibt den Schülerinnen und Schülern freier Gestaltungsraum; sie können den Song mit klischeehaften Bildern illustrieren, sie können aber auch durch Kontrastierung (ähnlich wie *„Wonderful World“* in *„Good Morning Vietnam“*) eine kritische Verfremdung erreichen.

Worksheet 2

© Konrad Wothe/LOOK-foto

Activities

1. Look at the picture.
- Describe what you see.
- Would you like to be the person on the horse? Explain why.
2. What comes into your mind when you see such a picture? Draw a mind map.

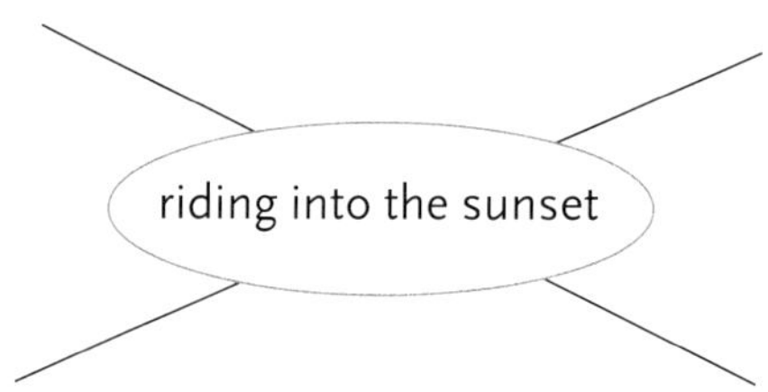

3. The following song is called "Wild West Hero." Design a concept (pictures/text) for a poster with that title.
4. Listen to the song and take notes to be able to summarize the main elements.
5. Compare the message of the song to what you have learned about the American West so far. Discuss your findings and prepare a presentation of your results.
6. Project: There are many videos produced by YouTube users illustrating the message of a song as they see it. Design a storyboard for such a video clip.

Worksheet 2

Wild West Hero

Jeff Lynne

Wish I was, yeah, a Wild West hero.

Sometimes I look up high
and then I think there might
just be a better life.
Away from all we know,
That's where I wanna go,
out on the wild side
and I wish I was,
o-oo-o-oh, a Wild West hero.

Ride the range[1] all the day
till the first fading light,
be with my western girl
round the fire, oh, so bright.
I'd be the Indians' friend,
let them live to be free,
ridin' into the sunset,
I wish I could be.

I'd ride the desert sands
and through the prairie lands,
tryin' to do what's right.
The folks would come to me,
They'd say, we need you here.
I'd stay there for the night.
Oh, I wish I was,
o-oo-o-oh, a Wild West hero.

Ride the range all the day
till the first fading light,
be with my western girl
round the fire, oh, so bright.
I'd be the Indians' friend,
let them live to be free,
ridin' into the sunset,
I wish I could be.

Oh, I wish I was,
o-oo-o-oh, a Wild West hero.
I wish I was,
o-oo-o-oh, a Wild West hero.
Oh, I wish I was,
o-oo-o-oh, a Wild West hero.
Wish I was,
o-oo-o-oh, a Wild West hero.
Wish I was,
o-o-oo-o-o-o-oo, a Wild West hero.

[1] **range** *Gebirgszug*

Worksheet 2 Solution

1. **Look at the picture.**
   – Describe what you see.
   – Would you like to be the person on the horse? Explain why.
   A man riding into the sunset
   Individual answers

2. **What comes into your mind when you see such a picture? Draw a mind map.**

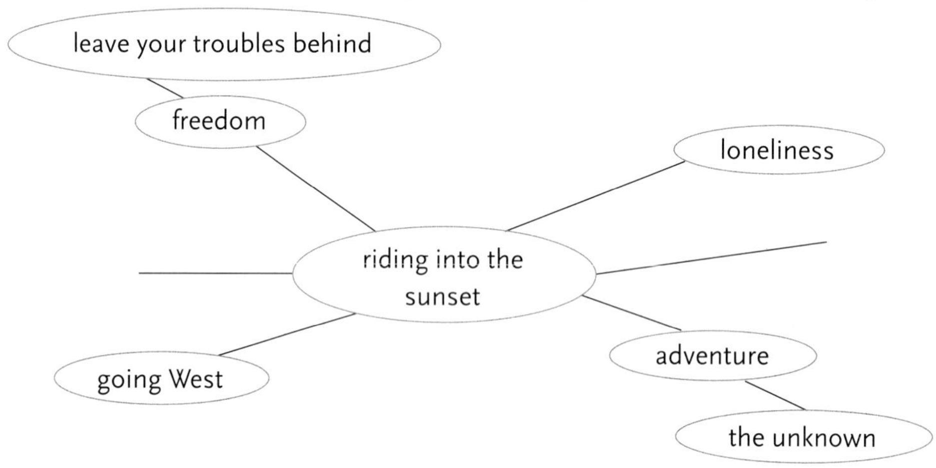

   Individual answers

3. **The following song is called "Wild West Hero." Design a concept (pictures/text) for a poster with that title.**
   The poster should show "a hero" (individual concept); the typography could consist of typical "Western" typefaces, as used in movie titles.
   Individual solutions

4. **Listen to the song and take notes to be able to summarize the main elements.**

1st stanza: – a better life – away from all we know – out on the wild side – be a Wild West hero
Chorus – ride the range all the day – be with my western girl – be the Indians' friend – let them live to be free – riding into the sunset
2nd stanza – riding the desert sands – riding through the prairie lands – do what's right – folks come to me – be needed

Worksheet 2 Solution

5. Compare the message of the song to what you have learned about the American West so far. Discuss your findings and prepare a presentation of your results.

Wild West Hero	The True West
1st stanza – a better life – away from all we know – out on the wild side – be a Wild West hero	– Life was difficult, "The West", SB p. 23, l. 56 ff. – Civilization followed the settlers, "Frontier", SB p. 20, l. 19 f., "Telegraph Road", SB p. 25, l. 24 f.
Chorus – ride the range all the day – be with my western girl – be the Indians' friend – let them live to be free – riding into the sunset	– Indians were killed by the settlers, "American Progress", SB p. 18
2nd stanza – riding the desert sands – riding through the prairie lands – do what's right – folks come to me – be needed	– "one mile to hell", "The West", SB p. 24, l. 70 – "then there was the hard times, then there was a war", "Telegraph Road", SB p. 25, l. 14

6. Project: There are many videos produced by YouTube users illustrating the message of a song as they see it. Design a storyboard for such a video clip.
Individual answers

In the Wake of a Dream

Immigration from 1850 to 2000

Source of Data

As the Constitution of the United States stipulates that the population should be counted at least every ten years to determine the number of members from each state in the House of Representatives (see *Constitution of the United States*, Article 1, Section II, Clause 3), an agency had to be founded to this purpose. This led to the establishment of the Bureau of the Census, responsible for gathering all sorts of demographic data. The US Census has always been one of the most modern in the world, using electric counting machines, designed by Herman Hollerith, as early as 1890. A wide array of demographic and economic data can be found at www.census.gov

Unterrichtsempfehlungen

Die „Einheitlichen Prüfungsanforderungen in der Abiturprüfung" (EPA) sehen als eine Aufgabenart „Sachtexte, Statistiken, Diagramme, Cartoons usw. aus Zeitungen, Zeitschriften, allgemein verständlichen ökonomischen Werken" (S. 24, Beispiel auf S. 27) vor. Die Versprachlichung statistischer Daten ist eine unabdingbare Kompetenz in vielen Berufszweigen (Wirtschaftswissenschaften; Naturwissenschaften etc.). Um die Kenntnisse in diesem Bereich zu festigen, wurden hier zur Einführung in den Themenkomplex zwei Graphiken (ein *bar chart* und ein *graph*) eingebracht. Ausführliches Besprechungsvokabular wird auf dem Arbeitsblatt 3 zur Verfügung gestellt.
Besonders die erste Graphik (*Immigration from 1850 to 2000*) lässt neben den Aufgabenstellungen im Schülerbuch eine Reihe weiterer Fragestellungen zu. Das für die Besprechung notwendige Vokabular findet sich auf **Worksheet 3** am Ende dieses Kapitels.
Die untenstehenden Lösungen beschränken sich auf die begrenzte Fragestellung der Aufgaben und können natürlich so im Unterricht bearbeitet werden. Wenn genügend Zeit ist kann hingegen auf der Basis des Arbeitsblattes eine wesentlich ausführlichere Versprachlichung der Grafiken erfolgen. Hierbei wäre an eine Präsentation von Gruppenergebnissen mit der *Bar Chart* bzw. dem *Graph* auf Folie zu denken, wie sie in beruflichem Umfeld zum Tagesgeschäft gehört. Dabei kann auch zugleich das notwendige Besprechungsvokabular umgewälzt werden. Aufgabe 3 eignet sich als Hausaufgabe zum individuellen Training. In Aufgabe 4 wird eine eigene statistische Erhebung notwendig, die z. B. in Form einer *Pie Chart* visualisiert werden könnte. Die letzten beiden Aufgaben gehören in den Anforderungsbereich II, da hier Reorganisation von Ergebnissen zu einer neuen Schlussfolgerung erwartet wird. Die letzte Aufgabe kann als *Placemat Activity* zu einer Präsentation von Thesen führen, die als Basis für weitere Texte dieses Kapitels in Form von Postern festgehalten werden sollte, sodass dann an geeigneter Stelle auf die eigenen Vermutungen und Hypothesen über die Einstellung gegenüber der Immigrationsproblematik zurückgegriffen werden kann. Alle nachfolgenden Texte des Kapitels haben einen direkten Bezug zu den Daten, sodass ein mehrperspektivischer Rückbezug sinnvoll ist, aus dem ein vielschichtiges Bild unterschiedlicher Migrationsgeschichten erfahrbar wird.

Solutions

Activities p. 32

1. **Describe the bar chart with regard to the development of immigration from Europe.**

The vertical axis, which stands for the number of immigrants within a decade, clearly indicates a rise of immigration from Europe until the 1930s. A decrease can be detected until the end of the century with numbers rising slightly after the turn of the century. Europeans used to be the largest group of immigrants until the 1970s, when Asians and Latin Americans began to immigrate in higher numbers. The blue segment reveals that Europeans are currently the third biggest group of immigrants to the USA.

2. **Analyse the data of immigrants (a) from Asia and (b) from Latin America.**
(a) After the Second World War the number of Asians immigrating to the USA began to rise significantly, surpassing the number of Europeans in the 1980s. Today Asians are the second largest group of immigrants.
(b) Latin Americans began to settle in the USA at the end of the 19th century. Their numbers began to steadily increase in the 1970s, and they represent over half of the immigrants in the USA today.

3. **Write a short "History of Immigration" using the most important data from this bar chart.**
The first immigrants to reach North America were the Europeans. They crossed the Atlantic in ever-increasing numbers, reaching their peak before the Second World War. After the war the USA became a new home for many people from Asia and Latin America. The slight increase of African immigrants, shown by the growth of the yellow segment, becomes notable from the 1980s onward.

4. **Find out how many in your class/group are "foreign born".**
Individual answer; Students may want to make their own graphs/bar charts using Open Office Calc or MS Excel.

5. **Compare the graph to the bar chart above. What do they have in common?**
The number of foreign born Americans is given in a line graph; the y-axis represents percentage levels of the total population. The line graph steadily rises to the end of the 19th century with three peaks at 1870, 1890 and 1910. The graph falls sharply until 1970, when only about 4% of the population of the United States was foreign born. The sharp rise beginning in 1990 is equal to the rise of Latin Americans in the bar chart and reveals that the USA is once again becoming a country of immigrants with more than one in ten being a foreign born American citizen.

6. **What may be the implications of the rising figures in the present discussion about "immigration"?**
Immigration was lower in the 1970s than at the end of the 19th century. With just one in 25 American citizens still being foreign born, the population felt they were no longer a country of immigrants. The sharp rise of immigrants, especially from South America, may be seen by some Americans as a threat to their way of life, especially because immigrants from Latin America do not always assimilate as quickly as former immigrants from other countries, who sought to adapt as soon as possible. Historically speaking the USA was a country of immigrated Europeans and is now beginning to change into a land of Latin Americans.

The New Colossus

Emma Lazarus

Author and text

Emma Lazarus, born in New York on July 22, 1849, was a member of an old Jewish family who had lived in New England since colonial times. In New York the Lazarus family

belonged to the respected families, representing traditional republican values. Coming from a very rich family she was privately taught, and learned French and German as well as Italian. She had a profound knowledge of European culture and tradition. With the arrival of Russian Jews escaping the pogroms in Russia at the beginning of the 1880s, she became more interested in her own Jewish heritage and was one of the first advocates for a Jewish homeland. Emma Lazarus had not seen the "teeming shores" of old Europe when she wrote the poem, but she later travelled twice to Europe (in 1885 and 1887).
The poem was written as a donation for the Art Loan Fund Exhibition, a fundraiser for the pedestal of the Statue. The poem was read at the exhibition, but soon forgotten afterwards. Due to the efforts of a friend, the poem was engraved on a plaque at the base of the Statue in 1903 and then rose to national fame. Nevertheless, when Emma Lazarus died at the age of 38 in November 1887, she had no idea of her future glory.
The poem was long taught and praised in the American school system; nobody reviewed the text critically until 1949, when Walcot Gibbs wrote that the sonnet "may be the most lamentable collection of words ever thus preserved for the ages" (*The New Yorker*, July 23, 1949, p. 49). The poem is in fact overdone with regard to stylistical devices. Its hyphenated adjectives and nouns (sea-washed, beacon-hand etc.) as well as the numerous alliterations lack the subtle elegance of other sonnets (e. g. by Christina Rossetti) of the 19th century.
Today Emma Lazarus has been rediscovered as a female Jewish writer. Her other poems and plays, that long stood in the shadow of the "New Colossus", have been re-edited.

Unterrichtsempfehlungen

Das Gedicht von Emma Lazarus gehört zum amerikanischen Kulturerbe und ist unverzichtbar in jeder Reihe zum *American Dream*.
Die Beschäftigung mit der *Statue of Liberty*, also dem Objekt des Gedichts, sollte auf jeden Fall in privater (häuslicher) Vorbereitung durch eine Internetrecherche erfolgen (*pre-reading*). Den besten Zugang bieten folgende Websites:
www.nps.gov/history/worldheritage/liberty.htm
Sehr lohnend ist die nachstehende „E-Tour" durch die Statue, die viele bildliche, z. T. historische Eindrücke bietet: www.nps.gov/stli/photosmultimedia/virtualtour.htm
Diese letzte Seite auf Flickr sammelt alle Fotos von Liberty Island und der Statue of Liberty, natürlich viele eher private Urlaubsbilder, aber auch einige hochprofessionelle Fotos, die zusätzlich den Sockel und die Umgebung gut zeigen:
www.flickr.com/photos/statuelibrtynps
Das Gedicht wird in den üblichen drei Schritten (*Comprehension – Analysis – Evaluation*) bearbeitet.
Als Vorbereitung (Hausaufgabe) dient Aufgabe 1, die bereits ein erstes Verständnis des Textes begründet. Die zweite Aufgabe übt ein weiteres Mal die stilistische Analyse, angesichts des Stellenwertes in den Abiturklausuren erscheint hier Routinebildung sinnvoll, wenngleich das Gedicht trotz seiner zahlreichen rhetorischen Figuren sicherlich nicht den literarischen Stellenwert hat, den es postuliert. Diese Aufgabe lässt sich am schnellsten in Partnerarbeit lösen, die Ergebnisse werden, wie in den Lösungen abgelegt, auf einer Folie notiert und ggf. im Gedichttext farbig markiert.
Die letzte Aufgabe (AFB III) greift auf das Vorwissen der Schülerinnen und Schüler zurück und verlangt vor diesem Hintergrund (Schwerpunkt Kapitel 1) einen Perspektivenwechsel und eine begründete Stellungnahme. Um das notwendige Wissen zu reaktivieren, bietet sich eine einleitende Gruppenarbeit an, welche die besten/schlagkräftigsten Argumente in einer *Placemat*-Arbeit sammelt, sodass alle Lernenden ausreichend Stichpunkte für eine anschließende Ausarbeitung (Hausaufgabe) haben. Die Ergebnisse sollten abschließend gesammelt und von der Lerngruppe hinsichtlich ihrer Argumenta-

tionsstärke bewertet werden. Den „besten" Brief könnte die Lerngruppe als europäischen Einwurf an den National Park Service schicken, vielleicht bekommt man ja eine Antwort.

Solutions

Activities

Before you read p. 33

Find out more about the history of the Statue of Liberty.

The Statue of Liberty was designed by the French sculptor Frédéric-Auguste Bartholdi, born in Colmar in 1834. When Alsace became a German province after the Franco-Prussian War in 1870/71, he began working on a project to commemorate the old republican links between the USA and the newly forming French Republic. He sailed to New York in 1871 and found the perfect place for his gigantic statue on Bedloe's Island at the entrance of the New York harbour. Shortly afterwards he began promoting his idea, discussing his plans with prominent politicians, including President Ulysses S. Grant. On the other side of the Atlantic Ocean the French politician Laboulaye, who had already kindled the idea of a "present" for the USA in 1865, helped raise funds. It was decided that the French would pay for the statue whereas the Americans had to build the pedestal. The time was too short to finish the statue by 1876, but the arm and torch of the statue were displayed in Philadelphia that year. For 50 cents visitors could climb to the top on a ladder, thus raising further funds for the completion of the statue. The novel concept of a statue people could climb inside generated new enthusiasm. In June 1884 the statue was finished, but in the beginning only few people dared climb the narrow steps inside, though the metal frame supporting the structure had been designed and built by the famous French engineer Gustave Eiffel. Lady Liberty stayed in Paris for a further year, becoming an attraction for tourists. In 1885 the statue was taken apart to be shipped to the New World in 214 wooden boxes. When the statue arrived the pedestal still had not been finished. American publisher Joseph Pulitzer started another fundraiser in his paper *The World* which finally earned the necessary funds. The foundation, on which the 11-pointed-star-shaped pedestal was to be constructed, required more than 24,000 tons of concrete. The reassembly and mounting of the statue onto the pedestal was supervised by General Charles P. Stone. The statue was unveiled by Bartholdi himself on October 28, 1886, in an ostentatious ceremony that united American and French politicians as well as more than a million spectators on the shores.

Activities p. 34

1. The basic concept of this poem is contrast. Begin by making a list of the things attributed to "old" Europe and those belonging to the "new" world.

Old	New
– a brazen giant – conquering – storied pomp – tired [...] poor [...] huddled masses – yearning to breathe free – wretched refuse – teeming shore – homeless – tempest-tost	– a mighty woman – a torch – imprisoned lightening – mother of exiles – beacon-hand – world-wide welcome – mild eyes – air-bridged harbor – golden door

Leuchtfeuer

2. Analyse the stylistic devices used in the sonnet. How do they underline the message of the poem?

Alliteration	**l**and to **l**and (2); **s**ea-washed, **s**unset (3) **w**orld-**w**ide-**w**elcome (7); **t**empest-**t**os**t** (13) **l**ift my **l**amp (14)

Antithesis	keep [...] your .../give me your ... (9/10)
Assonance	mild eyes (7) twin cities (8) storied pomp (9) breathe free (11)
Enumeration	your tired, your poor,/your huddled masses (10/11)
Including 'we'	Here at **our** sea-washed (3)
Inversion	cries she (9)
Metaphor	imprisoned lightening (5) The air-bridged harbor (8) wretched refuse (12)
Metonymy	golden door (14)
Oxymoron	cries she/with silent lips (9/10)
Personification	conquering limbs (2) cries she (9)
Simile	Not like the brazen giant (1)

There is no "Lyrical I" (speaker) in the poem, except for the first person plural (3). On the other hand the statue herself is speaking in the second part of the poem. The form is that of an Italian sonnet, two quatrains that form an octave (a/b/b/a/a/b/b/a) and two tercets united into one sestet (c/d/c/d/c/d). The form underlines the content in several ways: Beginning with a negation of any link to European history, the poem develops a unique American interpretation of the Statue. Following the first description (ll. 3 – 8) the turn is introduced in direct speech, filling the last six lines of the poem. The argumentative structure of the text is thus underlined.

3. **The statue was given by the French people to the American people in commemoration of the common republican origins of the Enlightenment (see chapter 1). The poem, written to raise funds for the socket of the statue, was misconstrued interpreting the significance of the statue in a different, even anti-European way. Imagine you were a French citizen reading the poem. Write a letter to the Statue of Liberty National Monument at *National Park Service* responsible for the monument today, stating your (European) point of view.**

falsch auslegen
missverstehen

This is a combined task that (1) requires the reproduction of facts given in the text (AFB I & II) and (2) evaluation and statement of a personal opinion (AFB III) blended in a re-creation-of-text exercise.

The student	
uses the form of a letter	AFB I
refers to the main assertions of the poem: Europe as – conquering – pompous – refusing freedom to its "huddled masses" – mistreating human beings (wretched refuse)	AFB I & II
evaluates the historical development and states his/her personal opinion – Enlightenment was brought by Europeans to America – The ideas of Hobbes, Locke and Rousseau which were essential for the Declaration of Independence came from Europe – The Statue is a gift of the French people to the American people commemorating the common bonds between these two countries – The Statue should stress the common interests and beliefs and not state a negative view of Europe – The student should question the actual attitude towards immigration in the USA and point out the discrepancy with Lazarus' verses.	AFB III

E Pluribus Unum – the Motto on the Great Seal of the United States

Creator and text

The development of the Great Seal has a long history, beginning in 1776, when the Continental Congress agreed that the new nation needed a symbol of sovereignty. Three committees worked on the design. Some of these men had only little knowledge of heraldry, so the drafts are interesting results of personal ideas and concepts, but they do not comply with the highly compressed form required by heraldic standards.
The motto "E Pluribus Unum" was already featured in the first draft designed by Benjamin Franklin, John Adams and Thomas Jefferson, accompanying the symbols of the nations from which the country's immigrants had come, i.e. England, Scotland, Ireland, France, Holland and Germany.
The motto itself has a rather trite history that, although long ushered away, is meanwhile recognized by the official government presentation: The motto was featured on the title page of the *Gentleman's Magazine*, published in London since 1732 and read by most of the committee members, a paper that reprinted texts from different magazines. After the fruitless efforts of the three leading politicians to come up with an acceptable proposition, two further committees worked on the design of the seal. The last version of the third committee, mainly designed by William Barton, was presented in Congress in 1782.
The final version, designed by Charles Thompson, secretary to Congress (see his portrait in the painting on SB p. 6) in the same year, includes elements from all three former drafts, but draws most of the heraldic concept from the third version designed by William Barton. There is only one remaining early draft of Thompson's final version, as the seal presented to Congress was entirely described in words with no graphical support.
The full history and interpretation of the Great Seal can be found on the governmental website: www.state.gov/www/publications/great_seal.pdf
Another very detailed analysis of all elements and their history is given on:
www.great-seal.com/

Unterrichtsempfehlungen

Heraldik ist sicherlich keine typische Kompetenz des Englischunterrichts. Dennoch soll an dieser Stelle ein kurzer Blick auf diese Wissenschaft geworfen werden, da sich in Siegeln und Wappen auch das Selbstverständnis einer Nation ausdrückt. Der Zugang wurde daher auch nicht über das offizielle Siegel, sondern über die Ein-Dollar-Note gewählt, ein Stück Papier, das jede Schülerin und jeder Schüler vielleicht schon einmal in der Hand gehalten hat, oder halten wird (Anschaulichkeit: → konkretes Exemplar mitbringen). Der Lernzuwachs dieses Abschnitts liegt in der Beschäftigung mit dem Motto, unabdingbare Kenntnis für viele Texte. Es wird daher auch nur die Vorderseite (*obverse*) des Siegels analysiert, die Symbolik der Rückseite (*reverse*) mit der dreizehnstufigen Pyramide, dem „*eye of providence*“ sollte besser unerwähnt bleiben, denn hier schießen die okkulten Spekulationen im Internet nur so aus dem Boden.
Bereits zur Vorderseite finden sich zahlreiche Websites, welche tiefgreifende freimaurerische Verschwörungstheorien zu belegen versuchen. Dass der Begriff „*American Dream*“ auch dreizehn (!) Buchstaben hat, sei hier als letztes nur am Rande erwähnt.
Die Analyse setzt (1) mit der Beschreibung der Symbole und (2) anschließend ihrer Deutung ein. Dies lässt sich am Besten konzentriert mithilfe einer Folie zur Ergebnissicherung gestalten. Die Darstellung im Schülerbuch wurde mit Absicht so stark vergrößert, dass alle Elemente gut erkennbar sind.

Die zweite Aufgabe zielt auf eine Internetrecherche. Google listet für „*Great Seal*" mehr als 200 000 Sites. Daher sollten aus den o. g. Gründen primär die beiden oben aufgeführten Webseiten, welche detaillierte Informationen anbieten, zu Grunde gelegt werden. Der Fokus der Analyse liegt dabei auf dem Motto und nicht so sehr auf den anderen Symbolen.

Die dritte Aufgabe stellt die heutige Interpretation des Mottos ins Zentrum der Überlegungen. Hierbei ist der Rückgriff auf die Statistiken vom Beginn des Kapitels sinnvoll, da sich hieraus das heutige Verständnis des Mottos durch viele Amerikaner erfahren lässt.

Solutions

Activities p. 35

1. This picture is taken from a one-dollar bill. Make a list of the symbols you can find. What do they stand for?

symbol	explanation
13 stars radiating through a cloud	The thirteen stars, according to official explanation, are breaking through the cloud thus forming a new nation on the firmament. The thirteen stars represent the thirteen founding states.
an **eagle**	The eagle is an old heraldic element, representing power; the eagle's head is turned to the left (the "peace" side).
an **olive branch** in the eagle's right (stronger) talon	The olive branch is an ancient symbol for peace.
in the eagle's left talon a **bundle of thirteen arrows**	The bundle of arrows represents the power of war.
in its beak a **scroll** with the **motto "E PLURIBUS UNUM"**	The motto was meant to signify that out of many (thirteen) states a new nation was born.
a **shield**, consisting of a blue horizontal bar and 13 vertical stripes, seven white and six red	The shield is an old heraldic element, too, symbolizing defence, but also readiness to take up a fight. The blue horizontal bar could be interpreted as the "Union", based on the thirteen federal states. The colour blue in heraldry symbolizes "justice", red stands for "boldness" and white for "innocence". There are seven white and six red stripes, whereas in the American flag there are seven red and only six white stripes.
(the number **thirteen**)	The olive branch has thirteen leaves and thirteen olives; there are thirteen arrows and thirteen stars, as well as thirteen stripes; the motto "e pluribus unum" consists of thirteen letters. The use of the number thirteen can be explained by the number of the federal states, but has been subject to numerous, sometimes strange explanations, especially involving the theory of freemasonry being behind the symbols.

2. **"E Pluribus Unum" is Latin. It translates "out of many, one." It was adopted as a motto for the Great Seal of the United States in 1782 and first used on a gold coin in 1795 and has since been used on coins and paper bills. Considering your results, what did this motto signify back in 1782?**
   Though the first committee used the motto to represent the different national origins of the American people, it was reinterpreted in the context of the Great Seal describing the "Union" of the thirteen independent states to form a greater whole.

3. **Today the motto is often referred to with regard to immigration. How would you translate its meaning in this context?**
   Students should consider what they have read so far, i. e. have look at the statistics at the beginning of the chapter. This context opens up another, different meaning: "From many nations into one."

Ellis Island

Joseph Bruchac

Author and text

Joseph Bruchac (born 1942) is a writer of poems, plays, short stories, novels and songs. The focus of his works is on north-eastern Native American and Anglo-American life and folklore. He is from Saratoga Springs, New York, and he is of mixed Abenaki and Slovak origin. Joseph Bruchac lives with is wife, Carol, in Greenfield Center, New York. His work draws on that land and his American Indian heritage.
Bruchac has a Ph.D. in Comparative Literature and is an editor of literary magazines. He has published more than 70 books, many of them for children, and has won numerous prizes.

Unterrichtsempfehlungen

Bevor das Gedicht von Joseph Bruchac bearbeitet werden kann, sollte die zweite historische Insel in der Hafeneinfahrt von New York erforscht werden. Die beiden historischen Orte scheinen heute untrennbar miteinander verbunden; Ellis Island wurde allerdings etwas später eingerichtet, als die *Statue of Liberty* schon stand. Millionen von Einwanderern, welche die „*Liberty*" aber als erstes Willkommenszeichen in der neuen Welt gesehen haben, begründen aber eine nicht mehr trennbare Verbindung der beiden Orte.
Auch hier ist der Zugang über die offiziellen Websites ein guter Start. Beide unten angegebenen Seiten bieten viele Links und Informationen. Die Ergebnisse sollten auf Postern gesammelt werden, weil sie bei der späteren Lektüre des Amy Bloom-Textes noch einmal tragend werden, weil dort sehr präzise, literarisch verdichtet, der Weg einer Einwanderin durch die Stationen von Ellis Island erlebbar gemacht wird. Alle drei literarischen Texte zu Beginn dieses Kapitels beleuchten aus verschiedenen Blickwinkeln die Entstehung der amerikanischen Nation als ein Volk von Immigranten – *E Pluribus Unum.*
Das Gedicht von Joseph Bruchac steht in schroffem Kontrast zum bombastischen Sonett von Emma Lazarus. Mit Lyrik wenig erfahrene Schülerinnen und Schüler könnten fragen: Ist das überhaupt ein Gedicht? Dabei steht Bruchac stilistisch in einer alten amerikanischen Tradition, wie man sie z. B. auch bei Carl Sandburg findet.
Schwerpunkt der Textarbeit soll die Beschäftigung mit der „geteilten" Persönlichkeit (*double identity*) des Sprechers sein, welche die des Autors spiegelt. Hierzu wird in

einem ersten Schritt die Identität, so wie sie sich im Gedicht widerspiegelt, erarbeitet. Die erste Aufgabe beschränkt sich auf eine nur auf diesen Aspekt reduzierte *Comprehension*, die von den Schülerinnen und Schülern schnell selbstständig geleistet werden sollte. Aufgabe 2 untersucht in Partnerarbeit die wesentlichen stilistischen Merkmale des Textes, sodass die Lernenden erfahren können, dass auch ein auf den ersten Blick scheinbar schmuckloser Text sprachlich hoch verdichtet sein kann. Auf der Basis beider Lösungen kann jetzt ein weiterer Schritt erfolgen, in welchem die Thematik und grundlegenden Aussagen des Gedichts für die Lerngruppe visualisiert werden. Hierzu sollte das Gedicht in drei Teile zerschnitten auf Folie präsentiert werden (s. u.). Die Schülerinnen und Schüler haben bereits in Aufgabe 1 die Dreiteilung erarbeitet, jetzt wird die sprachliche Vernetzung verdeutlicht. Der Speaker erscheint in jeder Strophe einmal (*first person singular*), in der ersten und dritten als „*my*" und in der mittleren, verbindenden als „*lyrical I*". Ebenso werden andere Themen wieder aufgegriffen (*own – owned*) und der große Kontrast *man-made – nature*, der die Aussagen in beiden Strophen stützt, erkennbar. Dazwischen, hier auf der Sicherungsfolie unten herausgenommen (entsprechend dem Ergebnis von Aufgabe 1), steht der Sprecher des Textes, der „*answerer of dreams*" (16 f.).

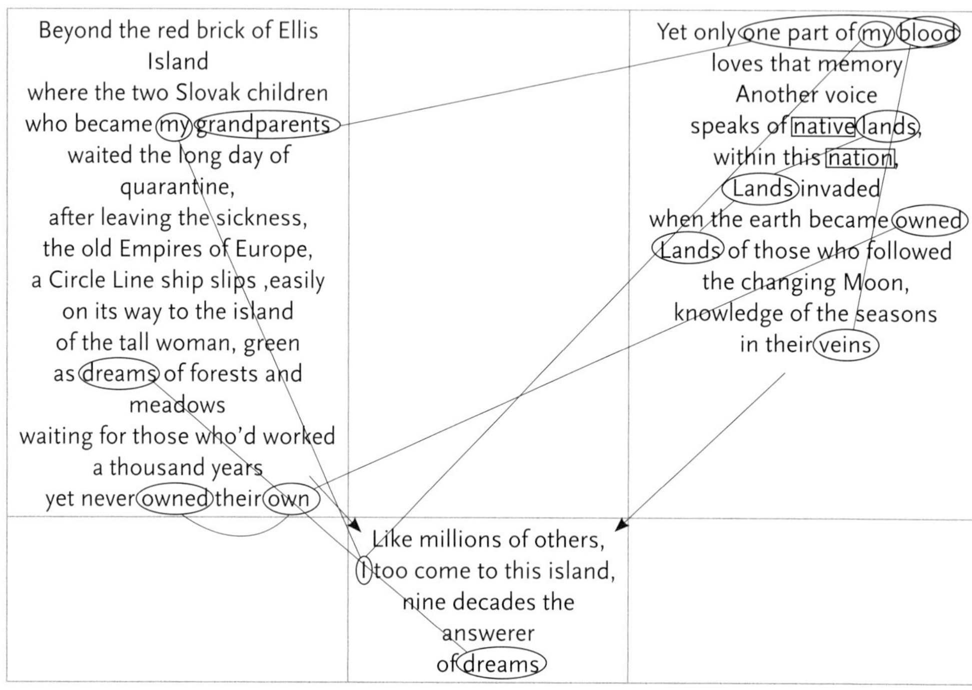

Die letzte Aufgabe lässt sich auch gestützt auf die oben dargelegte Erschließung zügig erarbeiten. In der letzten Aufgabe ist wiederum ein Transfer unter Berücksichtigung des bisher Gelernten geplant, wobei die Lernenden zusätzlich zur Reorganisation wiederum eigenes Urteilen belegen sollen (AFB III). Die Lösung entspricht wegen der individuellen Gestaltungsmöglichkeit den kriterialen Beschreibungen des Abiturs.

Solutions

Before you read p. 36

In groups gather all information you can get about Ellis Island. Make a poster using photos and historical information.

Located in the New York Harbour, approximately 12 million steamship passengers who entered the United States through the port of New York were legally and medically inspected at Ellis Island between 1892 and 1954. At peak times in 1907 11,747 persons were "processed" on one day. Immigrants who were considered sick received a chalk mark on their clothes and were sent back to where they came from. After 1924 only war

refugees and displaced persons passed through Ellis Island. The main part of the island became a detention and deportation centre. Later it was used by the US Coast guard. In 1990 Ellis Island was renovated and transformed into a museum dedicated to educating visitors about the immigrant experience. More than 100 million Americans can trace their ancestors to Ellis Island. Like all historic sites it is administered by the National Park Service.
Useful information can be found at:
www.nps.gov/elis
www.ellisisland.org

1. Take evidence from the text and define the origins of the speaker. You may try to sketch a rough family tree.

Activities p. 37

European	Native American
two Slovak children (2) who became my grandparents (3)	another voice speaks/of native lands/ within this nation (19 f.)
↓ (father?/mother?)	↓ (father?/mother?)
↓ speaker nine decades the answerer/of dreams (16 f.)	

2. The poem consists of four more or less complex sentences. Nevertheless there is a number of stylistic devices enhancing the meaning of the text. Make a list of those you think most striking. Compare with your neighbour and agree on a common presentation (think – pair – share).

Alliteration	**B**eyond the red **b**rick (1)
Anaphora	yet (13) ... Yet (18) Lands invaded (22) ... Lands of those (24)
Assonance	sh**i**p sl**i**ps **easily** (7) my bl**oo**d l**o**ves (18) **ow**ned (23) f**o**ll**ow**ed (24)
Metaphor	the answerer of dreams (16 f.)
Metonymy	the red brick of Ellis Island (1) the island/of the tall woman (8 f.) Lands of those who followed/the changing Moon (24 f.)
Paradox	never owned their own (13)
Personification	the changing Moon (25)
Repetition	of native lands ... Lands invaded ... Lands of those (20 ff.)
Simile	green/as dreams of forests and meadows (9 f.)

3. Analyse the images that express the speaker's divided identity. Which part of his identity do you think predominates?
The first stanza (sentence 1) contrasts the two islands (Ellis Island and Liberty Island). The first is described as an artificial man-made place ("red brick", l. 1), a sorrowful place of transition between the old world and the new, whereas Liberty Island ("the Island/of the tall woman, green", l. 8 f.) reminds the speaker of dreams of forests and meadows. The third stanza (sentences 3 and 4) describes the land of the Native Americans, living in harmony with nature (ll. 24–27). It becomes clear that this part of his identity, which longs for a natural life according to nature's laws, is predominant.

4. **To describe the American nation the metaphor of "the melting pot", describing the multicultural American society, is often used. Evaluate the image from the point of view of the speaker of this poem.**

The student	
describes the United States as a nation built by people from different countries underlines his/her statement with statistical data relates the metaphor of the melting pot to the motto "E pluribus unum"	AFB I & II
points out that part of the speaker is glad that the United States is a nation where his ancestors could finally live in peace and freedom and realize their dreams (quote ll. 10–13)	AFB III
contrasts this to the feeling of being invaded and robbed of one's land (quote ll. 22–23)	AFB III
points out that the speaker criticizes the loss of the Native American identity within the American nation (quote "native lands within this nation" 20 f.)	AFB III
adds a personal statement about being torn between these two sides	AFB III

And Lost There, a Golden Feather in a Foreign, Foreign Land

Amy Bloom

Author and text Amy Bloom (born in 1953) has worked as a social worker and psychotherapist before becoming a writer. She teaches creative writing at Yale University. *Away* is her second novel, published in 2007, which earned her a nomination for the National Book Award. The epic novel tells the story of a Russian immigrant (Lillian Leyb) arriving in New York in 1924 after her family was killed in an anti-Jewish pogrom. Lillian first settles among the Yiddish theatre community, before she once again sets off to cross the continent westward in an attempt to reach Siberia via Alaska, hoping to find her lost daughter again.

Unterrichtsempfehlungen

Dieser Romanausschnitt steht inhaltlich in direktem Bezug zu dem Gedicht von J. Bruchac und den statistischen Daten. Es wäre möglich, in der Datenbank von Ellis Island (s. o.) nach jemandem mit dem Namen „Leyb" zu forschen, der/die in den 1920er-Jahren in Ellis Island angekommen ist, und den Herkunftsort/das Herkunftsland zu ermitteln, um die Geschichte an die konkrete historische Situation anzubinden.
Ebenso spiegelt der Ausschnitt zahllose Berichte von Immigranten über ihre Erfahrungen und Gefühle bei der Ankunft in Ellis Island (Aufgabe 1).
Die beiden ersten Aufgaben sollten zur häuslichen Vorbereitung gegeben werden und stellen die Rezeption des Textausschnittes sicher. Das kontrastierende Prinzip der Sammlung eröffnet die Möglichkeit zur Diskussion über die Fragestellung *„American Dream – American Nightmare"*, die bisher in diesem Kapitel noch nicht aufgegriffen wurde.
Die dritte Aufgabe wiederholt und vertieft die analytischen Kompetenzen (*point of view*) der Schülerinnen und Schüler und kann knapp im Unterricht behandelt werden.
Die letzten beiden Aufgaben sind offen und kreativ angelegt, wobei Aufgabe 4 noch einen konkreten Textbezug verlangt, während die letzte Aufgabe auch Raum für emotionale Ausarbeitung (*hopes and fears*) lässt. Die Aufführung dieser kurzen Spielszene (in Gruppen- bzw. auch in Partnerarbeit) vorbereitet kommt der Forderung nach Stärkung der Mündlichkeit im Fremdsprachenunterricht nach. Daher sollte auch auf einen möglichst freien Vortrag geachtet werden.

Solutions

Activities p. 39

1. **Write down the pieces of advice Lillian has to keep in mind while passing through Ellis Island.**
   – Step lively
   – When you see something like this (*SCRATCH YOUR RIGHT EAR*) scratch your right ear
   – Don't show that you can't speak English

2. **Complete the list of the things Lillian expected about America and those that surprised her:**

expected	unexpected
– anyone can buy anything – enough food (flour, condensed milk, powdered cacao) – hairpins that matched the color of your hair – very good stockings at low prices	– people who can't read – men with signs on their fronts and their backs – women in short skirts – colored boys with chairs on their backs and pictures of shiny shoes – people selling shoelaces, fans, pencils and salted twists of dough – a desperate woman evicted from her home in her nightgown and a china plate on her lap

3. **Analyse how the point of view contributes to the atmosphere of this passage into a new life.**
   The point of view is that of a third person limited narrator. The reader sees the "new world" through Lillian's eyes, who is often surprised and does not understand everything she observes. This subjective description contributes to the atmosphere of adventure, astonishment and surprise.

4. **Imagine being Lillian who writes her first impressions into her diary.**
   Students should mention:
   – the long hours of waiting
   – the different procedures to get registered on Ellis Island
   – the surprise that not everybody seems to be happy and rich
   – the astonishment that many people can't read or seem to be uneducated
   – the shock of how brutal life can be if you haven't enough money to pay your debts
   – the friendly accommodation offered by her cousin Frieda
   – ...

5. **Enact a dialogue between Frieda and Lillian discussing their hopes and fears. First make notes, but try to act it out freely.**

Lillian	Frieda
– find work, make a living – get her own room/home – become an American citizen – afraid because she can't speak the language – fear of being rejected – scared to end up on the street – anxiety about not fitting in and becoming a burden for Frieda – ...	– offers help – assures Lillian that she will help her – promises to help find her a proper job – suggests how to learn the language – afraid that Lillian might feel patronized by her – ...

Republican National Convention Address (2004)

Arnold Schwarzenegger

Author and text

The speech was given at the Republic National Convention (2004), held in New York City from August 30 to September 2. The convention had been timed to take place just a week before the third anniversary of the attacks on the World Trade Center. Beginning the day before the convention massive protests took place in New York (for a literary account of these see Don DeLillo, *Falling Man*, part 3, chapter 10). Schwarzenegger was one of the speakers on the second day of the conference. He had been elected Governor of California the year before and was facing difficult problems with regard to his re-election in 2006. It was an important step in his political career to be listed among the top group of Republican politicians, especially since he had opposed some issues that had been supported by the Bush administration and vice versa (i. e. his support of the Kyoto protocol). His immigration-friendly attitude changed just eight months later, when he declared at the annual meeting of the Newspaper Association of America: "Close the borders in California and all across Mexico and in the United States" (April 20, 2005). A year later, struggling for re-election he changed his opinion again and stated that "walling off hundreds of miles of the California-Mexico border is a strategy from the Stone Age."

Unterrichtsempfehlungen

Die Schwarzenegger-Rede ist allein wegen seiner Herkunft für das Thema interessant. Der Österreicher verkörpert in der Tat alle Elemente des amerikanischen Traumes, so wie ihn sicherlich tausende von Menschen haben, die jährlich versuchen, eine „Green Card" zu bekommen.

Die Rede ist sprachlich recht einfach und kann in die häusliche Vorbereitung gegeben werden (Hinweis auf die Randfragen!). Ebenso kann bereits Aufgabe 1 und 2 vor dem Unterricht schriftlich bearbeitet werden und dann als Anknüpfung und Einstieg in die Textarbeit dienen. Die Rede selbst kann als MP3 bei www.americanrhetoric.com herunter geladen werden, wobei zu beachten ist, dass der Text im Schülerbuch gekürzt ist. Es ist aber ohne Zweifel für die Schülerinnen und Schüler interessant, den Governor zumindest auszugsweise Englisch reden zu hören.

Die Textarbeit gliedert sich in zwei Teile: Der erste Teil fokussiert auf eine genaue Analyse seiner Aussagen über Österreich. Im ersten Schritt (Aufgabe 3) wird dabei noch rein reproduzierend eine Gegenüberstellung der Aussagen über Österreich im Gegensatz zu den USA erarbeitet. Schülerinnen und Schüler, die schon einmal in Österreich waren, werden das hier von Schwarzenegger vermittelte Bild der Alpenrepublik bestimmt mit Verwunderung zur Kenntnis nehmen. Übertrieben gesprochen, hat er die sozialistische Hölle verlassen und den kapitalistischen Himmel gefunden, so zumindest muss diese Passage auf die Zuhörer wirken, deren eigenes konkretes Bild von Österreich als recht unscharf angenommen werden darf. Dass Schwarzenegger hier Geschichtsverzerrung betreibt, wird in der nächsten Aufgabe (4) erarbeitet. Sie kann nur gelöst werden, wenn die Lernenden sich zuvor in historischen Werken über die Nachkriegszeit und die 2. Republik informiert haben (→ Sprachmittlung). Die Fragestellung für die Diskussion führt dabei mehr in die Richtung, warum er diese wissentlich falsche historische Darstellung seines Heimatlandes gibt.

Die fünfte Aufgabe führt wieder zurück zum Thema und sammelt zunächst einmal alles, was er zum *„American Dream"* sagt. In einer Pyramidendiskussion etwa könnte in Gruppen eine Definition erarbeitet werden, die dann mit den anderen Lösungen im Plenum verglichen werden kann.

Der Typ der letzten Aufgabe ist bereits mehrfach in verschiedenen Bundesländern im Zentralabitur vorgekommen und soll daher auch hier entsprechend geübt werden. Dies müsste den Schülerinnen und Schülern leichter fallen, als bei anderen Politikern, da die Mehrzahl eine recht konkrete Vorstellung von der Person des Politikers hat und sich somit leichter in die Interviewsituation denken kann. Es ist dabei denkbar, die Aufgabe auch erst nach der Besprechung der folgenden beiden Texte zu stellen, da dann ein noch wesentlich detaillierteres Meinungsbild zum Diskussionsstand vorhanden sein sollte. Die Lösung der Aufgabe wurde dem kriterialen System des Abiturs angepasst.

Solutions

Activities p. 42

1. Outline the main elements of this autobiographical text.

Today	Governor of California; Speaking on behalf of President G. W. Bush
21 years ago (1983)	Became an American citizen
As a boy (1950s)	Lived in Austria in fear of the Russian occupation
1968	Came to the United States with empty pockets but full of dreams Watched Nixon on TV and decided to become a Republican
Today	Believes that the USA holds many chances for immigrants like himself

2. Make a list of the historical events Arnold Schwarzenegger refers to in his speech.

1940s to 1955	Austria occupied by Russian army until the Russians left (1955)
1950s/1960s	Austria becomes a socialist country
1968	Presidential campaign in the USA (Nixon – Humphrey)
November 1989	The Germans bring Berlin Wall down
June 1989	Tiananmen square; students protest in China
1994	Nelson Mandela, set free from prison, wins general elections in South Africa

3. On a poster draw and complete the following clusters:

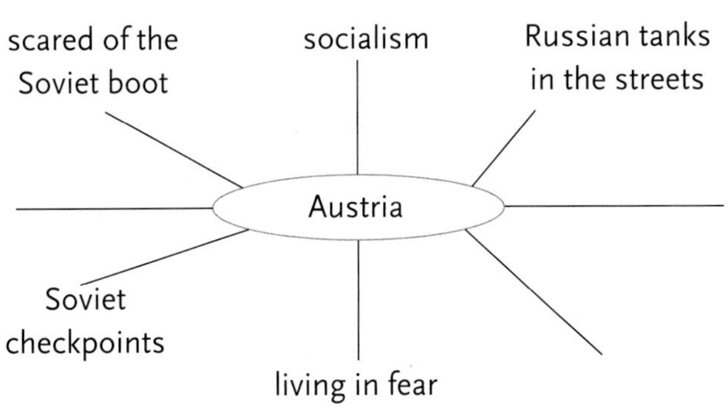

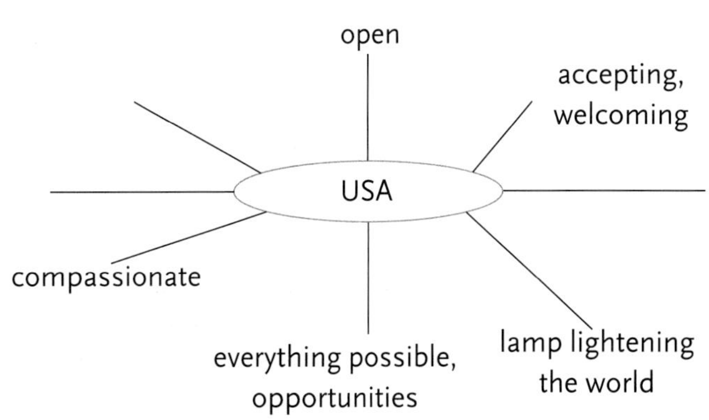

4. Do you think that what Schwarzenegger says about Austria is still relevant? Discuss.

Students should first gather additional information about Austrian history. They will find out that Schwarzenegger's presentation of the facts is partly wrong. Austria was was occupied from 1945 to 1955. It is true that the Soviet Union established a strict rule in their sector (compare to East Germany).

Austria nevertheless did not become a "socialist" country when the Allies left. From 1955 to 1966 Austria was governed by a coalition of the conservative "Peoples' Party" (ÖVP) and the Social Democrats (SPÖ), then the ÖVP ruled for four years. In 1970 the first Social Democratic chancellor was elected (Bruno Kreisky, 1970-1983). Kreisky, who received many international honours, can hardly be said to have been a hard-boiled socialist, so this part of Schwarzenegger's speech distorts historical facts. Apparently he wants to establish a contrast that explains his emigration, possibly an allusion to "your poor, your huddled masses, yearning to breathe free", but nevertheless a false historical abstract.

5. **Try to write a definition of the "American Dream" as Schwarzenegger sees it.**
The definition should refer to the following elements in the speech:
– a scrawny boy from Austria becomes Governor of California (5)
– (an immigrant) can speak in Madison Square garden on behalf of the President of the United States (6 f.)
– free enterprise (47)
– if you work hard and if you play by the rules, this country is truly open (59 f.)
– you can achieve anything (60)
– it doesn't make a difference where you were born or who your parents were (62 f.)
– America gives opportunities (66)
– you can respectfully disagree and still be patriotic (75)
– no matter the nationality, no matter the religion, no matter the ethnic background, America brings out the best in people (90 f.)

6. **You are a journalist from a Latin American country. Write an interview with Governor Schwarzenegger reflecting his attitude towards immigration.**

The student	
explains as "the Journalist" – that he will base his/her questions mainly on what Schwarzenegger said in his speech – states that the main topic of the interview should be Schwarzenegger's attitude toward immigration	AFB III
develops questions according to his/her role as a iournalist, referring to – Schwarzenegger's own experience as an immigrant (4–43) – the governor's attitude towards immigration from Latin America (56–65) – clearly puts the focus on the Latin American aspect of immigration – uses different interviewing techniques, e. g. factual provocative, contradictory or affirmative questions/statements.	AFB III
as "Schwarzenegger" answers the questions – in accordance with Schwarzenegger's general attitude as shown in his speech – aware of the discussion about the stop of immigration and his role as the governor of a border state – with regard to legal issues ("if you play by the rules", 59)	AFB III

The Tortilla Curtain

T. C. Boyle

Author and text

T. C. Boyle was born in 1948 in Peekskill, NY. After finishing school he studied history and English literature at the State University in Potsdam, NY. At the age of 20 he earned his BA in English and literature and began teaching. He was accepted at the Iowa Writers' Workshop at the University of Iowa in 1972 and got a job as a fiction editor for the

Iowa Review and began to publish his first works of fiction. In 1977, having finished his PhD in English Literature, Boyle received a Creative Writing Fellowship from The National Endowment for the Arts and became Assistant Professor (1978–82), Associate Professor (1982–86), and since 1986 has taught as Professor of English at the University of Southern California. He has written more than a hundred short stories and a dozen novels, earning him numerous awards.
The Tortilla Curtain was published in 1995 and tells the story of two very different couples (one illegal Mexican immigrants, the other well-off white American citizens), whose paths cross at several instances. The story depicts a white urban community and their racist attitude towards the Mexican immigrants, who are seen and treated as a nuisance and danger to the American way of life.

Unterrichtsempfehlungen

Obwohl der Roman 1995 geschrieben wurde, ist die Thematik bis heute aktuelle Tagespolitik in den USA. Der Einstieg über den Cartoon (auf Folie kopieren) ermöglicht bereits eine Erweiterung der bisherigen Perspektive auf die Problematik, da hier jetzt auch die mexikanische, bzw. die Perspektive der lateinamerikanischen Immigranten berücksichtigt wird. Der Cartoon wird in drei Schritten bearbeitet: zunächst erfolgt eine sachliche Beschreibung, im zweiten Schritt wird die Textaussage analysiert und in der letzten Aufgabe die Hauptaussage zusammengefasst.
Als weitere *pre-reading*-Aktivität wäre ein *Brainstorming* zu dem gelben „*Caution*"-Schild mit der laufenden Einwandererfamilie (S. 43, rechter Textrand) denkbar. Dies könnte sehr offen geschehen (Schild auf Folie) und vielleicht können auch erst einmal Fragen gesammelt werden (*What does this sign signify? Why are they running? Where do they come from? Where do they want to go?* Etc.). Als weiterer Denkanstoß wäre das deutsche Verkehrszeichen für „Wildwechsel" fruchtbar. Die Fragen könnten auf Postern festgehalten werden mit dem Ziel Antworten (durch diesen und die folgenden Texte) zu finden.
Die fünf Aufgaben zum Text decken wiederum alle Anforderungsbereiche ab: Aufgaben 1 und 2 sind reproduzierend (*Comprehension*) angelegt (Aufgabe 1 zur häuslichen Vorbereitung, Aufgabe 2 in arbeitsteiliger Gruppenarbeit im Kurs). In Aufgabe 3 wird Reorganisation und Bezugnahme auf bekannte Tatsachen verlangt (AFB II und III). Die vierte Aufgabe ist textanalytisch (AFB II) konzipiert. In der letzten Aufgabe wird eigenes Werten (*Evaluation*, AFB III) erwartet. Hier muss der/die Unterrichtende entscheiden, wie viel Zeit investiert werden soll. Die Schülerinnen und Schüler sollten bereits auf der Basis der bisher bearbeiteten Texte in der Lage sein, sich eine eigene Meinung zu bilden und, auch im Hinblick auf den Perspektivenwechsel, die Grundeinstellungen beider Seiten zu übernehmen. Als Hilfestellung können die Listen aus Aufgabe 2 als Poster im Klassenraum dienen. Eine zusätzliche Internetrecherche (in arbeitsteiliger Gruppenarbeit) zur Vorbereitung und ggf. die Aufteilung in weitere Interessengruppen brächte natürlich eine noch tiefere Durchdringung der Thematik. Bei knapperer Zeit können auch nur die letzten Texte dieses Kapitels bearbeitet werden und die Debatte im Anschluss daran durchgeführt werden. Die möglichen Regeln für die *debate* sind bei den Lösungen exemplifiziert. In den gesellschaftswissenschaftlichen Fächern hat es sich als aufmerksamkeitssteigerndes Element bewährt, nach Abschluss der Debatte die besten Argumente der jeweiligen Gegenpartei herausstellen zu lassen. Dieses Mittel der gegenseitigen Wertschätzung verlangt von den Debattenteilnehmern ein genaues Zuhören und wirkt lernförderlich.

Solutions

Before you read p. 43

1. Describe the Cartoon.

(note: for the analysis of a cartoon see **Worksheet 4**, p. 123)

The description should be factual, just naming the elements without further interpretation:

- A man (Uncle Sam) is standing on a high wall. The top of the wall is protected by barbed wire.
- On one side of the wall (left side) is the American flag, on the other side there is a sign saying "Mexico".
- The man is holding a sign in each hand. One sign says "HELP WANTED", the other, in the octagonal form of a STOP sign, reads: "STOP ILLEGAL IMMIGRATION".
- A group of (9) people (men and women) are looking up at him from below.
- One of them asks "Is he schizophrenic?" and a woman behind him answers "Borderline."

2. In a dictionary look up the word "borderline." Also check medical use as in "borderline syndrome".

borderline, adjective:
"not clearly belonging to a particular condition or group; not clearly acceptable"

Oxford Advanced Learner's Dictionary

Emotionally Unstable (Borderline) Personality Disorder is a condition characterized by impulsive actions, rapidly shifting moods, and chaotic relationships. The individual usually goes from one emotional crisis to another. Often there is dependency, separation anxiety, unstable self-image, chronic feelings of emptiness and threats of self-harm (suicide or self-mutilation). This disorder is only diagnosed when these behaviors become persistent and very disabling/distressing.

www.mentalhealth.com

3. Summarize how the cartoonist presents the state of discussion about immigration in the USA.

Presenting Uncle Sam holding two contradictory signs depicts the state of the discussion as controversial, or even as "schizophrenic". On the one hand the US needs cheap labour; on the other hand the large numbers of illegal immigrants create problems, especially with regard to health care and schooling.

Activities p. 45

1. Summarize in your own words what the discussion between Delaney Mossbacher and Jack Jardine is about.

In the first part of the abstract (1–30) the discussion circles around two closely linked topics:

1. the gate:
   - Mossbacher doesn't want to be locking himself away (9 f.)
   - Jardine thinks that this is just a measure of safety and self-protection (11 f.)
2. the borders
   - Jardine insists the US should get control of the borders (15 f.)
   - He says that this a question of national sovereignty (21)
   - He points out that those people coming across the border are uneducated and unskilled and aren't really needed, as modern machinery can do the same job (25–30)

The second part (31–70) presents a discussion of the question of immigration:

- Mossbacher underlines that the USA is a nation of immigrants (34)

- Jardine points out that not all immigrants are equal, referring to his ancestors who fought the Revolutionary War (36 f.)
- Mossbacher questions whether you should differenciate between immigrants, as he is only a third-generation immigrant (38 f.)
- Jardine shifts the discussion to illegal immigration and its costs, quoting a newspaper article (48–56)
- Mossbacher concedes to Jardine, though he thinks that Jardine's point is not right (57–70)

2. **Make two lists: one of Jack Jardine's arguments against immigration and one of Delaney Mossbacher's in favour of immigration.**

Delaney Mossbacher	Jack Jardine
- we live in a democracy - immigrants are the lifeblood of this country – we're a nation of immigrants (34 f.) - everybody is an immigrant from somewhere (38) - [thinks] that everyone deserves a chance in life and that Mexicans will assimilate just like the Poles, Italians, Germans, Irish and Chinese (57 f.)	- need to control the borders (16) - question of national sovereignty (21) - U.S. accepted more (legal) immigrants last year than all the other countries of the world (21–23) - the illegal immigrants are killing us; no education, no resources, no skills (25 f.) - there's a point of saturation (36) - [Immigrants] are costing us [...] tax dollars for social services. (43 f.) - the illegals in San Diego county contributed 70 million in tax revenues and at the same time used up 240 million in services (49–51)

3. **Compare the two opinions to Arnold Schwarzenegger's arguments. Living in California, which of the two might vote for Governor Schwarzenegger? Give reasons.**
Looking at the list it becomes evident that Mossbacher would vote for Schwarzenegger, as he represents the same (positive) attitude towards immigration.

4. **Analyse the techniques of persuasion Jack uses to convince Delaney.**
Jack Jardine is a lawyer and he knows how to convince people. At the beginning of the discussion he is not sure of Delaney Mossbacher's opinion, so he opens with
- a positive message concerning his own state of mind (1 f.)
- when he finds that Delaney opposes his view he
- shifts the argument from a general level (the gate) to a personal, more private level ("Safety ...car ... front door", 11 f.)
- quotes someone else's opinion (Jack Cherrystone) (13 f.)
- introduces a new aspect (the borders) (16)

Now he has completely changed the topic from "the gate" to the national scale (border security). In this new line of argumentation
- he once again quotes an external authority (without naming a source), arguing by citing statistical data (21–23)
- he then contrasts legal and illegal immigration (24–30)
- he furthermore implicitly differentiates between different groups of immigrants (36 f.), putting Delaney in an inferior position
- he once again quotes statistical data, this time giving a renowned newspaper as his source (44–55)
- adds a well-placed reference to Delaney's own negative experiences with illegal immigrants (54–56)

Feeling that he has made his point he ends his argument by
- assuring Delaney that he understands his arguments and feelings and that he himself shares Delaney's point of view (63 f.)

– telling him that he will reverse his decision if the situation changes (66 f.)
– closing with a pessimistic view of the future (67 f.)

5. **Stage a panel discussion. Find more arguments for both sides. The motion might read: "We believe that the USA are saturated and immigration to the USA should be stopped."**
   The panel discussion should follow the general rules of debating: two persons speaking in favour of the motion, two against it, each person has about a minute to put forward their arguments. A chairperson should moderate the debate and watch the time and behaviour of the two sides. The rest of the class may join in with additional contributions after the initial statements. After that each group presents a final statement and then the whole group votes.

Migrate, then Integrate

Gregory Rodriguez

Author and text Gregory Rodriguez studied sociology at UCLA. He has written many articles and books on national identity and social cohesion. He is one of the contributing editors of *The Los Angeles Times*, but also writes for *The New York Times*, *The Washington Post* and other publications. Rodriguez is director of the California Fellows Program and an Irvine Senior Fellow at the New America Foundation. He has recently published a widely-praised study on the cultural and political influences of Mexican-Americans on the American nation, entitled *Mongrels, Bastards, Orphans, and Vagabonds: Mexican Immigration and the Future of Race in America*, Vintage, 2008.

Unterrichtsempfehlungen

Der Artikel von Gregory Rodriguez spiegelt eine moderne soziologische Analyse der Situation in Kalifornien aus der Feder eines anerkannten Experten wider. Der argumentative Text ist Quelle und zugleich auch Modell für die Textsorte. Daher werden zunächst der Aufbau und der Inhalt erarbeitet. Die letzte Aufgabe verlangt dann als Transfer das eigenständige Verfassen eines argumentativen Textes.
Aufgabe 1 dient zur Vorbereitung und kann in die häusliche Arbeit gegeben werden. Die genaue Strukturierung des Textes sollte in einer Einstiegsphase mit der gesamten Lerngruppe besprochen werden, sodass allen Schülerinnen und Schülern der Aufbau transparent wird.
Aufgabe 2 eignet sich zu einer arbeitsteiligen Gruppenarbeit (Sicherung auf einem Poster, ggf. auf Folien). Die Ergebnisse sind wichtig für die spätere Argumentation, daher sollten sie im Klassenraum ausgestellt werden (und bleiben).
Die dritte Aufgabe ist schnell erledigt; es ist möglich unterschiedliche Wörterbücher zu verwenden, die Definitionen sind vergleichbar. Neben der Übung im Umgang mit monolingualen Wörterbüchern ist an dieser Stelle für die Lernenden die Erkenntnis wichtig, dass man auch auf der Basis von Referenzwerken argumentieren kann. Die Wichtigkeit semantischer Bedeutungen in einer Argumentationskette wird dadurch für die Kursteilnehmerinnen und Teilnehmer transparent.
Aufgabe 4 entspricht der Klausuraufgabe der *Analysis*. Methodisch angebracht wäre eine *placemat activity* (EA/GA), bei welcher zunächst in den Gruppen alle Elemente gesammelt und vorgestellt werden. Im zweiten Schritt ist dann unter Anleitung der Lehrkraft eine Systematisierung aller gefundenen Elemente notwendig, die auch wieder allen (etwa als Kopie einer Masterfolie) zur Verfügung stehen sollte, damit sie in Aufgabe 5 selbst angewandt werden können. Die Lehrkraft sollte bei der vertiefenden

Textarbeit die linguistischen Mittel, welche Rodriguez einsetzt, betont ansprechen, da diese Elemente ja auch von den Schülerinnen und Schülern beim Abfassen ihrer Klausuren bepunktet werden und leider nur allzu häufig fehlen, weil sie sich der Bedeutung z. B. der *Connectives* nicht ausreichend bewusst sind.
Für die letzte Aufgabe wurde wieder eine Lösung entsprechend den Abiturvorgaben erstellt, die eine Beurteilung unterschiedlicher individueller Lösungen erlaubt.

Solutions

Activities p. 47

1. Structure the text and give appropriate headlines.

Lines	Headline
1–18	The number of immigrants to L.A. is going down
19–47	Beginning in the 60s society became split into two parallel communities
48–62	Today second generation immigrants become ethnic Americans
63–73	There is a need for integration and full inclusion

2. Summarize the most important pieces of information of this article on a poster: use two columns, one labeled "first generation", the other "second generation."

First generation	Second generation
- had a tenuous toehold in U.S. society (24) - sought to re-create the sounds and smells and networks of home in their new land (26 f.) - formed distinct communities (35) - the (monolingual) Latino population was separated (39 f.) - less-educated immigrants (56)	- begins to eclipse their parents (54 f.) - [is] often bilingual (55) - plays the role of mediators (55) - actively negotiates the gap between their parents' home culture and the American mainstream (57 f.) - schooled in English (59) - goes beyond the cultural enclave (60) - not immigrants but ethnic Americans (60 f.) - demand full inclusion in their country of birth (65)

3. Look up the word "community" in a monolingual dictionary. Compare to the definition given by the author in the last paragraph of his article.

Community

1. the people who live in the same area, town, etc.	1. the people who live together in any given location (70f.)
2. a group of people who have the same interests, religion, race, etc.	2. ethnic or other minority group (70)
(Longman DCE, 2005)	*(G. Rodriguez)*

Rodriguez's definition is nearly identical with the dictionary definition (stressing that 1 comes first), compared to his use of the word in l. 35, where only definition 2 applies.

Activities p. 48

4. Examine the style of the article and point out which elements show that this is an argumentative text.

Argumentative texts are the most common type of texts in leaders, letters to the editor, political speeches and essays. They usually deal with a controversial topic. The writer wants to win the reader's support. Argumentative texts also contain informative and persuasive elements.
Argumentative texts are usually structured into three parts: an **Introduction** followed by a **Development**, which generally consists of two opposing views or the

presentation of controversial facts (Development 1 and Development 2). The second part contains the arguments supported by the writer. At the end the writer summarizes his/her opinion in the **Conclusion** and points out the intended consequences of his/her argumentation.
The structure of the text, as developed in task 1, reflects the division into Introduction, Development (1) and Development (2) and Conclusion.
Students should also point out the typical linguistic markers of a contrastive text structure:

– Contrast	stuck (1) – move (2) increase (7) – actually lost (8) incorporates (67) – segregates (67) cross-ethnic ties (67 f.) – group-specific appeals (68)
– Connectives	even as (6) and now (8) No (14) but (15) Particularly (38) Because (41) For example (43) Likewise (45) But (48) Indeed (51) In other words (63)
– first person plural (including 'we')	we're getting ready (2) tells us (9) our region (15) our city (49) require us (66) should remind us (69) we now have (72)
– addressing the reader	Consider (19)
– use of the 'will-future' to point out future action	will be less (51) will not settle (64) will increasingly demand (65) will require (66)
– giving advice	should remind us (69)

At the beginning (and only at the beginning) of the text the author uses short forms (It'**s** too bad l. 1; we'**re** getting ready l. 2) to introduce a more colloquial style. Note that the first person plural is only used in those passages to underline his opinion (Introduction, Development 2 and Conclusion). The implicit use of a dictionary definition in his last paragraph is meant to reinforce his whole argumentation.

5. Imagine you are Delaney Mossbacher and you have just read the article in the *LA Times*. Write a letter to the editor stating your opinion on the subject.

The student	
presents his/her opinion as an inhabitant of the Arroyo Blanco Estates in L.A. in form of a letter to the editor with clear reference to the article written by Rodriguez (i.e. quotes, references)	AFB III
states that in his community the majority want to build a gated fence around their estate	AFB III
points out the evident problems of illegal immigration as seen by the neighbourhood he lives in	AFB III
voices his opinion that everyone deserves a chance and gives reasons (personal experience/American history – e.g. Declaration of Independence) for this	AFB III
demands that the newspaper should write more often about the positive influence and fruitful contribution of the new immigrants	AFB III
uses stylistic and rhetorical devices to convince the readers of his opinion	AFB III

Border Security and Immigration Reform

John McCain

Author and text

John Sidney McCain III, born in 1936, has twice run in a presidential campaign. After he lost in 2000 against his party opponent George W. Bush he was nominated candidate of the Republican Party in 2007, but lost to Democratic candidate Barack Obama.
John McCain is known as a war hero, as he was shot down in his plane over Vietnam and spent more than five years in prison camps. He was often tortured because the Vietcong knew that his father was the commander of the US naval forces in the Pacific. His poor physical condition after his release from imprisonment in 1973 prevented him from continuing his career in the military so he turned to politics. He won a seat in the House of Representatives in 1982. In 1986 he became Senator of Arizona, an office he still holds today. John McCain has supported all Republican presidents, though he has been known to openly question issues if he doesn't agree with the Republican opinion. He did not agree with G. W. Bush on global warming, same-sex marriage and illegal immigration. In his first attempt to win the presidential nomination in 2000 he was largely supported by Democratic crossvoters in the New England states. Many Americans like John McCain because they find his "straight talk" refreshing and different from other politicians. He led a tough campaign against Barack Obama in 2008, but lost by a large percentage.
The text is taken from John McCain's Presidential campaign homepage www.johnmccain.com.

Unterrichtsempfehlungen

Der Text von der Wahlkampf-Webseite des republikanischen Kandidaten sollte von den Schülerinnen und Schülern zuhause vorbereitet werden, wobei die Bearbeitung von Aufgabe 1 zur Sicherung des Textverständnisses sinnvoll ist. Die beiden nächsten Aufgaben dienen zur Vernetzung mit bereits bearbeiteten Texten. Zur weiteren Bearbeitung in der Lerngruppe sollten die Ergebnisse auf Folie gesammelt werden (s. Anschrieb u.). Da Mossbacher und Jardine (*Tortilla Curtain*) prototypisch für bestimmte Wählergruppen sind, kann diese Aufgabe recht schnell gelöst werden. Es bietet sich eine kurze *Think–Pair–Share* Arbeitsphase an, in welcher zunächst jede/r Lernende die fünf Thesen von McCain mit den bekannten Argumenten der beiden fiktiven Charaktere abgleicht und sich anschließend mit dem Partner/der Partnerin austauscht. An-

schließend wird mit der gesamten Lerngruppe auf der Folie markiert ob Mossbacher (M) oder Jardine (J) diesen Thesen zustimmen würde. Es wird sich dabei herausstellen, dass John McCain mit seinen Thesen eine relativ breite Wählerschicht anzusprechen weiß, da beide (M & J) einer Mehrzahl von Forderungen zustimmen würden.
Aufgabe 3 wird in arbeitsteiliger Gruppenarbeit diskutiert und die Ergebnisse (siehe Anschrieb unten) auf einer Folie zusammengetragen. Auch hier können wiederum Gemeinsamkeiten der beiden Politiker, aber auch Differenzen innerhalb desselben politischen Lagers herausgearbeitet werden.
Die letzte Aufgabe verlangt eine intensive Vorbereitungsphase, die, wie unten beschrieben, in arbeitsteiliger Gruppenarbeit zu bewerkstelligen ist. Zugang zum Internet wäre für die Vorbereitung (ggf. zuhause → Sammlung von Argumenten) sinnvoll, um ein höheres Diskussionsniveau durch vertieften Erkenntnisstand zu erreichen.

Solutions

Activities p. 49

1. Make a list of the measures concerning immigration John McCain wants to implement if he is elected president.

1) secure the border (6)
2) help Mexico and Latin America to build strong domestic economies (13 ff.)
3) help build flexible labour market to provide skilled ... immigrants with opportunity (20 ff.)
4) facilitate the assimilation of the immigrant population, which includes learning English, American history and civics, and respecting the values of a democratic society (26 ff.)
5) border security and the immigration system need to be reformed (32 ff.)

2. Would either Delaney Mossbacher or Jack Jardine (or both) vote for him? Give reasons.

Delaney Mossbacher in his more liberal attitude might oppose 1), but would probably agree on 2) to 5);
Jack Jardine would also agree on 1) to 4). He would question 5) depending on what the reform would entail.
So both might vote for John McCain.

3. Schwarzenegger and McCain are members of the same political party (Republican). Which ideas do they share and where do they differ?

Schwarzenegger	McCain
– *not mentioned/disagree?*	– secure the border
– it doesn't matter where you were born or who your parents were – if you work hard and if you play by the rules, this country is truly open – you can achieve anything – America gives opportunities	– recognize that America will always be attractive for immigrants seeking a better life built on hard work and optimism – flexible labour market to provide skilled ... immigrants with opportunity
– you can respectfully disagree and still be patriotic	– respecting the values of a democratic society
– no matter the nationality, no matter the religion, no matter the ethnic background, America brings out the best in people	– *certainly too extensive*
– *implied?*	– importance of assimilation of the immigrant population, which includes learning English, American history and civics

Schwarzenegger and McCain agree on a number of important topics. The greatest difference lies in the openness of the borders: McCain clearly wants stricter regulations, whereas Schwarzenegger shows a more liberal attitude.

4. **Under the heading "The shining City upon a hill" stage a hot chair discussion questioning John McCain on his attitude towards immigration and the promise of the American Dream.**
A hot chair discussion should be well prepared. One student (plus a "shadow" for help) and a number of questioners should prepare for the hot chair session, while the rest of the class acts as observers (→ assessment sheets). For this hot chair discussion the following groups (besides John McCain) should prepare questions:
– Legal Latin American immigrants
– Illegal Latin American immigrants seeking permanent residence
– Employers in search of cheap labour
– Residents of border communities (like Delaney Mossbacher and Jack Jardine)
– American citizens in general (not directly afflicted by the problem)
The person taking the hot seat will need to do special preparation with the help of a group (3 or 4 students) to turn him/her into the character ... of "John McCain". It is a good idea to think of possible questions (and answers), to take some notes based on the text and to gather some additional information about the politician and his character.
The other groups collect questions based on the text, but also on what they have learned about the American Dream so far. More information could be found by doing (limited) Internet research. The groups will decide in a pyramid discussion about the best questions (4 or 5) to be asked, avoiding an excessive number of trivial questions. During the discussion the questioners pay attention to the questions asked by other groups (same or opposite attitude?).
The assessment group (there should be at least 5 students doing this job) develop (with the help/hints of the teacher) an assessment sheet and will give their results after the discussion when everybody is back in his/her student role.

Worksheet 3

How to Analyse Charts

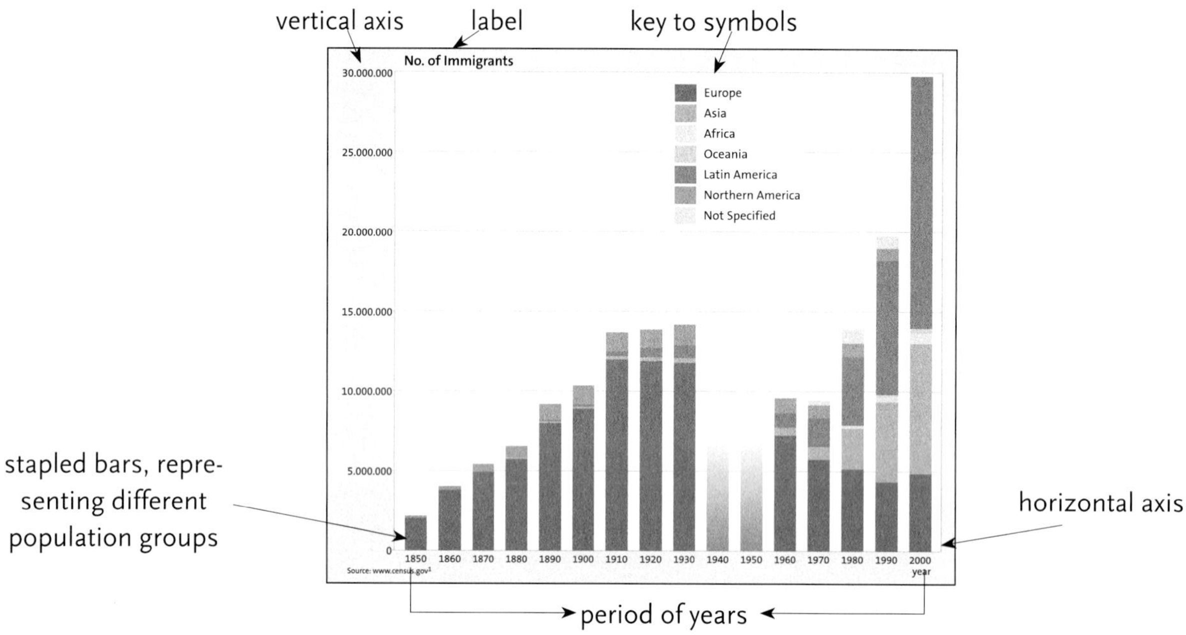

Bar Charts			
The vertical bar chart	shows uses	two axes one horizontal (x) and one vertical y-axis	
The y-axis The red/blue/green/yellow/ salmon/magenta/segment The vertical axis	represents gives shows indicates	numbers of ... percentages percentage levels	
	is labelled runs from (0 to xy)		
The x-axis The horizontal axis	stands for shows gives indicates is divided into	years/decades/periods (of time) ...	
The divisions on the horizontal axis	represent indicate		
The bar chart	helps to compare shows reveals	the development of a trend towards	two/three [...] groups
Line Graphs			
The line graph	represents shows indicates	the number of ... the increase/decrease in ...	from ... to ... over a period of ... years
	falls/rises	more/less sharply slowly/ gradually/steadily	during the period from ... to ... between ... and ... (years)
	shows gives evidence of	a clear/underlying trend towards	
	reaches	a (first/second) peak	in ... (year)

Worksheet 3

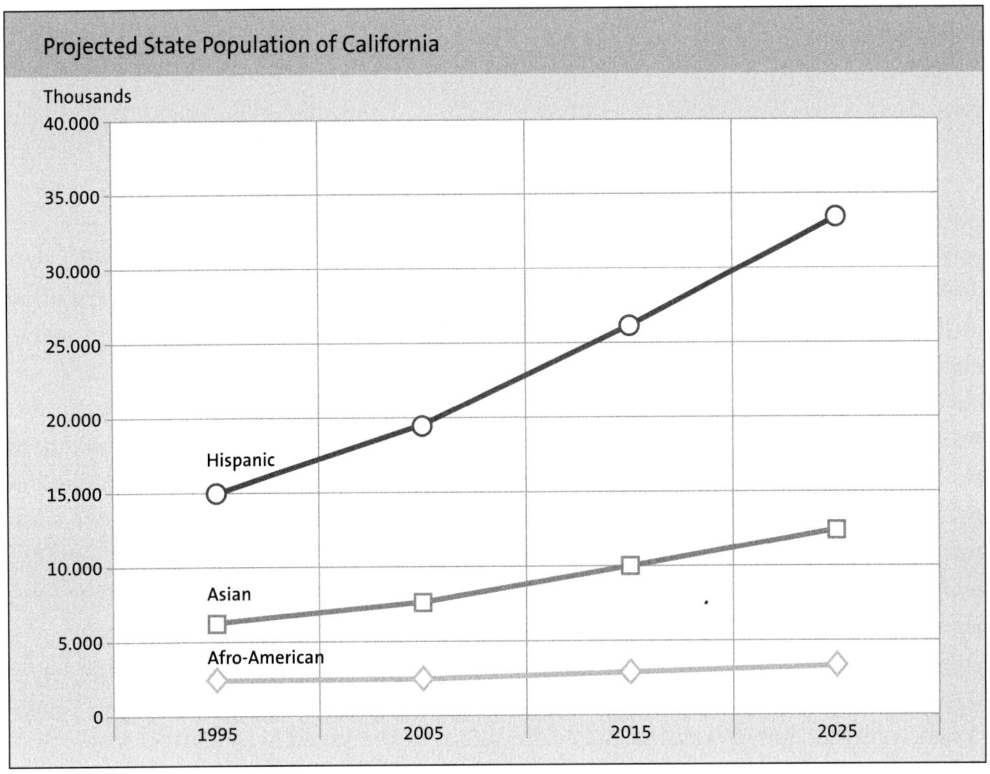

Activities

1. **Describe the line graph of the "Projected State Population of California".**
2. **Which demographic development becomes evident?**

The Grapes of Wrath

John Steinbeck

Author and text

John Steinbeck (1902–1968) was born in Salinas, California. He studied at Stanford University but never finished his studies. In 1925 he settled in New York, where he tried to establish himself as a writer, but was not able to get his works published. So he went back to California. His first three novels were hardly noticed by literary critics. He lived in Pacific Grove with his wife, where he gathered most of his material for his first widely known novel *Tortilla Flat* (1935). After this humorous novel his style and writing attitude changed into a more serious approach, dealing with social problems, especially among rural labourers. *In Dubious Battle* (1936) and *Of Mice and Men* (1937) are set in the world of migratory workers. In 1939 he published what is considered his finest novel, *The Grapes of Wrath*, a "Dust Bowl novel" narrating the story of Oklahoma tenant farmers who, unable to earn a living from the land, move to California to become migratory workers. This novel earned him the Pulitzer prize in 1940. His books were soon turned into successful films starring great American actors (*Tortilla Flat*, 1942; *Of Mice and Men*, 1939; and *Grapes of Wrath*, 1940, starring Henry Fonda and directed by John Ford) and so became known to the great American public.
During the war Steinbeck served as a war correspondent for *The New York Herald Tribune*. He returned home wounded in 1944. The next year he published another "Pacific Grove novel", *Cannery Row*, written once again in the more lighthearted style of his early novels. As he had become quite popular among movie producers, he participated in script writing for several films. The best known work of his later writing is *East of Eden* (1952), turned into a film starring James Dean. In 1962 Steinbeck won the Nobel Prize for Literature. He died in New York City in 1968.

Unterrichtsempfehlungen

Steinbecks Romanauszug öffnet einen neuen Aspekt des amerikanischen Traums, der in den letzten Jahren immer stärkere Beachtung gefunden hat: das trügerische Versprechen der unendlichen Weiten, die scheinbar nur erschlossen werden mussten, die sich dann aber schnell wieder in staubige Wüsten verwandelten und enttäuschte Lebensträume zurückließen. Die Beschäftigung mit den *„Great Plains"*, besonders unter ökologischen Fragestellungen, greift auch in der Fachliteratur gerne auf die Erfahrungen der *„Grapes of Wrath"* zurück. David Laskin zitiert in einem Beitrag der New York Times den Umweltautor Timothy Egan: „[It was] the nation's worst prolonged environmental disaster, [...]. Aside from Katrina, it's also probably the most familiar." Kein anderes Umweltdesaster ist so gut dokumentiert. Unter dem Suchbegriff *„dust bowl"* lassen sich Hunderte von Websites finden.
Im vorliegenden Buch wurde die Thematik bereits im Text „The West" im Schülerbuch (S. 22–25) angerissen. Daneben können zur Vertiefung der Problematik aktuelle Sachtexte herangezogen werden. Hier bieten sich an:
www.nytimes.com/2002/05/03/us/dry-high-plains-are-blowing-away-again.html
Co-ed Beitrag von Timothy Egan, in welchem die historischen und aktuellen Klimagefahren im mittleren Westen analysiert werden.

www.nytimes.com/2005/12/17/books/17lask.html
Buchbesprechung von David Laskin, der verschiedene Darstellungen, einschließlich Steinbecks Fiktion heranzieht.
Sehr umfassend informiert Stephanie LeMenagers Buch *Manifest and Other Destinies: Territorial Fictions of the Nineteenth-Century United States* (Postwestern Horizons, 2008)
In Steinbecks Romanauszug treffen verschiedene Wertesysteme aufeinander, die sich alle in der Tradition des *„American Dream"* sehen: zum einen das hart von der Familie erarbeitete Stückchen Glück, an dem, trotz aller Widrigkeiten, verzweifelt festgehalten wird; zum anderen die fortschrittsgläubige Einstellung des besser, effizienter und größer. Beide finden sich in den Versprechen des Traums, aber beide stehen, wenn sie aufeinandertreffen auch in unüberbrückbarem Widerspruch. Steinbeck kontrastiert diese im Dialog des *„Tenant"* mit dem Traktorfahrer, wobei beide Seiten mit guten Argumenten aufwarten und die Frage letztlich nur durch die Gewalt der Maschine gelöst wird.
Steinbeck wie auch Bruce Springsteen (s. u.) thematisieren in ihren Texten ein Amerika, das von vielen ignoriert wird. Es sind die Menschen, die dem Versprechen des amerikanischen Traumes gefolgt sind, der sich für sie kurzfristig zu realisieren schien, die dann aber von der Macht der sozialen und industriellen Veränderung überrannt werden, die keine Rücksicht auf den individuellen *„pursuit of happiness"* legt. Diese große schweigende Bevölkerungsgruppe, die sich mal diesem, mal jenem Leitidol anschließt, ist schwer fassbar. Barack Obama konnte sie in seinem Wahlkampf (2008) für sich mobilisieren, sie ist aber volatil, was den schnellen Absturz in der Zustimmung begründet. Diese Bevölkerungsgruppe existiert seit den frühen 1930er-Jahren. Roosevelt hat sie umworben, aber auch mit seinem „New Deal" nicht binden können.
Die Bearbeitung des Romanauszuges konzentriert sich auf die Kontrastierung der beiden Grundeinstellungen, welche in diesem Falle gar nicht weit auseinander liegen, denn beide, Traktorfahrer (Moderne) und *Tenant* (Tradition) wollen nur in der sich ändernden, unerbittlichen Welt überleben. Keiner will eigentlich dem anderen sein Glück, bzw. seinen Job wegnehmen, aber jeder muss sich um sein eigenes Überleben kümmern. Steinbecks literarischer Stil ist in dieser Passage gut zu erkennen, emotionslos, beschreibend, und damit aufwühlend stellt er die Situation da. Das Urteil bleibt dem Leser vorbehalten.
In der ersten Aufgabe, die sinnvollerweise als vorbereitende Hausaufgabe gestellt wird, geht es darum, sachlich die geschilderten Fakten zusammenzufassen. Hierauf baut Aufgabe 2 auf, die versucht, die sozialen und ökonomischen Zusammenhänge/Machtstrukturen zu visualisieren, ohne dabei schon eine Wertung anzustreben.
Die dritte Aufgabe, für die sich eine Gruppenarbeit anbietet, zielt auf die Empathie, der Schülerinnen und Schüler, welche sie gefühlsmäßig in diese für uns heute schwer vorstellbare Situation (Hunger) einführen soll. Aufgabe 4 kann ebenfalls in Kleingruppen gelöst werden, wobei jeweils zwei Gruppenmitglieder ihren Dialog vorspielen sollten. Der Perspektivwechsel sollte durch eine vorhergehende Sammlung der Argumente des Traktorfahrers vorbereitet werden. Wichtig ist die Einsicht, dass der Mann nicht aus niederen Motiven handelt, sondern auch lediglich seine Familie ernähren will. Er steht allerdings für die moderne industrielle Zeit (siehe sein „Outfit"), in welcher der Mensch Teil der Maschine zu werden scheint. (➔ Chaplin, *Modern Times*)
Nachdem jetzt beide Seiten beleuchtet wurden, kann in Gruppenarbeit die Diskussion von Aufgabe 5 vorbereitet werden. Die Argumente finden sich nur zum Teil im Text; moralisch haben natürlich die *Tenants* die Oberhand, ökonomisch allerdings die Gegenseite. Es sollte daher die Gelegenheit gegeben werden, sich mit der Sachlage (Industrialisierung vs. ökologischer Anbau in der Landwirtschaft) zu beschäftigen (➔ Internet).

Die Probleme im mittleren Westen berühren auch heute nur selten die Haltungen der Führungseliten. Aufgabe 6 versucht dies aufzugreifen und durch einen Kommentar zu erschließen. Welche Resonanz ein solcher Zeitungsbeitrag in den mittleren 30er-Jahren gehabt hätte, könnte abschließend im Plenum diskutiert werden.
Die gesamte Problemstellung ist bis heute relevant: in allen Ländern stellt sich die Frage, wie viel „Bio" unsere landwirtschaftlichen Produkte sein sollen und wie viel Industrie wir zugunsten des günstigeren Preises akzeptieren wollen. Die Besprechung dieser Frage, die am sinnvollsten in einer Debatte gelöst würde, ist von aktueller Relevanz und lässt sehr unterschiedliche Haltungen und Einstellungen zu. Die angebotenen Websites sind nur ein erster Beginn, man sollte aber überlegen, wie viel Zeit man auf diese Fragestellung verwendet und ob sich dies nicht auch als Projekt (fächerübergreifend) eignet.

Solutions

Activities p. 53

1. Write a short summary of the excerpt. Remember to use a neutral style.

The student	
uses the neutral style of a summary	AFB I
describes the lunch scene – the driver eating – the children watching	AFB I
outlines the main arguments of the discussion between the tractor driver and the tenant; it can be divided into three parts: 1. the change (16–48) – farming has become a big industry – if you want to earn money you have to fit in – property becomes alienated from the property owner 2. the individual problems of the driver and the tenant (49–69) – tractor driver has to follow orders or he loses his job – tenant refuses to leave the property he has built with his own hands 3. who is responsible? (70–89) – the tenant wants to shoot the person responsible. – neither man knows who gave the orders or who is to blame.	AFB I
describes how the tractor driver destroys the tenant's house and leaves the family homeless	AFB I

2. "Who can we shoot?" Who is responsible for the situation? Draw a pyramid of responsibility, starting with the driver at the bottom.

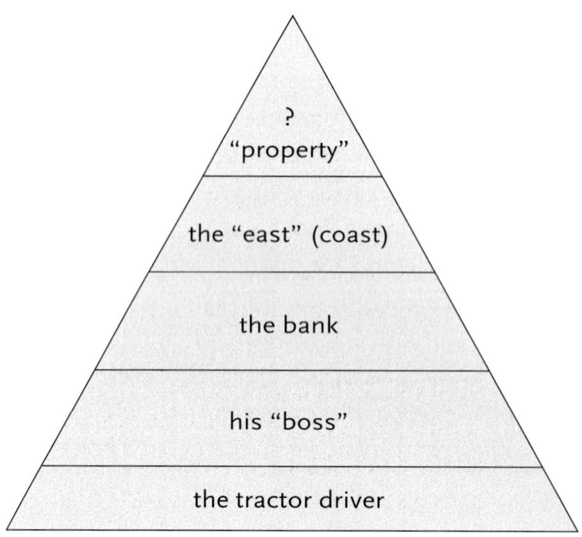

3. **Build a freeze frame of the children watching the driver.**
The freeze frame should reflect the information given in ll. 9 – 14.

4. **Back home, the driver tells his wife about the argument with the tenant. Retell from his point of view.**

The student	
uses the style of a personal narration	AFB I

narrates from the tractor driver's point of view
– the work he did in the morning (filled in the well to keep the lines straight)
– that he had lunch (some friendly words about how nice the sandwiches and the pie were)
– the argument he had with the tenant
  – that the tenant accused him of working against his people
  – how he explained the changes in modern farming
  – that the tenant still stuck to old fashioned views
  – that the tenant threatened to shoot him
  – how he explained to the tenant that it wasn't a personal affair but that he was only doing his job to earn his living
  – how they both tried to figure out who was responsible
– that he tore down the house
– that they might get a couple of dollars more because he destroyed the farmhouse and drove away the farmers.
	AFB II

5. **Stage a panel discussion between the tenants and the new owners. First, in groups, collect arguments for or against industrial farming. Then choose two speakers for each side.**

For industrial farming	Against industrial farming
– Higher efficiency – Technical equipment can be used – Higher revenue – Better overall use of the land – ...	– Individual use of the soil – Less need for chemical treatment – Decisions are made by more individuals – Less risk of mismanagement – Feeds more families

6. **Imagine you are a journalist working for a newspaper on the east coast. Write a comment on what is going on in the Midwest. Don't forget to make your opinion clear.**

The student	
uses the formal style of a newspaper comment	AFB II
describes the problems in the Midwest (aridity)	AFB III
points out the two opposing attitudes (individual farming vs. industrial farming)	AFB III
expresses sympathy/doesn't express sympathy towards the farmers	AFB III
questions/supports the use of industrial farming	AFB III
states his/her opinion regarding the future development of the region	AFB III

7. **The conflict between traditional and industrial farming is still relevant today. Gather information about the present situation.**
Here are some websites that contain information both for and against industrial farming:
www.farmsanctuary.org/issues/factoryfarming
www.humanesociety.org/issues/campaigns/factory_farming
http://en.wikipedia.org/wiki/Industrial_agriculture
http://eh.net/encyclopedia/article/gardner.agriculture.us

The Ghost of Tom Joad

Bruce Springsteen

Author and text

Bruce Springsteen, born September 23, 1949, is an America rock singer and songwriter. Due to his roots and his first successful albums he is still linked to the blue-collar life of the Jersey Shore. He is a multiple Grammy Award winner (20 times), earned two Golden Globes and also won the Oscar in 1994 for his song "Streets of Philadelphia", featured on the soundtrack to the film *Philadelphia*. He had his greates success in 1984 with the best-selling album *Born in the USA* that sold more than 15 million copies in the USA. The title track, a bitter commentary on the treatment the Vietnam veterans received at home, has often been misinterpreted, though the lyrics are clear and unambiguous. The Livealbum box set (1975–1985) sold the following year, which chronicles the first ten years of his career, is still the most successful live recording ever sold, selling more than 13 million copies. Despite his earlier success his fame faded in the nineties. His solo project after the split-up with the E-Street Band had become too political for some fans in his country, though European fans continued to buy his records. "The Ghost of Tom Joad" dates back to the nineties (1995), a decade Springsteen later referred to as "lost years". The style of the song is more reminiscent of Dylan or Seeger than of Springsteen, and the minimal vocals and the twangy music (harmonica and minimal guitar) were not appreciated by the wide public. Nevertheless the album of the same name gave voice to minorities in the USA, such as immigrants and homeless people. Continuing to sing about political topics he participated in the 2004 Vote for Change tour, participating with the E-Street band and other famous American pop stars (R.E.M., John Mellencamp, The Dixie Chicks, etc.) trying to gain a Democrat majority against George W. Bush. Following his new protest song concept he recorded the *Pete-Seeger Sessions* in 2006, paying homage to arguably the greatest American protest singer-songwriter ("We shall overcome") of the 20th century. Beginning in April 2008 Springsteen supported Senator Barack Obama in his presidential campaign, offering free concerts for the candidate and using his fame to help Obama gain a majority of votes. He explained his political involvement by pointing out that he was (still) fighting for "Truth, transparency and integrity in government, the right of every American to have a job, a living wage, to be educated in a decent school, and a life filled with the dignity of work, the promise and the sanctity of home." In 2009 Springsteen was given the Kennedy Center Honors, an annual award to personalities from the world of arts for their contribution to American culture.

Unterrichtsempfehlungen

Bruce Springsteen ist auch heute noch ein sehr bekannter Künstler in Deutschland, seine Konzerte sind regelmäßig ausverkauft, auch wenn die Zielgruppe/Fangemeinde deutlich über dem Alter der Schülerinnen und Schüler liegt. Der gewählte Song entspricht wahrscheinlich nicht dem Hörgeschmack einer größeren Anzahl der Lernenden, er schließt andererseits nahtlos an den vorhergehenden Text an und unterstreicht dessen Aussagen in ihrer aktuellen Relevanz. Der Song ist als Hörverstehensübung geeignet, da er sprachlich nicht sehr schwierig ist. Dazu ist allerdings die Vorbereitung durch den *Pre-reading Task* notwendig.

Die Sammlung der inhaltlichen Aussagen (Aufgabe 1 und 2) kann auch noch im Unterrichtsgespräch, möglichst ohne Textvorlage erfolgen. Dabei können die Schülerinnen und Schüler in einer *Placemat Activity* die wesentlichen, von ihnen erfassten Informationen sammeln. Dies kann nachfolgend mit dem Text abgeglichen werden.

Für Aufgabe 3, die in der Klasse, allerdings auch als Hausaufgabe bearbeitet werden kann, sollte die zweispaltige Tabelle (s. u.) vorgegeben werden. In der Collage werden affektive Lernziele stärker evoziert, als dies häufig bei der reinen Textarbeit geschieht. Die Lernenden vergegenwärtigen sich die Szene und suchen passende Illustrationen, ergänzen vielleicht auch selbst zeichnerisch. Beim Museumsrundgang kann zudem der individuelle Sprachanteil gesteigert werden, indem in jeder „Besuchergruppe" immer jeweils möglichst nur ein „Künstler" ist, der den anderen sein/ihr jeweiliges Poster erläutert.
Durch die Collage ist die wertend-urteilende Aufgabe 5 ausreichend vorbereitet. Im Sinne der Lösung nach den Vorgaben des Zentralabiturs sollten dabei auch weitergehende Kommunikationsstrategien (Einbeziehung eigener Erwartungen und Erfahrungen) berücksichtigt werden.
Die letzte Aufgabe wird, dem jeweiligen Zeitgeschmack und den musikalischen Vorlieben der Lerngruppe entsprechend unterschiedliche Ergebnisse bringen. Hier bietet sich eine Sprachmittlungsübung an (*Explain to an American friend why you think this song treats a similar topic.*).

Solutions

Before you read p. 53

Search the Internet for references to Tom Joad. What does this character stand for? Quote/Present examples.
There are more than 240,000 hits for "Tom Joad" on Google. Besides the Wikipedia entry (http://en.wikipedia.org/wiki/Tom_Joad) it might be interesting to check: www.tomjoad.org/, a website that "in that spirit of solidarity with everyone, everywhere, expressed by the character Tom Joad [...] tries to provide a place [...] for political commentary and information regarding struggles for justice."
Another interesting website is http://tomjoadwashere.com. This site is "a selfinitiated street art project by a Denver, Colorado-based artist and graphic designer. The current state of our economy is in a severe crisis and is beginning to resemble the Great Depression of the 1930s. The purpose of this project is to spread awareness of the financial crisis by using various forms of visual communication and self-expression."
Note that a band from Münster has also chosen the name "The Ghost of Tom Joad".

Activities p. 54

1. **Outline what the speaker depicts in the first and second stanza.**

In the first stanza (ll. 1–8) the speaker depicts
– a group of men following the railroad tracks – a police helicopter watching/observing the scene – a long line of people waiting to get some warm soup served under a bridge – families that have no home and are sleeping in their cars
In the second stanza (ll. 13–20) he describes
– a preacher praying from his prayer book – he is sleeping/living in a cardboard box under a bridge/underpass – he is hungry – he has got a gun – he has no bed but has to sleep on the hard rock ground – he uses the city's sewer to wash himself

2. **How does he describe his own situation?**
The speaker seems to be one of the homeless people. He is sitting by a campfire.

3. Compare the text from Steinbeck's novel and the message of the third stanza. What do they have in common, where do they differ?

Steinbeck	Springsteen
I'll be – all around in the dark – everywhere you look – wherever there's a fight so hungry people can eat – wherever there's a cop beating up a guy – in the way guys yell when they are mad – in the way kids laugh when they are hungry and supper is ready – when our folks eat the stuff they have raised and live in houses they have built	Mom, (you'll see me) – wherever there's a cop beating a guy – wherever a hungry newborn baby cries – where there's a fight against the blood and hatred in the air – wherever there's somebody fighting for a place to stand or a decent job or a helping hand – wherever there's somebody struggling to be free
Both texts have many elements in common (hunger; violence; hatred), but they differ slightly in some aspects, though the overall message is the same:	
– The first two elements are very general. – The last two elements have a positive undertone (hope).	– No positive views, all elements are negative. – The aspect of "decent job" and "place to stand" are more general. – The concept of "freedom" goes further than anything mentioned in Steinbeck's text.

Activities p. 55

4. In groups make a collage (use newspapers/magazines) of the pictures evoked by this song. In a gallery walk explain to the others in your class what your collage shows.

The song evokes powerful images. The students should bring the necessary material (magazines/newspapers/pictures) from home and then in groups of four or five create a collage. When finished the students explain in a gallery walk what they have chosen/what aspects they have focused on etc.

5. As an exchange student you have, on your way to California, come across this band of people. Write a letter to your friends back home and tell them about your impressions.

The student	
uses the informal style of a private letter	AFB II
expresses his/her positive emotions/expectations about his/her trip to California	AFB III
expresses surprise/shock regarding the things he/she has seen – describing the scene – contrasting the situation with what he/she expected about the American Dream – perhaps compares the situation with something similar seen/lived at home/in another country – finally stating his/her opinion	AFB III

6. Do you know any German pop/rock songs that treat a similar topic?

Open answer. Students might mention songs by *Die Ärzte* or *Die Toten Hosen*, but also some rap singers (especially those from Berlin) might be named. It is important that the examples be explained and, if possible, compared to Springsteen's song.

A Divided Society

Daniel J. Kevles

Author and text

Daniel J. Kevles, born in Philadelphia in 1939, is Professor of History at Yale University. He is well known in the USA for his popular writing, as he summarizes and narrates historical findings and surveys in readable texts and thus opens scientific literature to a wider readership. The extract has been taken from the American history book *Inventing America* (New York, 2003), which he co-edited.

Unterrichtsempfehlungen

Der Text ist aus einem zweibändigen amerikanischen Geschichtsbuch entnommen, das sich an Schülerinnen und Schüler der High Schools sowie an Studierende richtet. Der Text verschriftlicht eine hohe Zahl von statistischen Daten und ist damit nicht leicht lesbar. An dieser Stelle wird der umgekehrte Schritt als im Kapitel 3 (SB S. 32 ff.) gegangen: Aus den vertexteten Informationen sollen Darstellungen in einem abstrakten, non-linearen Zeichensystem (Grafiken) entstehen. Diese Fertigkeit hat nicht nur im bilingualen Sachfachunterricht einen hohen Stellenwert, sondern ist in vielen Bereichen der universitären Ausbildung von großer Bedeutung.

Die erste Aufgabe, die erst nach der häuslichen Bearbeitung und Texterschließung zu behandeln ist, sollte zunächst in Partnerarbeit interessante Daten aus dem Text isolieren. Wenn es möglich ist, die so gesammelten Daten in einen Computer einzugeben (z. B. in *MS Excel* oder *OpenOffice Calc*), können die Schülerinnen und Schüler mit unterschiedlichen Formen der Visualisierung experimentieren. So erfahren sie gleichzeitig, dass dieselben Daten, unterschiedlich visualisiert, einen recht unterschiedlichen Eindruck hinterlassen und somit die Wahl der Präsentationsart auch eine Frage der Rezipientensteuerung ist.

Zusätzlich können weitere Informationsquellen genutzt werden, z. B.
http://en.wikipedia.org/wiki/Demographics_of_the_United_States_Congress
mit zahlreichen zusätzlichen Informationen);
http://baic.house.gov/ (die offizielle Seite der „*Black Americans in Congress*")
Zu allen anderen Daten finden sich vertiefende Ergänzungen unter:
www.census.gov (Achtung! Sehr umfangreich und detailliert, eine Vorauswahl ist unbedingt notwendig.)

Die zweite Aufgabe beschäftigt sich auf einem recht einfachen inhaltlichen Niveau mit der Auswertung der erstellten Datenübersichten. Die Bearbeitung kann im Unterrichtsgespräch erfolgen, wobei die Darstellung der Schülerinnen und Schüler auf den AFB III gerichtet sein sollte.

Die dritte Aufgabe bereitet auf die folgenden Texte, die sich zunächst auf den betrachteten Zeitraum der Fünfziger- und Sechzigerjahre beziehen, vor und schafft durch die Systematisierung eine thematische Vorentlastung.

Solutions

Activities p. 57

1. **There is a lot of data in this text from a history book. Structure the text into topical units and then, in groups, draw charts visualizing the data. Give appropriate headings.**

   The general problem you will encounter extracting the data is that the author sometimes doesn't give a clear reference group, i. e. "Members of Congress". It is alarming to read the "murder rate for black males [...] was between eight and fourteen times higher than the national murder rate (ll. 53–55), but the reader still doesn't know the exact national murder rate. The choice of graph to represent the data partly depends on what you want to express or underline: line charts describe a development, bar charts underline contrast and pie charts can show how big (or small) a portion is. Students might experiment with different types.

The first topical unit (ll. 1–10) is "acceptance of Afro-Americans". Note that, though a recent publication, the author uses the word "blacks" or "non-whites" (encompassing more than just Afro-Americans), which should be avoided in classroom discussion.

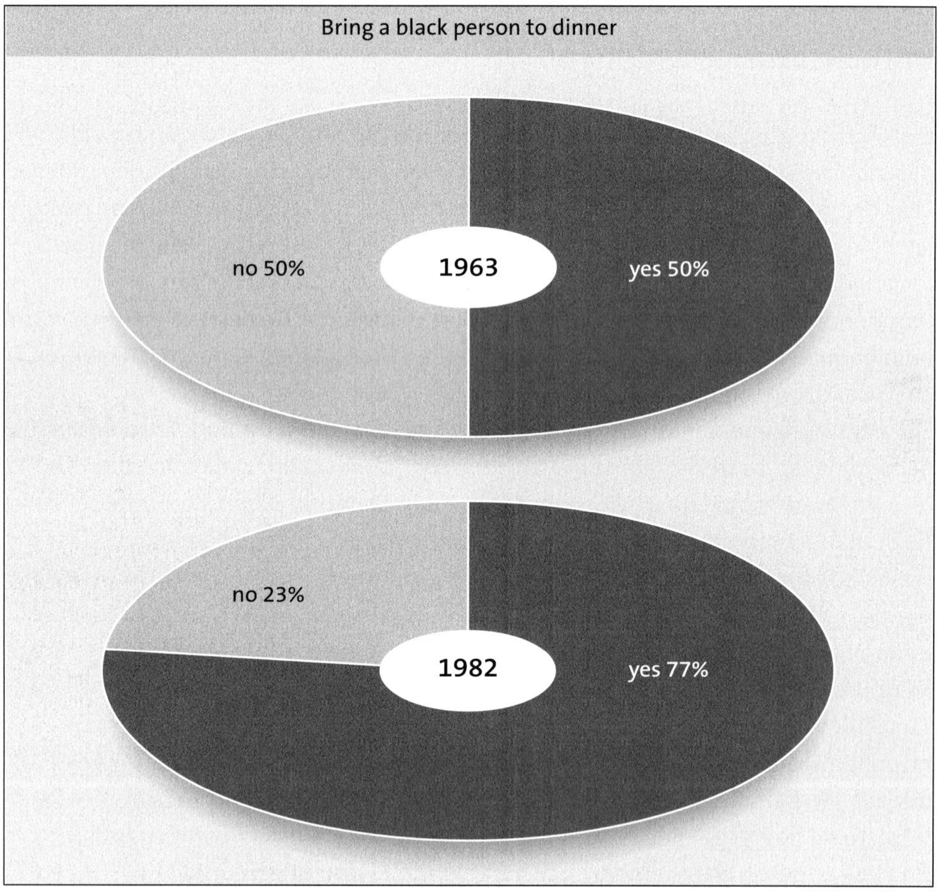

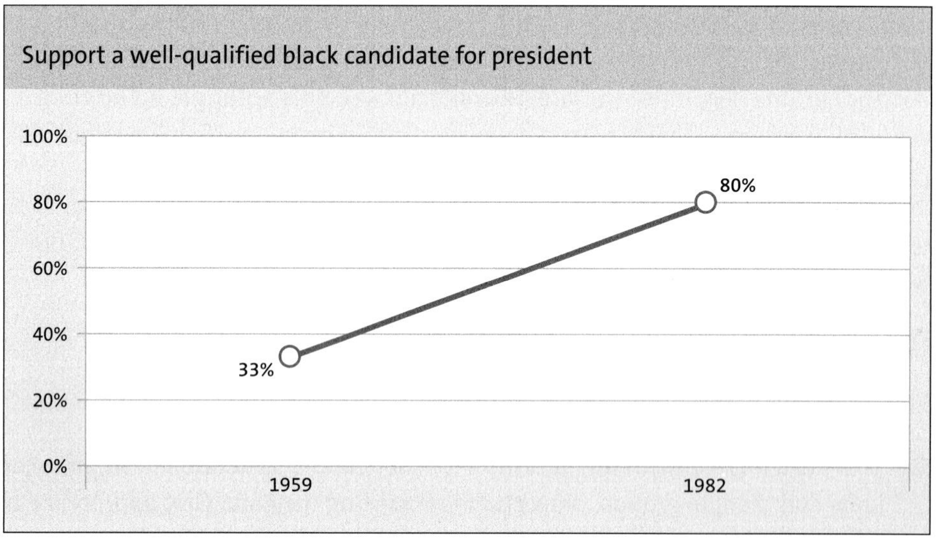

The second topic is "the division of the Afro-American society" (ll. 10–33).

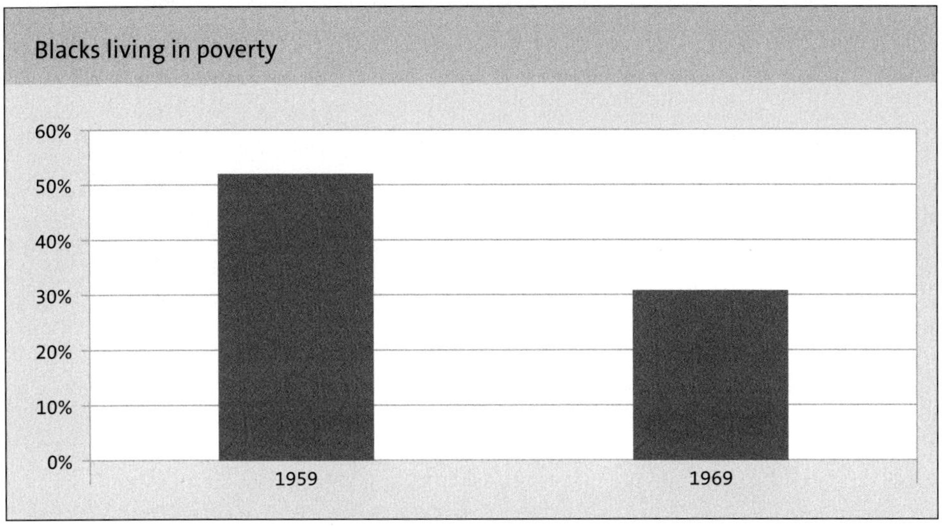

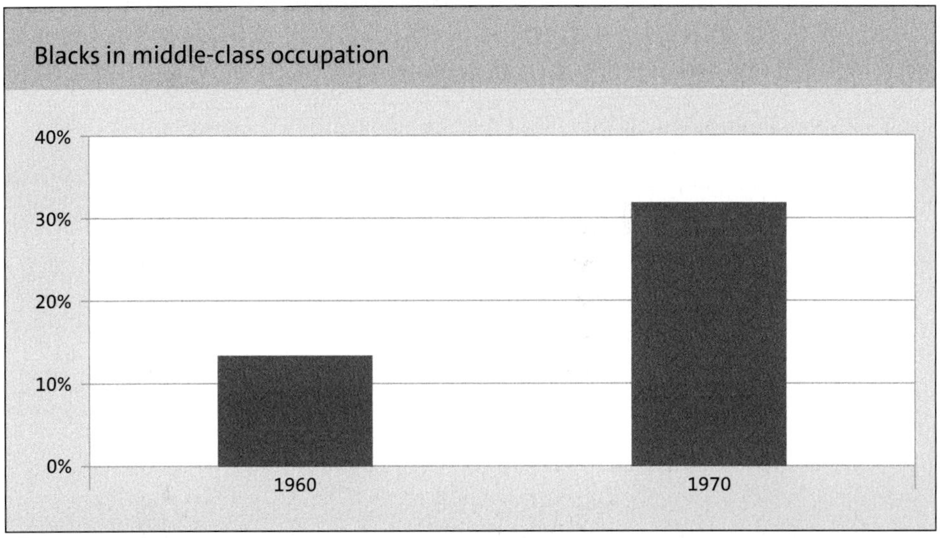

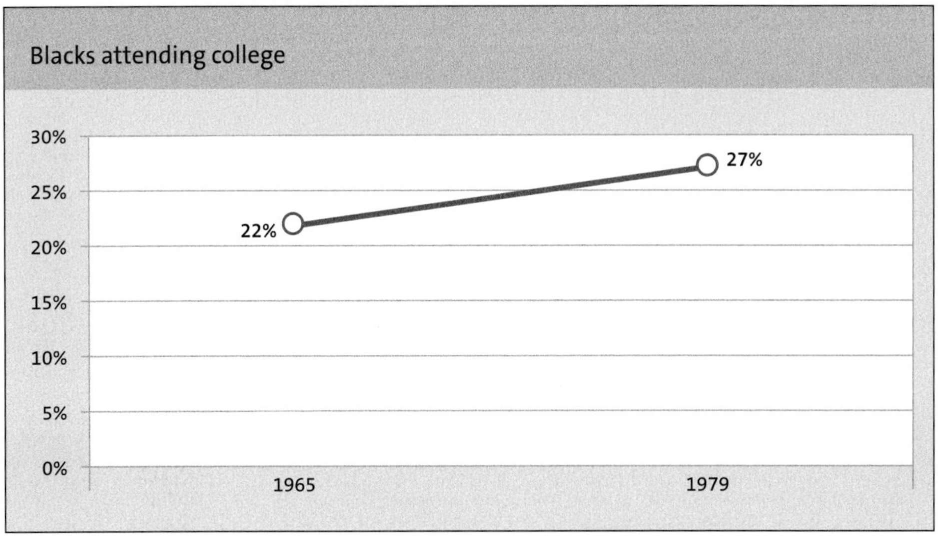

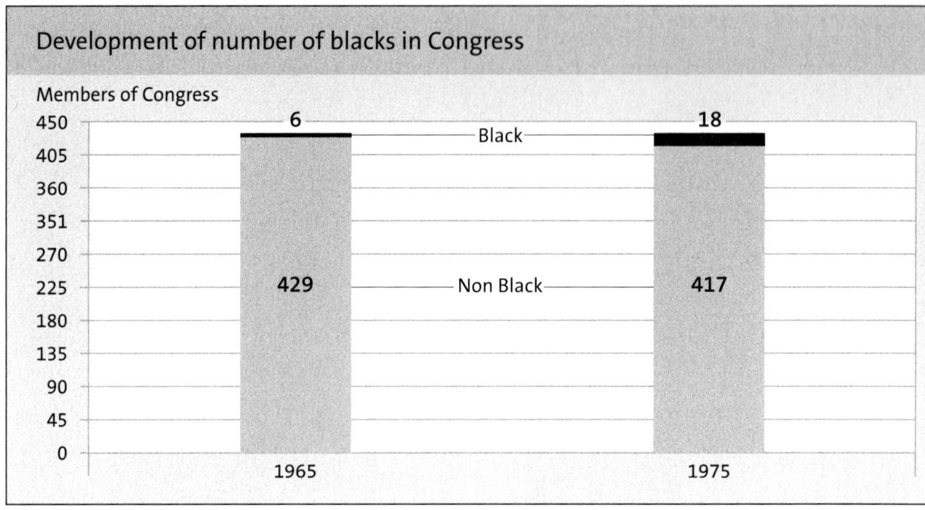

There are 435 members of Congress. Between 1870 and 2010 only 125 Afro-Americans became members of Congress. The information that the number of Afro-American members tripled (l. 30) is misleading, especially when you compare to the overall number of members of Congress.

The following topical unit is about "racism and discrimination" (ll. 34–49).

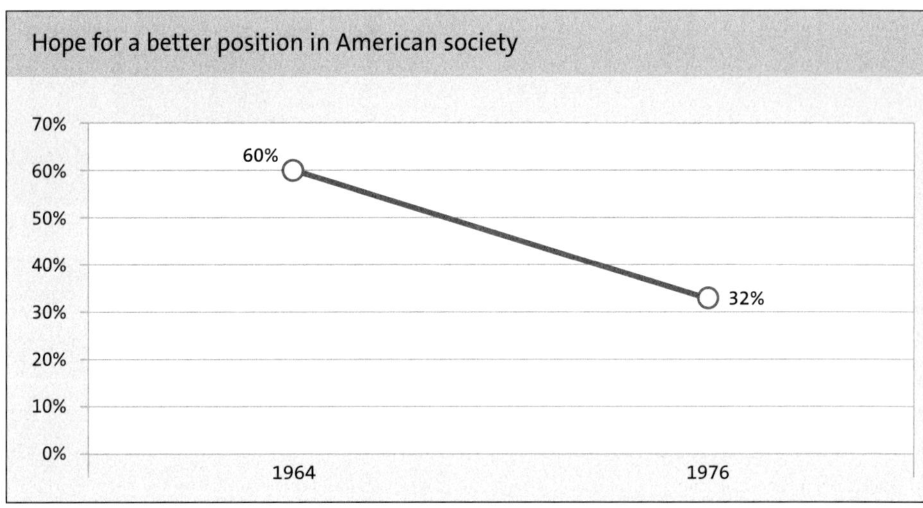

The last paragraph deals with "unemployment, crime and murder rates" but most data given there cannot be easily plotted on a graph.

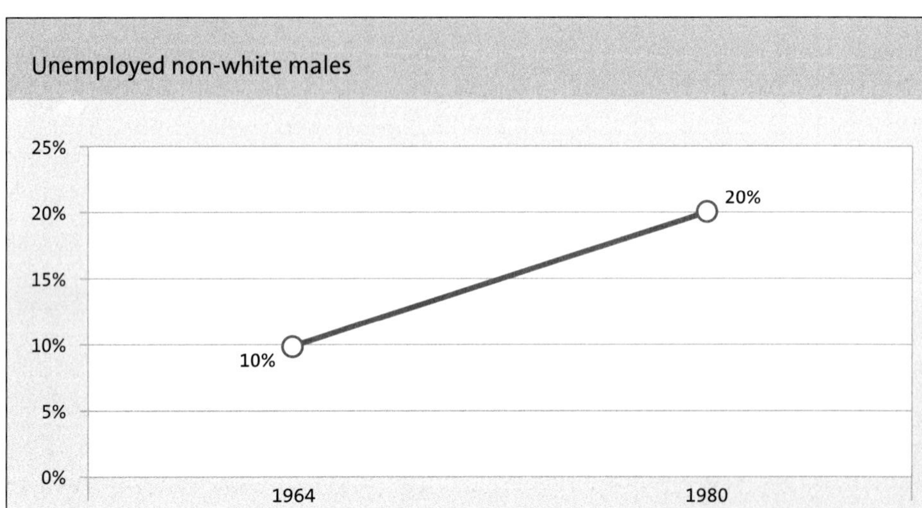

2. **Discuss the title of the text. Do your charts support this title?**
The society is doubly divided: for one the Afro-American society falls into two parts, the smaller being accepted and moving up on the social scale, whereas the greater part still lives on the fringes of society; on the other hand the data also show that the Afro-American population stays apart in many developments of American society as a whole (use "Members of Congress" as an example).

3. **Make a double list of things that have improved since the 1950s/60s and those that have worsened.**

Improved	Worsened
– tolerance towards Afro-Americans (bring black person to dinner) (7) – acceptance: Support a well-qualified black candidate for president (9) – schooling, college (28), obtaining better jobs (11 ff.) – fewer blacks living in poverty – rise to middle class occupation (26)	– rise of discrimination at workplace perceived (36) – no change in attitude of (white) American society (38) – rise of poverty rate among Afro-Americans in the inner cities (45) – rise of unemployed non-white males (51) – rise of crime and murder rate for black males (53)

Harlem

Langston Hughes

Author and text

Langston Hughes, born in 1902 in Joplin, Missouri, was one of the first Afro-American writers of the 20th century and certainly one of the most influential. He belonged to a very prominent family: his great uncle John Mercer Langston was the first black American elected to Congress (see picture and biography on http://baic.house.gov), and his maternal grandmother Mary Patterson was of African-American, French, English and Native American descent and one of the first coloured women to attend Oberlin College. Though a member of an elite and politically active family, his childhood was far from happy, as his father, no longer able to endure the hatred and racism of his country, left the family to live outside the USA. Langston Hughes grew up with his maternal grandmother Mary Patterson in Lawrence, Kansas. It was his grandmother who taught him literature and installed a deep pride for the Afro-American population. After the death of his grandmother he lived with his mother in Lincoln, Illinois. Still at Lincoln grammar school, he began writing poetry and short stories for the school newspaper. He asked his father to pay for tuition at a university and his father finally agreed, maintaining that his son should study engineering. Langston Hughes followed these studies at Columbia university for about a year, suffering from manifest racial discrimination. During this time he began to explore the university's neighbourhood and spent more and more time in Harlem, writing poetry again. Hughes later claimed his work during that period was mainly influenced by reading Walt Whitman and Carl Sandburg. His first collection of poems (*The Weary Blues*) was published in 1926 and he was soon acclaimed the "new black poet". After some travels and work in different jobs, he enrolled at Lincoln University, Pennsylvania, one of the first universities that offered higher education to students of Afro-American origin. He left the university after earning a B.A. In the same year he moved to Harlem in New York, a city he only left for some travels, mainly to Europe, afterwards.
Hughes' writings focus on "being black" in American society; although he was a member of the small Afro-American middle-class which some accused of ignoring the lives of the poorer classes, he tried to depict the struggles of the low folks, presenting power-

ful images of working-class people in his texts. His primal goal throughout his work was to establish the pride of an Afro-American nation, having its own clearly recognizable culture and tradition. His national and international career began in the thirties; he received numerous awards (Harmon Gold Medal; Guggenheim fellowship). Like other writers of his time (see John Steinbeck) he discovered the increasing influence of the cinema and wrote for the silver screen (*Way Down South*), though racial prejudice was stronger in that business than in other arts.
During the fifties Langston Hughes became a role model for many Afro-American writers. In 1952 the McCarthy committee questioned his open support of communist ideas in the early thirties, but this led to no further consequences. In the wake of the civil rights movement in the sixties he was honoured by many institutions: he became a member of the National Institute of Arts and Letters, and in 1963 Howard University awarded him an honorary doctorate. Langston Hughes died on May 22, 1967, due to complications after cancer surgery at the age of 65.
His fame grew further after his death, so in 1981, New York City Landmark status was given to his house in Harlem at 20 East 127th Street. His 100th birthday was commorated by a special stamp in February 2002.
The poem "Harlem" was published in 1951 in the collection *A Dream Deferred*, but might have been written some time earlier, probably in the thirties.

Unterrichtsempfehlungen

Das Gedicht von Langston Hughes ist ein Klassiker der afro-amerikanischen Literatur und nimmt bereits Jahre zuvor Martin Luther Kings „Dream" vorweg. Obwohl Hughes sich selbst zu den gemeinsamen Wurzeln der amerikanischen Lyrik bekennt, schafft er eine lyrische Aussage die außerhalb der „weißen" amerikanischen Lyrik steht.
Das Gedicht sollte im Unterricht den Schülerinnen und Schülern zunächst einmal zur Vorbereitung in Einzelarbeit präsentiert werden. Es ist sprachlich nicht sehr schwierig, sodass die erste Aufgabe nach einer kurzen Vorbereitungszeit (ggf. Klärung von Ausspracheschwierigkeiten) in der Klasse präsentiert werden kann. Interessant ist hier die Fragestellung, ob, und wenn wie lang, die Pausen nach Zeile 8 bzw. 10 sind.
Auch die zweite Aufgabe kann in einer von der Lehrperson moderierten Diskussionsrunde bearbeitet werden.
Aufgabe 3 sollte in Partnerarbeit mit anschließender gemeinsamer Sammlung gelöst werden. Die Besprechung führt thematisch bereits zur vierten Aufgabe, in welcher die Visualisierung im Vordergrund steht. Hierbei kann die Arbeit an den Plakaten in Gruppenarbeit im Unterricht beginnen, die Suche nach geeigneten Illustrationen erfolgt aber besser in häuslicher Arbeit. Dazu kann ebenfalls Aufgabe 5 bereits zur schriftlichen Bearbeitung gegeben werden. Mit den Postern und den Hypothesen zur Textaussage, kann abschließend in einer gemeinsamen Diskussion, die Bedeutung des Gedichts erschlossen werden, wobei die abschließende Rezeption sicherlich für die Einzelnen offen bleiben muss.
Die Wirkung auf die Zeitgenossen (historischer Hintergrund der frühen 50er-Jahre), sollte, als Vorbereitung auf die Besprechung des Dramenauszuges (*Raisin in the Sun*) diskutiert werden.

Solutions

Before you read p. 57

The stamp was published to commemorate his 100th birthday in 2002. What does this tell you about the author and his importance today?

To be commemorated by a stamp is a privileg and it shows that in the 21st century the United States valued one of its finest writers and poets. Hughes probably would have felt honoured, because the stamp didn't honour him only as a great American writer, but placed him in the context of "Black Heritage", his lifelong goal.

1. In a first step, read the poem silently and try to understand its meaning. Then read it aloud to your class. Compare different presentations.
Individual presentations

Activities p. 57

2. In a few sentences, try to say what the poem is about.
When your dreams are always denied this might lead to destruction.

3. Make a list of the most striking stylistic devices. Name the main differences between the first (ll. 1–8), the second (ll. 9–10) and the last (l. 11) stanza.

Activities p. 58

Alliteration	"**d**ream **d**eferred" (1) "**d**oes it **d**ry" (2) "**s**yrupy **s**weet" (8)
Metaphor	"a dream" ... "explode"
Repetition	"does it" (2) ... "does it" (6) ... "does it" (11) "like a" (3) ... "like a" (4) ... "like" (6) ... "like a" (8) ... "like a" (10)
Rhetorical questions	"What happens to ...?" (1) "Does it dry up?" (2) "Like a raisin in the sun?" (3) "Or fester [...]/and then run?" (4f.) "Or crust [...]/Like a syrupy sweet?" (7f.) "Or does it explode?" (11)
Rhyme	"sun" (3) "run" (5) "meat" (6) "sweet" (8) "load" (10) "explode" (11)
Simile	"Like a raisin in the sun?" (3) "Like a sore –" (4) "Like a syrupy sweet?" (8) "Like a heavy load." (10)

The first stanza is marked by a repetition of rhetorical question each answered with a new question. The second stanza changes, introducing a statement. The last line/stanza introduces a new question, leaving the answer (and interpretation) to the reader.

4. In groups write down the images of the poem on a poster. You may try to illustrate them with a drawing or a picture. What do they symbolize?
The similes in the first stanza are all, except one ("like a sore", 4), taken from the semantic field /food/. Food is essential for all living beings; when food gets wasted, it doesn't serve its purpose anymore and goes rotten, while people go hungry and suffer. A sore that festers often indicates that the body is no longer healthy, as it cannot cope with infection. A heavy load that sags usually means that the person carrying that load feels oppressed and may stumble.
The first question leads to the question in the last line, creating an all-encompassing metaphor, a dream that explodes (like a bomb).

5. The last line/stanza is in different print. Do you think that it contains a warning or a threat? Give reasons.
This last line has often been read as a warning. The dream referred to throughout the poem is comparable to Martin Luther King's concept of a dream. The last line, however, can be seen as a direct threat, bearing a revolutionary message as later expressed by Malcolm X. The consequences of "a dream deferred" as described in

the first two stanzas are unpleasant but nonetheless quiet and slow processes that do not affect outsiders. An explosion, however, poses a threat to everyone, and this difference is emphasized with italic print.

A Raisin in the Sun

Lorraine Hansberry

Author and text

Lorraine Hansberry (1930–1965) was an Afro-American playwright. Her partly autobiographical play *A Raisin in the Sun* was written in the mid-fifties while she worked in New York City for the black newspaper *Freedom*. Its imminent success was a big surprise, and she became the first female Afro-American playwright to be played on Broadway. The play earned her the New York Drama Critics Circle Award at the age of 29 and was turned into a successful movie in 1961. When she died at the age of 34 in 1965, she left some unfinished manuscripts, which were later completed by her husband. The most famous among these is the play *Young, Gifted and Black*.
The extract is one of the last discussions between Beneatha and her African boyfriend Asagai. Both represent the intellectual characters of the play, whose discussions reflect a broader, more critical view of the world than some of the other characters of the play.

Unterrichtsempfehlungen

Der hier ausgewählte Auszug aus dem Theaterstück unterscheidet sich in einigen Aspekten vom Rest des Textes; die beiden Charaktere sprechen korrektes Englisch, was für viele andere (lesenswerte) Auszüge nicht zugetroffen hätte. Des Weiteren ist der Textabschnitt, so wie er hier behandelt wird, ohne viele Begleitinformationen verständlich. Der Text spiegelt eine Situation, welche am Ende der 1950er-Jahre in Teilen der afro-amerikanischen Bevölkerung vorhanden war, die heute aber kaum noch Spuren zeigt. Angesichts der scheinbar unüberwindlichen Rassendiskriminierung träumten viele gebildete Afro-Amerikaner davon, in die ursprüngliche Heimat zurückzukehren, die gerade im Begriff war, sich von den Fesseln des Kolonialismus zu befreien. Den Zwiespalt der Frage des Bleibens und des Versuchs, auf dem afrikanischen Mutterkontinent den gleichen Traum zu initiieren, den die USA nach 1776 gelebt hatten, teilten besonders die Intellektuellen. Lorraine Hansberry zeigt durch die Figur der Beneatha prophetisch die drohenden Gefahren auf. Was Beneatha in den Zeilen 6–9 über die jungen Staatsgründungen auf dem afrikanischen Kontinent vorhersagt, ist leider so, und zum Teil noch viel schrecklicher, eingetreten. Hansberry hoffte auf die Realisierung des Traums in ihrem Heimatland, den USA, sah aber auch die Kluft zwischen dem rein materialistischen Traum und der umfassenderen Verwirklichung des Traums, wie sie Martin Luther King nur wenige Jahre später aufzeigen sollte. Für die weitere Bearbeitung des Themas wird als nächstes die letzte Rede (SB S. 60 ff.) des Friedensnobelpreisträgers in den Fokus zu rücken sein, denn auch er sieht 1968 mit kritischem Auge auf das Scheitern der jungen afrikanischen Nationen.
Der Dramentext soll daher schwerpunktmäßig unter diesem Aspekt, dem Streben nach dem „afrikanischen" Traum, behandelt werden. Hierzu werden in den Aufgaben 1 und 2 die beiden konkurrierenden Ideale erarbeitet. Beneatha ist in ihrem auf materielle Werte verkürzten Ideal des amerikanischen Traumes stecken geblieben und muss einsehen, dass sich ihr Leben nicht wie erträumt weiterentwickeln wird, Asagai träumt idealistisch noch von einer neuen besseren Welt auf dem afrikanischen Kontinent (Aufgabe 2). Beide Aufgaben konzentrieren sich schwerpunktmäßig auf das Textverständ-

nis und sollten von den Schülerinnen und Schülern in häuslicher Vorbereitung erarbeitet werden. Die Ergebnisse dieser Vorarbeit werden sukzessive in der Lerngruppe gesammelt und im Anschrieb (Folie/Tafel) festgehalten.
Die dritte Aufgabe benötigt eine recht zeitaufwändige Recherche, die bei Zeitmangel im Lehrervortrag zu bewerkstelligen wäre, ansonsten sollten die Schülerinnen und Schüler ihre Ergebnisse von der Lehrperson moderiert zusammen tragen.
Die vierte Aufgabe vernetzt wiederum mit den vorhergehenden Texten (Adams & Joplin) und den hier gewonnenen Erkenntnissen über die grundlegenden Konzeptionen des amerikanischen Traums. Die letzte Aufgabe kann knapp abgearbeitet werden (Gruppenarbeit mit *Placemat* und abschließender Diskussion), oder auch zeitintensiver in arbeitsteiliger Gruppenarbeit mit abschließender Präsentation (und Diskussion) bearbeitet werden.
Der interkulturelle Lernansatz liegt bei dieser Erörterung auf der in der Geschichte immer wieder gestellten Frage: „Warum geht ihr dann nicht fort?“ Thomas Mann hat Deutschland verlassen, aber Heinrich Böll ist trotz aller inneren Widerstände geblieben, einfach weil es seine Heimat war und er nicht wusste, was er woanders sollte. Beneatha und Asagai diskutieren genau diesen Zwiespalt.

Solutions

Activities p. 60

1. **Apparently Beneatha has lost all hopes and dreams. In your own words sum up her view of life.**
   Beneatha
   – doesn't believe in black leadership (5 ff.)
   – thinks that there is no progress or development, and everything is just turning in a circle (13 ff.)
   – thinks she has lost her future because her family has lost their money possessions.

2. **Asagai has an "African Dream." This dream is partly linked to ideas of the American Dream. Outline the main aspects of his dream.**
   – Independence (5)
   – The dream is a long line pointing into infinity. (20)
   – Doesn't want to give up being idealistic and believes in (positive) changes (22)
   – Dreams should not depend on material riches. (36 f.)

3. **Beneatha criticizes his dream and predicts that the only change will be that the crooks will be black instead of white (see l. 6 ff.). Has she been right or wrong? Check for Nigeria, the country he wants to return to, that became independent in 1960, just one year after the publication of the play.**
   Students will find a lot of websites (some biased!) concerning Nigeria. Its independence did not result in peace and prosperity, as there are, as in many English colonies, several different ethnic regions that are in conflict. In the year of independence the majority of the Nigerian nation lived in the north (Hausa and Fulani) and then began governing the rest of the country, which had developed its own structures and institutions. The Ibo in the eastern parts of the country felt even more oppressed by their new leaders than by the British. This resulted in the first bloody rebellion just six years after independence. Ibo soldiers killed the legal government in 1966, causing chaos throughout the young nation. In revenge Ibos living in the northern parts of the country were massacred by the local tribes. In May 1967 the Ibos declared their independence from Nigeria calling the new nation "Republic of Biafra". While Great Britain and the USA helped the federal government in Laos, the French supplied weapons to the secessionists in the east, thus

fueling an extremely bloody war that lasted three years and caused hundreds of thousands of civilian casualties and brought despair to the whole region. Facing starvation throughout their whole population the leaders of Biafra gave up the fight and fled to neighbouring countries and the eastern parts were reintegrated into the Nigerian nation. The military government succeeded in reorganizing the nation, now newly consolidated by the oil found on the territory, which soon made Nigeria one of the richest countries in Africa.

But the problem of the country, due to its different tribes and nations, persists, causing unrest. When the price of oil dropped at the end of the seventies, new rebellions began in different parts of the country. In 1993 the federal government, forced by international pressure, tried to re-establish a democratic republic by free elections, but the result did not please the military leaders, and the outcome was annulated and the military government continued to stay in office.

Nigeria consists of more than 200 different tribes, but its political direction hasn't been settled since its independence. Permanent civil war in different parts of the country rages on in one of the richest nations of the black continent, and corruption has been a distinctive trait of any government since 1960.

4. **Asagai questions the "dreams, good or bad" of the Younger family. What seems to be the main trait of their dreams?**
Even from this short abstract it becomes apparent that the Youngers' dreams are based solely on material wealth and not on wider idealistic concepts (see J. T. Adams, American Dream vs. Janis Joplin, Mercedes Benz).

5. **Asagai has been asked by a group of black students to talk about "The African Dream" in contrast to "The American Dream". Write down his main points and try to stage a presentation of his speech. You may add a discussion afterwards.**

The student	
uses the basic structure of an argumentative text to outline his/her arguments	AFB III
1. Presenting his view on the American Dream as too focused on material wealth and currently lacking idealism	AFB III
2. Developing his "African Dream" as a possible alternative for black Americans – Gaining independence from the colonial regimes (Great Britain) – A return to their native lands – The Dream of a positive change in the future (self-government) – Finding one's true identity (→ use of African names)	AFB III
3. Possibly inviting the students to join his movement	AFB III

I Have Been to the Mountain Top (April 3, 1968)

Martin Luther King

Author and text

Martin Luther King Jr was born on January 15, 1929 in Atlanta. His grandfather and father had been pastors at the Ebenezer Baptist Church in Atlanta. M. L. King chose to continue his family's tradition and first studied at Morehouse College in Atlanta; in 1948 he enrolled in Crozer Theological Seminary in Chester, Pennsylvania, where he graduated with a Bachelor of Divinity degree in 1951. Due to his outstanding qualifications he was granted a fellowship at Boston University, where received his doctoral degree in 1955. It was there that he met his wife Coretta Scott. The couple had two sons and two daughters.

In 1954, Martin Luther King became pastor of the Dexter Avenue Baptist Church in Montgomery, Alabama. When Rosa Parks was arrested in December 1955 for not giving up her seat to a white person King led the Montgomery bus boycott, the first powerful demonstration for equal civil rights. During the 385 days of the boycott King was arrested by the local police and later had his house bombed. During his lifetime Martin Luther King was arrested more than twenty times (see his manifesto: "Letter from a Birmingham Jail", 1963) and assaulted at least four times.

When the Supreme Court finally ruled out segregation on public transport in December 1956, King was recognized as the new leader of the black civil rights movement. His concept of nonviolent resistence, which he took from Gandhi, introduced a new period of the equal rights movement. In 1957 he co-founded the Southern Christian Leadership Conference (SCLC), over which he presided until his death in 1968. King's nonviolent protests against the racist laws of the southern states brought him larger media coverage and gave his movement the necessary power to achieve its aims.

In August 1963 he took part in the March on Washington, intended to bring attention to the injustice suffered by the Afro-American population. His concluding address ("I Have a Dream") to the 250,000 protesters in front of the Lincoln memorial has become a landmark in the fight for civil rights and the worldwide positive reception of this speech and the demands of the civil rights movement helped to get the Civil Rights Act of 1964 passed. In 1964 he was awarded the Nobel Peace Prize and thus became a worldwide figure of peaceful protest for civil rights.

In 1965 he began to openly object to the war in Vietnam, which was criticized by the mainstream media, which pointed out (e.g. *Washington Post*) that this was not a civil rights cause. In these later years King turned to more general political and social issues (Poor People's Campaign).

In April 1968 he travelled to Memphis in order to support a strike of the local (mainly black) garbage workers. Andrew Young, one of his close supporters, who later became a Congressman and then United States Ambassador to the United Nations, rememered that King did not feel well that night and at first did not want to address the audience in the Bishop Charles Mason Temple Church of God. His close friends Jesse Jackson, Benjamin Hooks and Ralph Abernathy nevertheless convinced him to give a speech. Martin Luther King spoke freely without any notes eventually using the traditional call and response interaction used in black preaching, that turns an address into a dialogue and creates an intense interaction between the orator and his audience. King spoke for more than 40 minutes. The Rev. Samuel Billy Kyles, who was in the Memphis church where King delivered his last speech, later said in a radio interview for NPR (National Public Radio): "Many of us, grown men, were crying. We didn't know why we were crying. We had no way of knowing that would be the last speech of his life. And then he took us to the mountaintop ...". Benjamin Hooks told an audience in a speech delivered ten years after Martin Luther King's death: "I remember that night when he finished, he stopped by quoting the words of that song that he loved so well, 'Mine eyes have seen the glory of the coming of the Lord.' He never finished. He wheeled around and took his seat and to my surprise, when I got a little closer, I saw tears streaming down his face. Grown men were sitting there weeping openly because of the power of this man who spoke on that night."

The next day King felt better; Young said that he was happy and joking. He went out of their hotel room onto a balcony to check whether he should take a coat, when he was shot and killed.

The text given in the SB is less then one third of the length of the original speech. The complete text can be found under: www.americanrhetoric.com/speeches/mlkivebeentothemountaintop.htm

Though our extract is often quoted and discussed, the fact that it is not the complete speech should nevertheless be taken into consideration. There are some video record-

ings available on the Internet, usually just the last paragraphs, which might be useful in class, because they transmit the atmosphere of the whole speech.
The audio recording is available from: http://americanradioworks.publicradio.org/features/sayitplain/mlking.html

Unterrichtsempfehlungen

Dr. Martin Luther King ist sicherlich eine der absolut unverzichtbaren Schlüsselfiguren des *„American Dream."* Den meisten Schülerinnen und Schülern wird er und seine berühmte Rede *„I Have a Dream"* bereits aus der Sekundarstufe 1 bekannt sein. Da diese Rede in vielen Schulbüchern (zumindest in Auszügen) bereits dort behandelt wird, soll an dieser Stelle die (in Deutschland) weniger bekannte letzte Rede des Friedensnobelpreisträgers in Auszügen behandelt werden. Um sicherzustellen, dass alle Lernenden denselben Informationsstand zu dieser zentralen Figur der amerikanischen Bürgerrechtsbewegung haben, wird eine *pre-reading activity* vorgeschaltet, bei welcher sich alle noch einmal ausführlich mit der Person und dem Wirken Martin Luther Kings auseinandersetzen. Hierbei kann, wenn nötig, auch noch einmal auf die *„Dream"*-Rede eingegangen werden, da sie zum Verständnis vieler Texte und Reden unverzichtbar ist. Das Material, welches an dieser Stelle vom Kurs erstellt wird sollte aufbewahrt (Poster/Folie) werden, da es später (➔ Kennedy Rede, SB S. 63 f.) noch einmal gebraucht wird.
Die Rede aus Memphis, von der niemand wissen konnte, dass es seine letzte sein sollte, fasst in ihren zentralen, hier wiedergegebenen Teilen, seine Botschaft und sein Vermächtnis zusammen. Sie ist mit 43 Minuten Redezeit sicherlich viel zu lang für eine Behandlung in der Schule. Sie ist in den hier ausgesparten Teilen biographisch interessant (z. B. das beinahe tödliche Attentat auf ihn in New York und die Reaktionen der Öffentlichkeit), in der Behandlung hier soll aber sein Vermächtnis und seine Vision der Zukunft im Vordergrund stehen.
Die erste Aufgabe dient der reinen Textrezeption, wobei die Schülerinnen und Schüler wissen sollten, dass es sich beim vorliegenden Text nicht um den Gesamttext handelt. Dennoch sind der Anfang und das Ende sowie entscheidende Teile des langen mittleren Redeteils abgedruckt, sodass die Entwicklung seiner Argumentation gut verfolgt werden kann. Nach der kurzen Begrüßung folgt ein längerer historischer Teil, der mehr dem *„past"* als dem *„present"* gewidmet ist, aus dem er aber auch für die Gegenwart Folgerungen zieht. Sollte die Bearbeitung im Unterricht, anschließend an die *pre-reading activity*, erfolgen, kann sie am besten in Partnerarbeit mit anschließender Sammlung/Sicherung durchgeführt werden.
Die Mind Map in Aufgabe 2 wird in Gruppen erarbeitet und im Tafelanschrieb gemeinsam konstruiert. Was hier deutlich wird, ist die vom Redner implizierte Vernetzung vieler Aspekte, welche seine in dieser Zeit forcierte Erweiterung seiner Handlungsschwerpunkte legitimiert.
Die dritte Aufgabe ist sehr umfangreich, bringt aber im Vergleich andere Ergebnisse als z. B. die Reden der Kennedys oder von Schwarzenegger. Dies liegt z. T. daran, dass Martin Luther King völlig ohne schriftliches Konzept sprach und in dieser Rede deutlich stärker auf das Konzept der Predigt zurückgreift, als bei seiner *„Dream"*-Rede, die ja nur in ihrem abschließenden Teil diese Mittel kennt. Wenn man sich die Aufnahme anhört, stellt man zudem fest, dass der Redner in einem ständigen Diskurs mit seinen Zuhörern, die ihn durch Zurufe bestätigen, steht.
Aufgabe 4 versucht eine reorganisierende Interpretation der Hauptaussage (AFB II), die notwendig für die letzte, sehr offene Aufgabe ist. Über die Botschaft dieser letzten Zeilen sind inzwischen viele Bücher geschrieben worden. Es ist beängstigend, dass ein Redner einen Tag vor seiner Ermordung so prophetische Worte spricht, zumal auch

seine Umgebung, die bei vielen Reden anwesend war, sich der Einmaligkeit dieser Worte bewusst war. Im Sinne einer hohen Schüleraktivierung und eines regen Meinungsaustausches könnte man diese Aufgabe entweder in Partnerarbeit (*Think – Pair – Share*) oder auch in Form einer *Placemat-Activity* lösen, wobei es offensteht, die endgültigen Ergebnisse zentral zu sammeln, oder lieber als offene Diskussion zu bearbeiten, aus welcher jede Schülerin/jeder Schüler ihre/seine eigenen Folgerungen zieht.

Solutions

Before you read p. 60

This is the last speech given by Martin Luther King. In groups search the main elements of his biography and draw a poster showing the main steps of his political career. What was the political situation in the USA in the spring of 1968 like?

There are more than 14 million websites concerning Martin Luther King. Students should be aware that not all websites furnish valid information, i. e. www.martinlutherking.org is an openly racist website slandering Martin Luther King.
The most detailed information is given by the King Centre in Atlanta, GA: www.thekingcenter.org/DrMLKingJr/Chronology.aspx
Another website created for educational purposes is:
http://mlk-kpp01.stanford.edu/
Wikipedia offers a well-structured biography, also presenting less well-known details about his life (esp. his extramarital affairs) and the conspiracy theory surrounding his death, which are, for evident reasons, usually neglected:
http://en.wikipedia.org/wiki/Martin_Luther_King,_Jr.
1968 is still considered one of the most difficult years in American history. The year began with a further escalation of the Vietnam War. The Tet Offensive began in January. Then the photo of a Vietnamese police officer executing a Vietcong fighter is printed on front pages of newspapers all over the world, discrediting the American policy in southeast Asia and showing the ugly face of war. Civil rights protests were brutally suppressed in some southern states of the USA; black demonstrators were shot and killed by police. In March the My Lai massacre caused a worldwide outcry of protest and antiwar demonstrations in many cities when it became known in November. The American nation was deeply divided over the Vietnam war. In March Black Power demonstrators started a new campaign of activism, which spread to other campuses. The assassination of Martin Luther King led to riots in many American cities causing much bloodshed. In May the humanitarian disaster in Biafra reached its terrible climax. May 1968 became a milestone date for its student protests in many Western cities outside of the USA as well. On June 5, Robert F. Kennedy, running for President, was shot and killed adding a further victim to the bloody record of that year.

Activities p. 62

1. Structure the speech and give appropriate headings.

1–3	Greeting the audience
4–26	A mental flight through history Ancient Egypt (Moses) Civil War (Lincoln) Great Drepression (Roosevelt) Fifties/Sixties (MLK?)
27–33	War or Peace/Nonviolence or Nonexistence
34–39	Bring the coloured people(s) out of their poverty
40–48	Assuming a just place in the world
49–66	An appeal to unity/to stand united
67–72	Recalling his troubled flight to Memphis

73–75	Threats against his life
76–85	I've been to the mountaintop = I believe that success is immanent

2. In this speech Martin Luther King is looking back at what has been achieved and puts the fight into a global perspective. In groups draw a mind map of his main ideas. Compare your findings and agree on a common result.

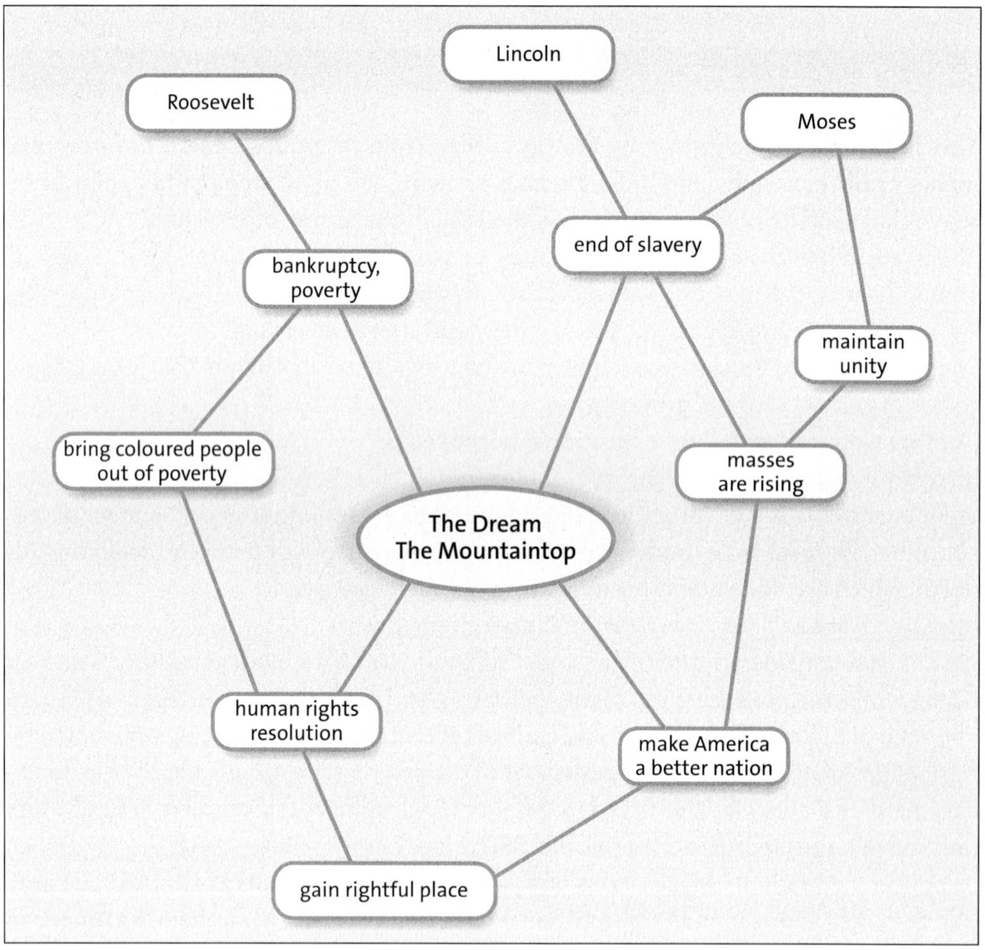

3. Outline the main stylistic devices used by Martin Luther King and explain their functions.

Alliteration	**str**ange **st**atement (17) **f**avourite, **f**avourite **f**ormula **f**or doing it. (52) **d**ifficult **d**ays (76)
Anaphora	**And** then I got to Memphis. **And** some began to say [...] (73) **And** He's allowed me [...] **And** I've looked over. **And** I've seen the Promised Land. (80–82)
Antithesis	a choice between violence and nonviolence (32 f.) it's nonviolence or nonexistence (33)
Chiasm	We are **saying** that we are **determined** to be [...] We are **determined** to be [...] We are **saying** that [...]
Epiphora	[...] I don't know what will happen **now**. [...] it doesn't matter with me **now**. [...] [...] I'm not concerned **now**. (76–79)
Geminatio	I can remember, I can remember [...] (40) he had a favourite, favourite formula (52)
Including 'we'	beginning l. 27 (passim)

Inversion	Only when it is dark enough, can you see the stars. (20)
Metaphor	the promised land (8)
Parallelism	**Scratching where they** didn't itch, and **laughing when they** were not tickled. (41 f.) **Let us** *rise up* [...] (62) **Let us** *stand* [...] (62) And **let us** *move* [...] (63) ➔ also described as a 'vertical metaphor' (rise – stand – move) **I'm not** worried about anything. **I'm not** fearing any man. (83 f.)
Paradox	Only when it is dark enough, **can you see** the stars. (20)
Personification	The nation is sick (18)
Quotation	"we have nothing to fear but fear itself" (Roosevelt) "Mine eyes have seen the glory of the coming of the Lord" (Battle Hymn of the Republic)
Repetition	Something is happening in Memphis, something is happening in our world (2 f.) something is happening in our world (22) I wouldn't stop there (9) I wouldn't stop there (12) I wouldn't stop there (15) Now that's a strange statement (17) That's a strange statement (19) We're going to have to grapple (28) have been trying to grapple (29) demands that we grapple (30) their long years of poverty, their long years of hurt (36) Whenever the slaves get together (53 f.) when the slaves get together (55) Now (5, 17, 31, 31, 37, 42, 49, 56, 57, 76, 77, 79) I will be **happy** (17) I'm **happy** (27) I'm just **happy** (37) And I'm **happy** (38) And I'm **happy** tonight (83)
Rhetorical Question	Now, what does all of this mean in this great period of history? (49) What was that? (52)

The strongest hook for the audience in this speech is based in the repetitions. This text is not highly elaborated but stands in the tradition of oral preaching. Anaphora and epiphora are simple techniques used to underline a topic; this applies to the parallelisms used in the text, too. A further element typical of sermons are quotations, usually from the Bible, but here taken from other contexts, and in both cases without further hint that this is a quote. Besides the listed devices there is a further all-encompassing metaphor in the text: ancient Egypt and the Pharaoh represent the slaveholders and the Israelites stand for the "Negroes" (to use King's word). This can be found in ll. 7 f. and 51 to 56. This implicitly likens King to Moses. The element of theophany (the revelation of God), an important element in the life of Moses, is also frequently alluded to by the speaker (first in line 6, then 15 f., 20 f. and 80 ff.). This last paragraph bears all elements of a eulogy, given by the "deceased" himself.

The second important metaphor is the "mountain top", taken from the Bible (Micah, 4,1 and Deuteronomy 34 1–5). Especially the latter is reflected in the last paragraph of the speech and might be consulted for the analysis of that part of the speech.

The last metaphor used by King in this speech (Road to Jericho) has been completely cut out from the text presented in this book.

4. **It is the foreboding message of the last part of this speech (ll. 76–85) that made it famous. What sentiment does he express in this last part?**
Martin Luther King expresses exactly what Moses felt when God led him onto the mountain top, showing him the future of his people. Like him, Martin Luther King believes that most of the hardships lay behind them and that his people will reach the "promised land". Like Moses (who died on the mountain top), he did not get there with them, but he was sure that he had fulfilled his task and that his death would be the ultimate sacrifice. The repetitious use of the phrase "I am happy" (cf. task 3) implies that he felt he had settled his affairs.

5. **In pairs discuss his possible motivation behind this message.**
There is no right or wrong answer to this question. Students should take into consideration, that:
   - getting involved in the new topic of the war in Vietnam he was drawing more critical response than before
   - people thought he had achieved all his "civil rights" goals
   - his "poor people campaign" was not unique and there were other politicians and public leaders working on that topic, which was not solely "black" (pupils might refer to the data from "Divided Society SB 55f.).

Announcement of M. L. King's Death (April 4, 1968)

Robert F. Kennedy

Author and text

Robert Francis Kennedy, born November 20, 1925, was the seventh of nine children of Senator Joseph Patrick Kennedy. He was the brother of President John F. Kennedy (1917–1963) and Senator Edward Moore Kennedy (1932–2009).
Robert F. Kennedy (also called "Bobby" Kennedy) graduated from Harvard University in 1948 and then continued his studies at the University of Virginia until 1951, when he was admitted as a lawyer. His first political engagement was his work as the campaign manager for his brother John F. Kennedy for senator in 1952. His very close ties to his brother, which made him the closest counsellor for the future President, date back to that time. In the 1950s he worked for different government counsels and commissions, among these the notorious McCarthy commission. When his brother entered the presidential campaign in 1960 Robert once again became his campaign manager. After the successful election John F. Kennedy nominated him Attorney General, although Robert had barely any experience that would qualify him for this difficult job. But Robert F. Kennedy soon proved that he was an efficient organizer and a very capable politician. His campaign against organized crime raised the number of convictions by 800% and confirmed his high competence and absolute will to lead and even to make difficult decisions. As early as 1961 he also became engaged in civil rights activities, appointing US marshals to guarantee free access for black students to university campuses. Though at that time he still questioned the efforts of Martin Luther King (whom he ordered to be wiretapped by the FBI at the same time) the two men progressively entered a closer relationship, as they understood they were both fighting the same cause. After the assassination of his brother, Robert Kennedy continued his work and got the Civil Rights Act signed by President Johnson in April 1964, but in the same year found it difficult to continue his work at the Department of Justice and resigned from his post in late 1964 because he openly opposed President Johnson's involvement in Vietnam. He stayed in the political business and immediately ran a campaign to become senator of the state of New York and was elected in 1964. During his time as senator he started introducing programmes for the poor, stretching his political interests and activities to include social issues. As a senator he began a worldwide campaign for human rights,

touring apartheid South Africa, Eastern Europe and South America. His second quest was his stance against the war in Vietnam, which he sought to bring to an end as soon as possible, proposing bilateral talks, including the North Vietnamese regime. In March 1968 he decided to run for the presidency, beginning a sweeping campaign trying to bridge the gap between the races and all social groups with the vision of a better America for all citizens. His campaign brought new hope for many Americans, who had already given up on the future of their nation.
During his campaign he was informed on his flight to a rally in Indianapolis that Martin Luther King had been assassinated. Arriving there police informed him that they feared riots and couldn't guarantee his safety in the inner city of Indianapolis. Kennedy nevertheless decided to speak from the platform of a truck to a mainly black audience. At the beginning of the recording you can hear him ask the organizers of the event "Do they know about Martin Luther King?" The answer is negative, so it was his first task to inform the public about the tragic news. The outcry heard on the recording testifies the emotions of those present.
His speech is still considered one of the most outstanding in American history, though completely impromptu, it convinced the audience of his faith. Indianapolis was one of the only big cities that night that did not suffer violent and bloody riots, an effect attributed to his speech.
Kennedy won Indiana and Nebraska in the following days, lost Oregon and then went campaigning to all-decisive California. He was shot after giving his victory speech in Los Angeles in the early morning hours of June 5. He suffered multiple shots and died a day later. His funeral included a heartbreaking ceremony and was very much like that of his brother. Parts of his famous Indianapolis speech are engraved on a marble stone at Arlington cemetery.
This speech can be read and discussed in class, but this will never render the message of the moment. The video is not entirely necessary and seems to be difficult to acquire, though it can usually be found on *YouTube*. The recording is more easily found, for example at www.americanrhetoric.com/speeches/rfkonmlkdeath.html
The spoken text better renders the atmosphere, as the sometimes faltering voice of Senator Kennedy more clearly underlines his sympathy than his words already do. Kennedy is talking to a crowd who has just learned that they lost their leader. Although he is on their side of the civil rights struggle, Kennedy is aware that his mainly black audience needs more than just condolences from a white speaker. This is the only speech in which he, though somewhat indirectly, refers to the assassination of his brother, and thus places himself within the group of victims of blind white violence. For the short time of this speech he becomes one with his audience, momentarily bridging the racial gap that was so apparent at that time in the USA. The speech, in its true sense, is not even a eulogy for Martin Luther King, but a pledge to continue the civil rights movement.

Unterrichtsempfehlungen

Die Rede Robert F. Kennedys zählt zu den herausragenden Texten amerikanischer Rhetorik. Es wird heute rückblickend darauf hingewiesen, dass nach Kennedy bis zum ersten prominenten Auftreten Barack Obamas (2004) kaum ein führender amerikanischer Politiker eine solche intellektuelle Rede, die dennoch breite Bevölkerungsschichten ansprach, halten konnte.
Da die Rede recht kurz ist und es gute Aufnahmen gibt, sollte die Rede beim ersten Zugriff auf jeden Fall als reiner Hörverstehenstext behandelt werden. Die *pre-reading/listening* Aufgabe (S. 63) kann in die häusliche Vorbereitung gegeben werden und wird dann mit Aufgabe 2 abgerufen. Um Aufgabe 1 bearbeiten zu können, müsste die Rede

zweimal abgespielt werden, beim ersten Mal als *„listening for gist“*, beim zweiten Mal (*„listening for detail“*) können dann Notizen gemacht werden, die danach bei der eigenständigen Lösung der Aufgabe helfen. Um eine hohe Schüleraktivierung zu erzielen und einen ersten Partneraustausch zu ermöglichen, könnte die Aufgabe im Kugellager (*double circle*) bearbeitet werden, wobei beim ersten Durchgang der Aussenkreis den Partnern den Inhalt wiedergibt und dann, nach der Rotation, der innere Kreis, jetzt doppelt informiert, dem äußeren Kreis den Inhalt berichtet. Eine abschließende Sicherung auf Folie bleibt fakultativ.
Der Vergleich der beiden Konzepte des Nachrufes in Aufgabe 2 erhellt eine Besonderheit der Rede, nämlich dass Kennedy nicht trauernd rückwärtsgewandt spricht, sondern, die Problematik und die Gefahren der Situation im Auge, vorwärtsgerichtet das geistige Vermächtnis M. L. Kings beschwört.
Aufgabe 3 erfüllt die Anforderungen einer formalen Analyse. Was an dieser Stelle erweiternd möglich wäre, ist die Reden der beiden Kennedy-Brüder zu vergleichen. Die Rede John F. Kennedys ist eine akribisch vorbereitete programmatische Rede und steht daher, z. B. im Einsatz rhetorischer Mittel, im Gegensatz zu dieser spontanen Rede, ohne dass die Rede Robert F. Kennedys dadurch in ihrem Wert gemindert wird. Die Lernenden könnten dadurch ihre Kompetenzen bei der Bearbeitung von Redetexten erweitern und lernen, woran man die Spontaneität bzw. die Elaboriertheit einer Rede erkennen kann.
Die letzten beiden Aufgaben sprechen auch affektive Ziele an. Von den beiden zuvor behandelten Redetexten (MLK und RFK) geht eine hohe emotionale Spannung aus, auf die sich die Schülerinnen und Schüler einlassen sollten und auf die nicht nur rational, sondern auch affektiv reagiert werden kann und soll. Es gibt hierbei kein „richtig“ oder „falsch“, sondern nur begründete Ich-Botschaften, die von den anderen Lernenden konstruktiv angenommen werden sollten. In der Diskussion sollte die Lehrperson eine rein moderierende Rolle einnehmen. Es ist zum Ende des Gesprächs aber auch denkbar, dass der/die Unterrichtende seine/ihre eigene Betroffenheit zur Sprache bringt.

Solutions

Before you read/listen p. 63

Imagine you are working for a newspaper and have just been informed about Martin Luther King's death. Use the information you have gathered before and write an obituary for him.

Students should use the elements assembled for the pre-reading task (p. 60 SB) and put these into the form of an obituary. Two authentic texts can still be found on the Internet:
http://topics.nytimes.com/topics/reference/timestopics/people/k/martin_luther_jr_king/index.html
www.guardian.co.uk/world/1968/apr/06/martin-luther-king-obituary-guardian-archive

Activities p. 64

1. **Imagine you were part of the audience. There was no written text of the speech. Tell a friend what Kennedy said.**

The student	
reports the atmosphere of shock and sorrow	AFB I
states that Kennedy thinks that this news is very bad for all people who seek peace and understanding	AFB I
outlines that Kennedy sees two possible developments for the future – hatred and bitterness – understanding, comprehension, compassion and love towards each other	AFB I

points out that Kennedy has sympathy for those who feel hatred and mistrust, as he himself has known such a situation	AFB I
states that Kennedy nevertheless refuses these attitudes and asks the audience to go beyond these feelings and urges them to turn towards love, wisdom and understanding, no matter what race they belong to	AFB I
reports that Kennedy asked the audience to pray – for the family of Martin Luther King – and for passion and understanding for the whole nation	AFB I
says that Kennedy has faith in justice and the improvement of life for all people in this nation	AFB I

2. **Compare your obituary with what Kennedy says. What are the common aspects and what is different? Make a list and discuss why Kennedy focuses on these aspects**

Possible Obituary	Kennedy
Born January 15, 1929	
Studies, doctorate at Boston in 1955	
1955 Minister in Montgomery	
Montgomery Bus Boycott (1955–56) beginning of non-violent action (protest marches)	
civil disobedience	Dedicated his life to love and justice between fellow human beings. (8 ff.) Replace that violence [...] with an effort to understand, compassion and love (19 ff.)
1963 March an Washington ("I Have a Dream")	
1964 Nobel Peace Prize	
1966 opposed the war in Vietnam	
1968 poor people's campaign	

Kennedy focuses solely on Martin Luther King's basic principles of non-violence and mutual respect. He reminds his audience of Martin Luther King's legacy, appealing to them to continue in that spirit, because he fears riots and bloodshed.

3. **In this impromptu speech Robert Kennedy uses a number of stylistic devices that underline the message of his words. Make a list and explain the intended effect.**

Alliteration	**l**ive to **l**ove (8) **d**ifficult **d**ay (10 f.)
Anaphora	What we need in the United States is not [...] what we need in the United States is not [...] what we need in the United States is not [...] (37 ff.) It is not the end of violence; it is not the end of lawlessness; and it's not the end of disorder. (47 ff.) Let us dedicate ourselves to [...] Let us dedicate ourselves to [...] (53 ff.)
Antithesis	We can move in that direction [...] Or we can make an effort [...] (18–22) whether they be black or whether they be white (41)
Chiasm	The **vast majority of [...] people in this country**,// **want** to improve the quality of our life,// and **want** justice// for **all human beings that abide in our land** (50 ff.)

Enumeration	you can be filled with **bitterness** and with **hatred**, and a **desire for revenge**. (15 f.)
Geminatio	the evidence evidently is (14)
Including 'we'	kind of a nation **we** are (12) and passim (25 times)
Metaphor	that stain of bloodshed that has spread across our land (20 f.)
Parallelism	**the vast majority of** white people and **the vast majority of** black people (50)
Quotation	"Even in our sleep [...] Aeschylus (31–36) "To tame the savageness of man and make gentle the life of this world." (53 f.)
Repetition	MLK **dedicated** his life (8) Let us **dedicate** ourselves [...] (53) Let us **dedicate** ourselves (54 f.) In this difficult day, in this **difficult time** (11) these rather **difficult times** (28 f.) We will have **difficult times**. (46) We've had **difficult times** (46 f.) And we will have **difficult times** [...] (47) to **say a prayer for** the family of Martin Luther King [...] to **say a prayer for** our own country **a prayer for** understanding [...] (42 ff.) **we can make an effort** [...] (19) with **an effort** to understand [...] (21) **we have to make an effort** in the United States, **we have to make an effort** to understand [...] (27 f.)
Rhetorical Question	It's perhaps well to ask what kind of a nation we are and what direction we want to move in. (12 ff.)
Synonyms	to understand and to comprehend (20)

There are two opposing concepts throughout this speech, which are repeated several times in similar contexts: (1) *love ... justice ... understanding ... compassion* which is opposed to (2) *hatred ... violence.*

As in many impromptu speeches, the speaker mainly relies on the stylistic devices of repetition (i.e. anaphora, parallelism, repetition, synonyms) as these serve as a hook for his audience to grasp his message. The two groups of ideas/concepts (mentioned above) stress the antithesis of his argumentation. The overall structure of the speech is that of an argumentative text, showing the counter-arguments (hatred, violence) and explicitly contrasting them with his pro arguments (compassion, love, understanding). The outstanding argument for the pro side is the reference to "a member of my family killed" (26) which underlines that he has personally suffered the same loss and has thereby come to the given conclusion.

This speech is often quoted as a perfect example of the Aristotelian concepts of "*ethos* (the character of the speaker), *logos* (the logic of the arguments) and *pathos* (the emotional appeal)", uniting all three in this short text.

Kennedy repeatedly uses the word "dedicate" (8, 53, 54). The repetition of this word is also a prominent feature in Lincoln's "Gettysburg Address." Just a day before, in his "Mountain top" speech, Martin Luther King spoke about "difficult days" (76). It is striking that Kennedy uses the same expression (10f.), though it may be assumed, that just a day later he hadn't yet heard a recording or read a transcript of that speech.

4. Checking Google or other search engines, you will find more than a thousand references to quotes from this speech using parts of it in blogs, articles or speeches. Which might be your favourite quote from this speech? Give reasons.

Two-thirds of the Robert F. Kennedy Memorial in Washington is covered by quotes from this speech, thus underlining the importance of its message. Those written on the marble are:

– Aeschylus once wrote: "Even in our sleep, pain which cannot forget falls drop by drop upon the heart, until, in our own despair, against our will, comes wisdom through the awful grace of God."
– What we need in the United States is not division; what we need in the United States is not hatred; what we need in the United States is not violence and lawlessness, but is love and wisdom, and compassion toward one another, and a feeling of justice toward those who still suffer within our country, whether they be white or whether they be black.
– Let us dedicate ourselves to what the Greeks wrote so many years ago: to tame the savageness of man and make gentle the life of this world. Let us dedicate ourselves to that, and say a prayer for our country and for our people.

5. Robert F. Kennedy was shot and killed only two months later (June 5, 1968). In an obituary, Time magazine (June 14, 1968) used a quote from Aeschylus as its motto: "When the height is won, then there is ease." This evokes the image used by Martin Luther King ("I've been to the mountain top"). Is this one of the core beliefs of the American Dream? Discuss.

Activities p. 65

The student	
discusses the image of "the height"/"the mountain top" and its symbolic meaning	AFB III
relates his/her findings to other texts, i.e. – F. S. Key, *Star-Spangled Banner*, (SB 12 f.): "What is that which the breeze, over the towering steep//As it fitfully blows, half conceals, half discloses." (11 f.) – John F. Kennedy, *The 'New' Frontier* ... (SB 26 ff.): "space is there, and we're going to climb it" (81) – J. T. Adams, *The American Dream* (SB 29 f.): "if the American Dream is to be reality, our communal spiritual and intellectual life must be distinctly higher than elsewhere" (22 ff.)	AFB III
presents a personal evaluation of the question.	AFB III

"A More Perfect Union" (March 18, 2008)

Barack Obama

Author and text

Barack Obama, born August 4, 1961 in Hawaii, is the first African-American President of the United States. His father is from Keyna and his mother is from Kansas. In his youth he was mainly raised by his grandparents. After college he moved to Chicago where he studied law and worked on several projects, helping homeless people. He graduated from Colombia University and Havard Law School. After earning his degree he worked as an attorney in Chicago, specializing in civil law suits. He became a member of the Illinois Senate in 1997, where he served three terms. Obama ran for the United States Senate in 2004. His successful campaign made him known for his inspiring speeches. His keynote address at the Democratic Convention in March 2004 brought him nationwide respect and attention. He began his presidential campaign in February 2007, first running against his own party opponent Hillary Clinton. He won the primaries and was nominated presidential candidate in 2008. In November 2008 he won by a vast majority against Republican nominee John McCain. Barack Obama was inaugurated as the 44th President on January 20, 2009. In October 2009 he was named Nobel Peace Prize laureate.

The speech was given during his presidential campaign (March 2008) and differs fundamentally from others given throughout his campaign. The place (Philadelphia) and the title, being a quote of the first lines of the Constitution of the United States, underline this fact.

Unterrichtsempfehlungen

Die vorliegende Rede Barack Obamas ist für eine Wahlkampfrede sehr zeitlos. Sie beschäftigt sich wesentlich stärker mit den historischen Grundlagen und Gegebenheiten, beschreibt den langen Weg der Veränderungen bis zu seiner Kandidatur.
Die Rede ist als Video-/Audiofile leicht zugänglich und sollte auch im Original gesehen/gehört werden, Quellen sind z. B.
www.youtube.com/watch?v=zrp-v2tHaDo
www.dailymotion.com/video/x5nr53_barack-obama-speech-on-race-tuesday_news
Zu beachten ist, dass im Schülerbuch allerdings nur der erste, mehr grundsätzliche Teil der Rede steht, die insgesamt wesentlich länger ist.
Der Einstieg in die Thematik (Präsidentschaftswahlkampf 2008) erfolgt über eine Karikatur (zur Bearbeitung im Kurs steht auf **Worksheet 4** umfangreiches Material zur Verfügung). Die Schülerinnen und Schüler lernen hier die beiden wesentlichen Akteure auf Seiten der Demokraten kennen (John McCain wurde bereits zuvor eingeführt, SB, S. 48f.). Der Artikel von Bill Maher (SB, S. 15 ff.) stammt ebenso aus dieser Zeit. Den beiden Protagonisten stehen in diesem Cartoon ihre *„shadows“* aus der Vergangenheit zur Seite und es ist leicht zu erkennen, welcher der Stärkere ist. Zudem wird der Begriff *„Dream“* von verschiedensten Seiten reflektiert, was eine erste Öffnung zum Rückblick über die gesamte Reihe (s. SB, S. 70) ermöglicht.
Aufgabe 1 ist reproduktiv ausgelegt und bringt die Kompetenz Sprachmittlung in das Blickfeld. Die zweite Aufgabe müsste schnell im Kursverband zu bearbeiten sein, da alle historischen Ereignisse im bisherigen Reihenverlauf thematisiert worden sind. Die dritte Aufgabe kann auf einem kleinen Poster oder einer Folie in Gruppenarbeit gelöst werden und sollte auch nicht viel Zeit beanspruchen. Es ist hierbei wichtig, dass die Lernenden sich bewusst werden, wie wichtig für Barack Obama auch sein „weißer“ Familienzweig ist und dass er nicht nur für den *„Dream“* der afro-amerikanischen Bürger steht. Die Analyse der stilistischen Redemittel ist festes (Übungs-)Element dieses Heftes. Hier kann man etwas weiter ausholen und nach der Bearbeitung, die sinnvollerweise als Hausaufgabe erfolgt, mit anderen Reden (John F. und Robert Kennedy, Martin Luther King, Abraham Lincoln) vergleichen. Obama wird von der Presse häufig mit Martin Luther King verglichen, ihre Redetechniken sind aber wenig ähnlich, da Obama aus einer juristischen Redetradition kommt, während Martin Luther King den unverkennbaren Stil des Südstaaten-Predigers (*audience response*) zur Perfektion beherrscht. Somit werden sich wesentlich mehr Parallelen zwischen den Kennedys und Obama finden. Die fünfte Aufgabe sollte zunächst in Einzelarbeit (Hausaufgabe/ Selbstlernzentrum) vorbereitet werden und dann z. B. in einer *Placemat-activity* gesammelt werden.
Die letzten beiden Aufgaben gehören in den Anforderungsbereich III und fordern eine persönliche Auseinandersetzung mit den Aussagen Barack Obamas. Aufgabe 5 wurde dabei ganz bewusst als kritische Auseinandersetzung gewählt, denn vieles, was Obama sagt, ist eindeutig mit der amerikanischen Sichtweise der Welt verbunden und so nicht haltbar. Er unterstellt hier eine amerikanische Überlegenheit (auch im Hinblick auf die Verwirklichung des Traumes), die in ihrer Einzigartigkeit gar nicht besteht, sondern eigentlich nur selbstverständliches Element aller modernen Demokratien und Basisaussage der Menschen- und Bürgerrechte ist. Zur letzten Aufgabe stehen bereits

die wichtigsten Hinweise zur methodischen Vorbereitung oben (s. S. 83f., John McCain).

Solutions

Before you read/listen p. 65

Carefully describe the cartoon (from left to right). Summarize the message of the cartoon in a few sentences. Published at midterm of the presidential nomination campaign, does it support one of the two candidates (Barack Obama – Hillary Clinton)? Give reasons.

(Note: use **Worksheet 4** for the analysis of the cartoon.)

The cartoon was drawn by "Darkow" for the Columbia Daily Tribune in 2008. The cartoon consists of four frames.

- In the first frame Martin Luther King is depicted stating "I have a dream."
- The second frame shows Barack Obama saying "I represent the American Dream".
- In the third element you can perceive Hilary Clinton, answering a frosty (icicled speech bubble) "In your dreams, kid!"
- In the last frame the artist has drawn former President Clinton in leisure wear, asking "Does anybody wanna hear about my wet dream?"

The message is mainly supported by the two middle frames, juxtaposing Obama and Hillary Clinton. The use of the derogative word "kid" to address her opponent underlines her unwavering will to win the race. Both characters are framed by other characters, contributing to their personal standing and acknowledgement. Whereas Martin Luther King seems to be a welcome supporter for a presidential campaign, Bill Clinton and the allusion to his sexual affairs can be seen as less helpful for the candidate Hillary Clinton.

Activities p. 67

1. **As an exchange student you watched the speech on TV. Write an e-mail in German to your friends at home, telling them what Barack Obama said.**

   Der Austauschstudent/die Austauschstudentin schreibt, die übliche Form einer E-Mail beachtend, dass Obama an historischer Stelle in Philadelphia, wo die Verfassung beschlossen wurde, gesprochen hat.

   Er/Sie benennt die wichtigsten Aussagen Obamas:
   - es erscheint immer noch unglaublich, dass die kleine Gruppe von Männern, die 1787 die Verfassung geschrieben hat, ein solch erfolgreiches Konstrukt erlassen haben;
   - die Verfassung war in der Sklavenfrage lange Zeit unentschieden;
   - die Lösung war bereits in der Verfassung selbst vorgegeben, indem sie allen Bürgern gleiche Rechte garantierte;
   - es hat Generationen von Bürgerrechtlern gebraucht, um die verfassungsmäßigen Rechte in der amerikanischen Gesellschaft zu verankern;
   - dieser Kampf ist noch nicht beendet und wird zentraler Aspekt der weiteren Kampagne sein;
   - das Vertrauen in die Größe der amerikanischen Gesellschaft spiegelt sich in seiner eigenen Biografie, als Sohn eines Kenianers und einer weißen Frau aus Kansas;
   - er kennt sowohl die besten Hochschulen des Landes als auch die ärmsten Länder der Welt aus eigener Erfahrung;
   - er glaubt nicht, dass in irgendeinem anderen Land dieser Welt dasselbe möglich wäre;
   - diese Nation ist mehr als die Summe ihrer Elemente.

2. **Obama's speech directly refers to American history. Make a list of the references and state why he has chosen them.**

   – 1787 signing of the Constitution
   – 1861–1865 Civil War (Lincoln)
   – 1957–1968 civil disobedience (Martin Luther King)
   – 2008 his own presidential campaign

   Besides the fact that he is running for President he has chosen what are arguably the three most important milestones of American history, beginning with the Constitution, then the Civil War and the Emancipation Proclamation signed by Lincoln. In June 1964 President Johnson signed the Civil Rights Act that finally established equality between the different races.

3. **Summarize in a drawing (genealogical tree) what Obama tells listeners about his family roots.**

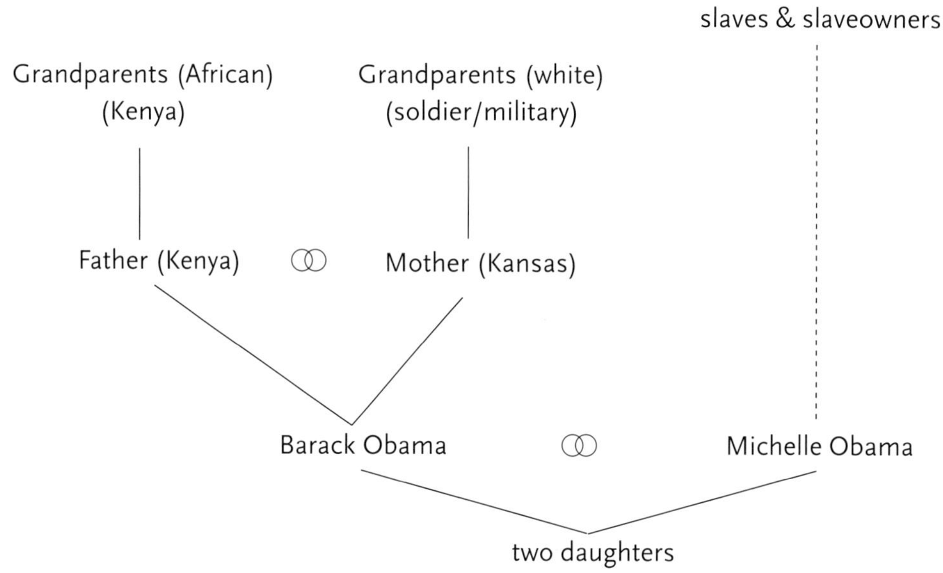

4. **Analyse the most important rhetorical devices used by the speaker to underline his message.**

Alliteration	**c**olor and **c**reed (18) **c**onventional **c**andidate (48)
Antithesis	we may not have come from the same place, but we all want to move in the same direction (32 f.) I have gone to some of the best schools ... and lived in the world's poorest nations. (41 f.)
Enumeration	Farmers and scholars; statesmen and patriots (4 f.) a more just, more equal, more free, more caring and more prosperous America. (27) brothers, sisters, nieces, nephews, uncles and cousins (44 f.)
Including 'we'	our Constitution (14); our ideals (23); 12 times *passim* (25 – 34); we are truly one (50)
Metaphor	was stained by this nation's original sin (9) the long march of those (26) has seared into my genetic makeup (49)
Metonymy	deliver slaves from **bondage** (18)
Paradox	The document [...] was eventually signed but ultimately unfinished (8) this nation is more than the sum of its parts (50)

Parallelism	a Constitution that ... (14) a Constitution that ... (15) a union that ... (16) a union that could and should be perfect. (16) through protests and struggle, on the streets and in the courts (21) civil war and civil disobedience (22) comes from my ... also comes from my (35 f.) a white woman ... a white grandfather ... a white grandmother (37 ff.)
Quotation	"We the people, in order to form a more perfect union." (1) Two hundred and twenty one years ago (2) (first lines of: Lincoln, *Gettysburg Address*/Martin Luther King, *I Have a Dream*) unless we perfect our union (30) (s. a.) out of many, we are truly one (50) (*e pluribus unum*)
Repetition	unless we solve ... unless we perfect (29 f.)
Synonyms	tyranny and persecution (5 f.) decency and generosity (35) every race and every hue (45)

Obama sets his speech within a historical context (1–25). Then follows the general appeal (high number of 'including we') (25–34) and his very personal story (35–49), followed by another quote in the last line (50).

5. **As Martin Luther King used a lot of allusions to the Bible in his speeches, Barack Obama directly or indirectly refers to other famous speeches, thus creating a net of persuasive ideas. Try to track down some of these references.**

"We the people, in order to form a more perfect union." (1) Constitution of the United States
Two hundred and twenty one ears ago (2) (first lines of: Lincoln, Gettysburg Address/ Martin Luther King, "I Have a Dream")
Farmers and scholars; statesmen an patriots (5) ("Let divines and philosophers, statesmen and patriots, unite their endeavors to renovate the age," Samuel Adams, *Letter to John Adams*, Oct 4, 1790)
men and women of every color and creed (18) ("King Nebuchadnezzar to everyone, everywhere – every race, color, and creed: 'Peace and prosperity to all!'" (*Bible*, Daniel 4,1)
to continue the long march of those who came before us (26) (no direct reference, but Martin Luther King as well as Mahatma Ghandi often referred to "marches" in their speeches; see SB, p. 62, 60)
unless we perfect our union (30) (s.a. Constitution)
slaves and slaveowners (43) (Martin Luther King, "I Have a Dream": "a dream that ... the sons of former slaves and slave owners will be able to sit down together at the table of Brotherhood.")
out of many, we are truly one (50) (*e pluribus unum*)

6. **Obama claims that "in no other country on Earth is my story even possible." Is that true? Discuss in groups and write down your arguments.**
The answer should be left open, but it is evident that this claim is not true. Political careers of people from an immigrant family or of different racial origin exist in all modern democracies. French President Sarkozy is of Hungarian origin, the German Minister Rösler (FDP) was born in Khánh Hung (Vietnam) and is of Vietnamese origin, just to name two out of many examples that could be quoted.

7. **Prepare and stage a hot chair discussion with Barack Obama questioning his positions and views.**
This hot chair discussion needs to be well prepared. One student (plus a "shadow" for help) and a number of questioners should prepare for the hot chair session, while the rest of the class acts as observers (➔ assessment sheets). The following groups (besides Barack Obama) should prepare questions:
– Afro-American civil rights activists
– Latin American immigrants
– Political opponents (McCain/Sarah Palin)
– Foreign students from Europe
– White American citizens
The person taking the hot seat will need special preparation with the help of a group (3 or 4 students), to turn him/her into the character of "Barack Obama". It is a good idea to think of possible questions (and answers), to take some notes based on the text and to gather some additional information about the politician and his character.
The other groups collect questions based on the text (but also on the following text and cartoon), as well as what they have learned about the American Dream and American history so far. More information might be found by a (limited) Internet search. The groups will decide in a pyramid discussion on the best questions (4 or 5) to ask, avoiding an excessive number of trivial questions. During the discussion the questioners pay attention to the questions asked by other groups (same or opposite attitude?).
The assessment group (there should be at least 5 students doing this job) develop an assessment sheet (with the help/hints of the teacher) and give their results after the discussion when everybody is back in his/her student role.

Obama Makes History

Robert Barnes and Michael D. Shear

Author and text

Robert (Bob) Barnes and Michael D. Shear are *Washington Post* staff writers. Both are responsible for front page reports and comments on political questions. The *Washington Post*, founded in 1877, is still the most important and influential newspaper in the United States. The paper has been awarded nearly 50 Pulitzer Prizes, underlining the high standards and the quality of research done by the journalists. It became famous worldwide when its reporters Woodward and Bernstein detected and unveiled the Watergate affair in the seventies. In the last years it has, like many other American newspapers, been losing readership and influence to online media.

Unterrichtsempfehlungen

Die grenzenlos positive Begeisterung, welche Barack Obama vor seiner Wahl in Europa erfahren hat, spiegelte nicht das z. T. kritischere Bild, welches viele Amerikaner hatten. Sein Wahlerfolg war zwar keine Überraschung, es gab aber auch damals schon zahlreiche kritische Stimmen, die seine Aussagen kritisch hinterfragten. Der Cartoon spiegelt genau diese Haltung und setzt damit einen Kontrast zum nachfolgenden Zeitungsartikel und öffnet auch für die Schülerinnen und Schüler eine distanziertere Sicht. Für die Bearbeitung des Cartoons (Präsentation im Kurs vielleicht auf Folie) bietet sich wieder die Verwendung von **Worksheet 4** an.

Die beiden Aufgaben sind reproduktiv angelegt und leiten durch ihre Systematisierung zur abschließenden Aufgabe hin, in welcher die Lernenden noch einmal alles, was sie in diesem Heft zum amerikanischen Traum erfahren haben, zusammenstellen können. Die sicherlich umfangreicheren Ergebnisse können anhand der Vorgaben (unten) ggf. systematisiert werden. Es bietet sich an, dass in Gruppen auf einem *Placemat* zunächst gesammelt wird und dann für die gesamte Lerngruppe, moderiert durch die Lehrperson, alle genannten Begriffe in eine große Mindmap einfließen. Dabei sollte das gesamte Heft zu Rate gezogen werden.

Solutions

Before you read p. 68

1. **Describe the cartoon. Remember to stick to an objective description, just giving facts and no interpretation.**
   (*Note:* use **Worksheet 4** for the analysis of the cartoon)
   The cartoon published by *Newsweek* in 2008 shows on the left side a man (Barack Obama), hands held high as if with great joy, holding a can of bubble soap in his right hand (marked "policies") and blowing soap bubbles from a pipe in his mouth. Three bubbles bear the writing "HOPE", two are marked "DREAM" and a third one "BELIEVE". There are several (three) bubbles that just exploded ("POP").

2. **Describe in your own words what the cartoonist wanted to express.**
   The cartoonist apparently wants to express that Barack Obama is uttering a lot of positive messages, based on the American Dream, giving hope and asking people to believe in his message. On the other hand it becomes apparent that all these ideas and policies are only soap bubbles that explode after just a short time. It is obvious that the artist does not believe in the ideas promoted by the democratic candidate and wants to express that these are only soap bubbles: brilliant, fascinating, but they will explode within a short time.

Activities p. 70

1. **Sum up the main reasons given in the article that helped Obama win the election.**
   – a reformist message of change (3)
   – an inspirational exhortation of hope (4)
   – President Bush's increasingly unpopular administration (9 f.)
   – advance of an economic and foreign policy agenda the Bush has largely blocked (29 f.)
   – melded the pride and aspirations of African-Americans with a coalition of younger and disaffected voters (43 ff.)
   – democrats worried about the economy and frustrated with the war in Iraq (45 f.)

2. **The election is called "historic" several times in the text. Make a list of the facts about Barack Obama mentioned in the article that are special or even unique.**
   – The first African-American to ascend to the White House (3 f.)
   – The first Democrat since Jimmy Carter in 1976 to receive more than 50 percent of the popular vote (40 f.)
   – Fifth-youngest man elected to a first presidential term (after Theodore Roosevelt, John F. Kennedy, Bill Clinton and Ulysses S. Grant) (47 ff.)
   – The 16th senator to ascend to the office, and the first since Kennedy's election in 1960 (49 f.)

3. **Listening to or reading the many speeches Obama has given during the 2008 presidential campaign you will come across the "buzz"-words used in the cartoon. These were "hope", "believe", "change" and "dream." Looking back at the texts in this booklet, first draw a mind map of what "dream" stands for and then explain why this is the most powerful concept to win a majority of voters in the USA.**

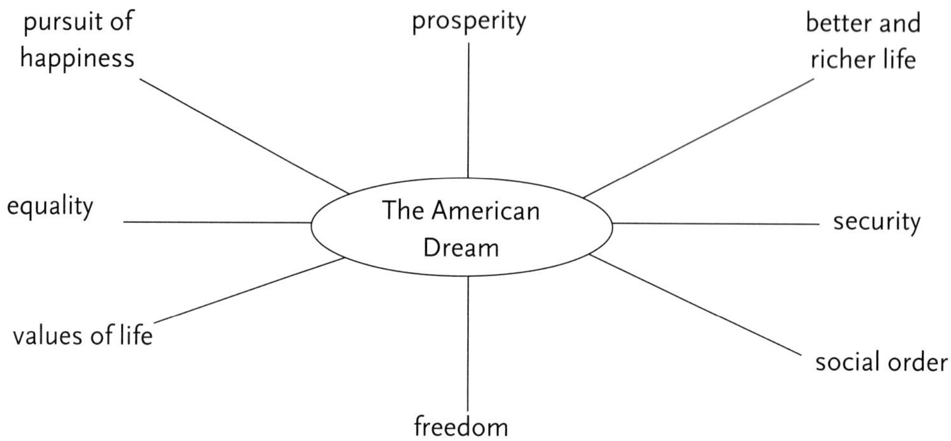

Worksheet 4

Der Cartoon kann in Einzelarbeit, bzw. als *Think – Pair – Share* analog der Aufgabenstellung bearbeitet werden. Es ist jedoch auch eine mehr zentrierende, dem Übungscharakter allerdings deutlich nähere Bearbeitung denkbar. Hierbei könnte die Lehrperson den Cartoon zunächst nur in einem Ausschnitt auf Folie zeigen und die Schülerinnen und Schüler den Karton und besonders die Aufschrift oben rechts in der Ecke beschreiben lassen. Im nächsten Schritt werden die Lernenden nach ihren eigenen Erfahrungen mit solchen „Preisen" befragt und berichten ggf., was sie schon in einer solchen Schachtel bekommen/gewonnen haben. Dieses durch echte Fragen und persönlichem Inhalt geprägte L – S-Gespräch bereitet auf die Hauptdiskrepanz des Cartoons vor.

Im zweiten Schritt kann nun der fast vollständige Cartoon beschrieben werden. Die Schülerinnen und Schüler sollten Barack Obama erkennen. Wichtig ist bei diesem Analyseschritt die genaue Beschreibung (a) der Situation und (b) der Figur selbst (Gesichtsausdruck/Kleidung). Jetzt kann wieder spekuliert werden, was denn nun für ein „*Prize*" in der Schachtel war, über den sich Obama so sehr freut.

Im letzten Schritt wird nun der vollständige Cartoon aufgelegt. Jetzt kann auch sofort der Schritt zur Deutung gegangen werden. Dieses Verfahren der verzögerten Rezeption stärkt vor allem die Übung der systematischen Beschreibung und Analyse nicht linearer Texte.

Worksheet 4

How to Analyse a Cartoon

General questions regarding the multi-layer text:

1. Who is the cartoonist?
   – additional information if available
2. Where was the cartoon published?
   – newspaper; magazine; Internet blog etc. (source? target group?)
   – place/country
3. When was it published?
   – date/season
4. What is presented?
   – topical event

Analysing a cartoon:

1. **Description (what you see):**
   – Give the number of frames (one or more?).
   – Describe all the objects or people in the cartoon.
   – Name (symbolic) characters (e.g. Uncle Sam)/persons/animals.
   – Describe the action depicted.
   – Name the devices the cartoonist uses (e.g. exaggerated physical features, facial expressions, size/position of figures, clothing).
   – Read the text (if any); there may be different text levels (speech bubbles/thought bubbles, signs/inscriptions, numbers, the caption).
2. **Interpretation (what it signifies):**
   – Use background knowledge, explain context.
   – Analyse associations/connotations evoked.
   – Analyse possible ambiguities (written text).
   – Interpret the meaning of symbols used'.
   – Explain what the cartoonist wanted to express in your opinion.

Words and phrases to describe cartoons:

<table>
<tr><td rowspan="4">The</td><td rowspan="4">cartoon
drawing
comic strip</td><td>was drawn</td><td colspan="2">by (xy)
by the cartoonist (xy)
by the artist/painter (xy)</td></tr>
<tr><td>published in […]</td><td>consists of</td><td>one frame
x pictorial elements/ frames</td></tr>
<tr><td>first appeared in
was published in</td><td>(xy) magazine
the (xy) newspaper</td><td>on (date)
in (month or year)
around (season)
during (the period of time)</td></tr>
<tr><td>refers to
depicts
shows
presents
alludes to</td><td colspan="2">(xy event)
the problem of …
the conflict between …
the topic of …</td></tr>
</table>

Worksheet 4

In the	foreground centre background bottom left/right hand corner	there is/are is/are shown/depicted you can perceive the cartoonist has drawn the artist has added	a/an [...] the ...
On the	left/right/bottom/top		
What strikes the eye is		the exaggerated presentation of the discrepancy between (a) and (b) the stereotypical presentation of the seemingly [...] atmosphere	
The attention is focused	on		
The	speech bubble thought bubble caption	reads ... states ... says ...	
The	object animal (lion/snake/donkey/elephant/...) person(s) symbolic figure of Uncle Sam way Mr/Mrs XY is depicted	symbolizes stands for represents shows	the fact that ... the character of ... the attitude of ...
The	double meaning ambiguity contradiction text words	of the caption of the speech bubble of the thought bubble	expresses ... underlines ... points out ... expresses the idea of ... forms a contrast to the picture ...
The	situation shown	epitomizes ... ridicules ... satirizes ...	
The	cartoon drawing comic strip	expresses ... conveys ... implies ...	
The	cartoonist artist	might want to express criticizes ridicules questions makes a sarcastic comment about	the idea that ... the situation in/of ... the fact that ... the position of ...

Worksheet 4

Henry Payne, The Detroit News, Michigan, Oct. 10, 2009

Activities

1. **Describe the cartoon published the day after the Nobel Prize Committee announced that President Obama had been awarded the Nobel Peace Prize.**
2. **What is the intended message of the cartoon?**

Worksheet 4 Solution

1. **Describe the cartoon published the day after the Nobel Prize Committee announced that President Obama had been awarded the Nobel Peace Prize.**
   The cartoon, drawn by Henry Payne and published in the Detroit News, shows Barack Obama finding the Nobel Peace Prize in a box of cereal. Obama has just opened a new box of Froot Loops, which is marked "Prize inside". Obama is depicted as a young boy with a T-shirt and braces on his trousers. He is obviously surprised and happy about this unforeseen prize. The effect of the cartoon lies in the discrepancy between the Nobel Peace Prize and what it stands for and its arrival in a plastic bag hidden within a box of cereal.

2. **What is the intended message of the cartoon?**
   The situation shown ridicules Obama's nomination and conveys the message that the choice of his person was not expected and that the prize was awarded to him as an unmerited present.

Klausur 1

"I, Too, Sing America" (1924)

Langston Hughes

I, too, sing America.

I am the darker brother.
They send me to eat in the kitchen
When company comes,
But I laugh,
And eat well,
And grow strong.

Tomorrow,
I'll be at the table
When company comes.
Nobody'll dare
Say to me,
"Eat in the kitchen,"
Then.

Besides,
They'll see how beautiful I am
And be ashamed –

I, too, am America.

From: *The Collected Poems of Langston Hughes*, edited by Arnold Rampersad, New York: Alfred A. Knopf, 1994, p. 46

Activities

1. **Present the situation of the speaker of this text.** (comprehension: AFB I)
2. **Examine the author's use of language and its significance.** (analysis: AFB II)
3. **Evaluate the author's view of American society in the mid-twenties and contrast this to Walt Whitman's poem "I Hear America Singing."** (evaluation: AFB III)

Klausur 1 Solution

Lernvoraussetzungen:
- Bearbeitung von **Worksheet 1** (Whitman, „I Hear America Singing", S. 32)
- Bearbeitung von Langston Hughes, "Harlem" (SB, S. 57)
- Bearbeitung der grundlegenden Texte zum *Civil Rights Movement* (SB, S. 55 – 70)

1. Comprehension:

The student	
portrays the speaker as an Afro-American (darker brother, 2)	AFB I
describes the present situation of the speaker: – he lives in his master's house (They send me ..., 3) – he is not treated as an equal human being (send me to eat in the kitchen ..., 3) – he is not unhappy with his situation (I laugh, 5) – and he takes care of himself (eat well ... grow strong, 6 f.)	AFB I
remarks that the speaker foresees a change of his situation for the future (Tomorrow, 8): – he will be part of society (I'll be at the table, 9) – and will have equal rights and powers (Nobody'll dare ... 11 ff.)	AFB I
points out that the speaker sees himself as superior to the others (They'll see how beautiful I am ..., 16 f.)	AFB I
observes that the speaker of the text is sure to be an entire member of American society (I, too, am America, 18)	AFB I

2. Analysis:

The student	
describes the structure of the poem – 5 stanzas – the first and last stanzas only consist of one single line	AFB II
delineates the language of the author as simple, straightforward statements	AFB II
analyses the use of a first person speaker	AFB II
analyses the use of the adverb "too" in the first and last line and points out that this signals the continuation of some sort of dialogue	AFB II
names and describes the rhetorical devices used in the poem: – Repetition: 1 and 18/3 and 13 (eat in the kitchen)/4 and 10 (when company comes) – Parallelism: 6 f. (and eat well,//and grow strong) – Anaphora: 1 f. (I/I) – Metonymy: 3 and 13 (kitchen ➔ representing the parts of the house designated for servants/slaves) – Synecdoche/Metonymy: 9 (table ➔ meaning the place where the "normal" people sit) – Alliteration: 4 and 10 (**c**ompany **c**omes) – Assonance: 2 (d**a**rker br**o**ther)	AFB II

– Enjambement: 3–4/5–7/8–10/11–13/16–17 – Frame: 8 (Tomorrow) and 14 (Then) (use of an adverb of time at the beginning of a sentence and at the end of the following sentence)	
analyses the use of the simple present (1–7) and the use of the will-future (8–17)	AFB II
analyses the symbolic meaning of "darker brother" (2) as different ("darker") but still the same ("brother" → belonging to the same family)	AFB II

3. Evaluation:

The student	
evaluates how the author presents the situation of the speaker of "I, too, ...": – someone who feels equal (brother, 2) but is not permitted to live a normal life – a person who accepts his present situation, but is working to change it (eat; grow strong, 6 f.) – a man who wants to take his rightful place in society (be at the table, 9) – a man who considers himself superior to those who mistreat him (see how beautiful I am/And be ashamed, 16 f.) – a person who considers himself a rightful member of the American nation (18)	AFB III
compares the main elements to those of Whitman's poem: – enumeration of different (manual) professions and groups who do their work while singing happily – poetic picture of numerous groups that constitute the American nation	AFB III
points out that the (former) slaves are not mentioned in Whitman's poem	AFB III
comments on the fact that Hughes directly links his poem to Whitman's text (I, too, sing America, 1, and I hear America singing, 1)	AFB III
points out that the Afro-Americans have been left out of the national heritage and now demand to be rightfully integrated	AFB III
considers these findings and concludes that Hughes is calling for integration and opposes the segregation of the Afro-American people	AFB III
(evaluates the process of integration from the 1920s until today)	AFB III

Klausur 2

Victory Speech (Nov. 4, 2008)

Barack Obama

The following speech was delivered by Barack Obama to supporters in Chicago on the night of his election (November 4, 2008) as the new President of the United States of America.

If there is anyone out there who still doubts that America is a place where all things are possible; who still wonders if the dream of our founders is still alive in our time; who still questions the power of our democracy, tonight is your answer. It's the answer told by lines that stretched around schools and churches in numbers this nation has never seen; by people who waited three hours and four hours, many for the first time in their lives, because they believed that this time must be different; that their voices could be that difference. It's the answer spoken by young and old, rich and poor, Democrat and Republican, black, white, Hispanic, Asian, Native American, gay, straight, disabled and not disabled – Americans who sent a message to the world that we have never been just a collection of individuals or just a collection of red states and blue states:[1] we are, and always will be, the United States of America. [...]
But above all, I will never forget who this victory truly belongs to – it belongs to you. I was never the likeliest candidate for this office. We didn't start with much money or many endorsements.[2] Our campaign was not hatched[3] in the halls of Washington – it began in the Backyards of Des Moines[4] and the living rooms of Concord[5] and the front porches[6] of Charleston.[7] It was built by working men and women who dug into what little savings they had to give five dollars and ten dollars and twenty dollars to the cause. It grew strength from the young people who rejected the myth of their generation's apathy; who left their homes and their families for jobs that offered little pay and less sleep; it drew strength from the not-so-young people who braved the bitter cold and scorching[8] heat to knock on the doors of perfect strangers; from the millions of Americans who volunteered and organized and proved that more than two centuries later, a government of the people, by the people and for the people has not perished from the Earth. This is your victory. [...]
The road ahead will be long. Our climb will be steep. We may not get there in one year or even in one term, but America – I have never been more hopeful than I am tonight that we will get there. I promise you – we as a people will get there. [...]
And to all those watching tonight from beyond our shores, from parliaments and palaces to those who are huddled around radios in the forgotten corners of our world – our stories are singular, but our destiny is shared and a new dawn of American leadership is at hand.
To those who would tear the world down – we will defeat you. To those who seek peace and security – we support you.
To all those who have wondered if America's beacon still burns as bright – tonight we proved once more that the true strength of our nation comes not from the might of

[1] **red states and blue states** red is the traditional colour of the Republicans, blue the colour of the Democrats
[2] **endorsement** money or support offered [3] **to hatch** *ausbrüten* [4] **Des Moines** capital of the state of Iowa; Obama won his first pre-election there [5] **Concord** there are more than 30 cities named "Concord" but Obama has used "Concord" in many speeches and refers to Concord, Massachusetts, where in 1775 one of the first battles of the Revolutionary War took place. It is the hometown of several American writers and poets, e.g. N. Hawthorne.
[6] **front porch** the space in front of a house, usually sheltered by the roof [7] **Charleston** city in South Carolina, once a cultural centre of the southern states [8] **scorching** burning hot

Klausur 2

our arms or the scale of our wealth, but from the enduring power of our ideals: democracy, liberty, opportunity, and unyielding[9] hope. [...]
This is our moment. This is our time – to put our people back to work and open doors of opportunity for our kids; to restore prosperity and promote the cause of peace; to reclaim the American Dream and reaffirm that fundamental truth – that out of many, we are one; that while we breathe, we hope, and where we are met with cynicism, and doubt, and those who tell us that we can't, we will respond with that timeless creed[10] that sums up the spirit of a people: Yes We Can. Thank you, God bless you, and may God bless the United States of America.

Source: http://elections.nytimes.com/2008/results/president/speeches/obama-victory-speech.html [05.11.2008]

[9] **unyielding** strong and unbreakable [10] **creed** sth you believe in, *Credo*

Activities

1. **Outline the main ideas of the speech.** (comprehension: AFB I)
2. **Analyse the speech (structure/stylistic devices). Which images and references does Obama use to refer to the American Dream?** (analysis: AFB II)
3. **Obama claims that "the dream of our founders is still alive in our time". Discuss.** (evaluation: AFB III)

Klausur 2 Solution

Lernvoraussetzungen:
Die Klausur steht am Ende der Reihe.
Bearbeitung von mehreren Redetexten
Bearbeitung von Barack Obama, „A More Perfect Union", SB, S. 65
Bearbeitung der grundlegenden Texte zum *American Dream* aus dem SB: Declaration of Independence; Bill of Rights; Lincoln, Gettysburg Address; Adams, "The American Dream"; Lazarus, "The New Colossus"; Motto on the Great Seal; Schwarzenegger, Republican National Convention Address; Kevles, Divided Society; Hughes, "Harlem"; M. L. King, "I've been on the Mountain Top"

1. Comprehension:

The student	
states the speaker, place and time of the given speech	AFB I
points out that Obama believes that the dream is still alive: – high turnout of voters from all groups of American society – America is united again	AFB I
outlines that he thanks his supporters: – for the high mobilization throughout the country – for the donations made by all members of society – for the many volunteers who helped him during his campaign despite all obstacles	AFB I
points out that Obama also addresses those listening to/watching him outside the USA: – political leaders/heads of state – terrorists – people seeking peace	AFB I
states that Obama affirms that the American ideals are still valid	AFB I
sums up the promises Obama makes: – to put people back to work – to restore prosperity – to promote the cause of peace – to renew the American Dream	AFB I

Klausur 2 Solution

2. Analysis:

The student	
structures the speech and glives headings/summarizes the content: 1–11 In the USA all things are possible 12–24 Victory of the people for the people 25–27 Promise to lead them to a better future 28–37 America is the beacon of the world 38–44 The American Dream is still alive	AFB II
names and analyses the stylistic devices used by Obama:	AFB II

Alliteration	**h**atched in the **h**alls (14) **b**egan in the **b**ackyards (15) **b**uilt **b**y (16) **b**raved the **b**itter (20) **p**arliaments and **p**alaces (28) **b**eacon still **b**urns as **b**right (34) **p**rosperity and **p**romote the cause of **p**eace (39) **w**hile **w**e breathe, **w**e hope (41)
Antithesis	young – old; rich – poor; Democrat – Republican; black – white; gay – straight; disabled – not disabled (7 f.) halls of Washington – backyards of Des Moines (14 f.) living rooms of Concord – the front porches of Charleston (15 f.) bitter cold – scorching heat (20 f.)
Assonance	c**o**ld and sc**o**rching (21) **o**pen d**oo**rs **o**f **o**pp**o**rtunity (38) w**e** br**ea**the w**e** hope (41)
Enumeration	the answer spoken by young and old, rich and poor, Democrat and Republican, black, white, Hispanic, Asian, Native American, gay, straight, disabled and not disabled (7 f.) five dollars and ten dollars and twenty dollars (17 f.) who volunteered and organized and proved (22) from the might of our arms or the scale of our wealth (35 f.) democracy, liberty, opportunity and unyielding hope (36 f.)
Including 'we'	*passim*: we (16 x); our (17 x); us (1 x)
Inversion	true strength of our nation **comes not** from (35)
Metaphor	the dream of our founders (2) men and women who dug into what little savings (16) The road ahead will be long (25) Our climb will be steep (25) new dawn of American leadership (30) America's beacon (34)

Klausur 2 Solution

Metonymy	schools (4) ➔ learning churches (4) ➔ religious faith/belief parliaments (democracy) and palaces (monarchy) (28 f.)
Parallelism	who still doubts ... who still wonders ... who still questions (1 f.) It's the answer told ... It's the answer spoken ... (3/7) who dug into (16) ... who left (19) ... who braved (20) ... who volunteered (22) to all those (28) ... to those who (29) ... To those who (32) To those who (32) ... To all those who (34) to restore ... to reclaim ... to reaffirm (39 f.)
Quotation	"government of the people ... perish from the earth" (23) (Gettysburg Address, SB, p. 14) "shores" – "huddled" – "beacon" (28–34) (Lazarus, "Brazen Giant" SB, p. 34) "out of many, we are one," Motto of the Great Seal (*E Pluribus Unum*, SB, p. 35) I promise you – "we as a people will get there" (27) (M.L. King, "Mountain Top", we as a people will get to the promised land", SB, p. 62)
Repetition	tonight (3/26/28/34) just a collection ... just a collection (10) It grew strength (18) ... it drew strength (20) hope(ful) (26) ... hope (37) ... hope (41) This is our moment. This is our time. (38)

analyses the images and references to the American Dream: – the dream of our founders is still alive (2) – we have never been just a collection of individuals ➔ "We, the people ..." *(Constitution)* – "a government of the people, by the people and for the people has not perished from this earth" (23 f.) reference to Abraham Lincoln, *Gettysburg Address* – we as a people will get there (27), reference to Martin Luther King's last speech ("Mountain Top") – shores – huddled – beacon (28–34) reference to Lazarus' poem, engraved on the Statue of Liberty ("Brazen Giant") – out of many we are one (40 f.) reference/translation of the Motto of the Great American Seal – young and old, ... disabled or not disabled. (7 f.) exemplifies "out of many, one" – destiny (30) clear reference to the thesis of the "manifest destiny" of the American people – democracy, liberty, opportunity (36 f.) ideals/elements of the American Dream	AFB II

Klausur 2 Solution

3. Evaluation:

The student	
points out that the fact that a black president with a multicultural background has been elected supports the thesis that the American Dream is still alive	AFB III
analyses which conditions and which change of attitude have made this possible	AFB III
questions whether the fact in itself shows a significant change in the attitudes of American society	AFB III
states that many problems (border – illegal immigration) have not been solved	AFB III
evaluates the meaning and importance of the dream for all groups within American society	AFB III
states his/her opinion for the future development of the USA	AFB III
individual answers	AFB III

Discover ...

Shakespeare-Textausgaben
Landeskundliche Themenhefte

Herausgegeben von
Klaus Hinz und Engelbert Thaler (ab 2007)

Africa – Postcolonial Experiences
Von Monika Teichmann
70 S. Best.-Nr. **978-3-14-040100-5**
Lehrerheft. Best.-Nr. **978-3-14-040101-2**

African-American Experiences – From Exploitation to Participation
Von Wiltrud Frenken, Angela Luz und Brigitte Prischtt
55 S. Best.-Nr. **978-3-14-040116-6**
Lehrerheft. Best.-Nr. **978-3-14-040117-3**

Australia and New Zealand – Neither Down nor Under
Von Rainer H. Berthelmann
95 S. Best.-Nr. **978-3-14-040104-3**
Lehrerheft. Best.-Nr. **978-3-14-040105-0**

British and American Youth Culture
Von Hannspeter Bauer und Gudrun Vesper
64 S. Best.-Nr. **978-3-14-040053-4**
Lehrerheft. Best.-Nr. **978-3-14-040077-0**

Canada – More than Mounties and Lumberjacks
Von Martin Kohn
56 S. Best.-Nr. **978-3-14-040082-4**
Lehrerheft. Best.-Nr. **978-3-14-040092-3**

Globalisation – Blessing or Curse?
Von Jürgen Einhoff, Klaus Hinz und Karl Heinz Wagner
68 S. Best.-Nr. **978-3-14-040059-6**
Lehrerheft. Best.-Nr. **978-3-14-040089-3**

Hispanics in America
Von Veronika Kaiser und James Martin
72 S. Best.-Nr. **978-3-14-040044-2**
Lehrerheft. Best.-Nr. **978-3-14-040064-0**

India – Tradition and Transformation
Von Michaela Banzhaf und Alexandra Peschel
51 S. Best.-Nr. **978-3-14-040098-5**
Lehrerheft. Best.-Nr. **978-3-14-040099-2**

Ireland – Changes and Challenges
Von Maria Eisenmann
55 S. Best.-Nr. **978-3-14-040110-4**
Lehrerheft. Best.-Nr. **978-3-14-040111-1**

Our Environment – A State of Emergency?
Von Stephen Speight
59 S. Best.-Nr. **978-3-14-040108-1**
Lehrerheft. Best.-Nr. **978-3-14-040109-8**

The American Dream – Inventing a Nation
Von Hanspeter Bauer
74 S. Best.-Nr. **978-3-14-040086-2**
Lehrerheft. Best.-Nr. **978-3-14-040087-9**

The American South
Von Jürgen Einhoff und Katharina Einhoff
72 S. Best.-Nr. **978-3-14-040052-7**
Lehrerheft. Best.-Nr. **978-3-14-040076-3**

The Different Faces of Britain
Von Stephen Speight
64 S. Best.-Nr. **978-3-14-040085-5**
Lehrerheft. Best.-Nr. **978-3-14-040095-4**

The Fascination and Risks of Technology
Von Stephen Speight
56 S. Best.-Nr. **978-3-14-040055-8**
Lehrerheft. Best.-Nr. **978-3-14-040079-4**

The Mass Media – From Gutenberg to Gates
Von Stephen Speight und Karsten Witsch
64 S. Best.-Nr. **978-3-14-040088-6**
Lehrerheft. Best.-Nr. **978-3-14-040096-1**

William Shakespeare: A Midsummer Night's Dream
Von Rainer Gocke und Angela Stock
104 S. Best.-Nr. **978-3-14-040058-9**
Lehrerheft. Best.-Nr. **978-3-14-040068-8**

William Shakespeare: Macbeth
Von Rainer Gocke und Angela Stock
136 S. Best.-Nr. **978-3-14-040041-1**
Lehrerheft. Best.-Nr. **978-3-14-040061-9**

William Shakespeare: Much Ado About Nothing
Von Rainer Gocke und Franziska Quabeck
110 S. Best.-Nr. **978-3-14-040118-0**
Lehrerheft. Best.-Nr. **978-3-14-040119-7**

William Shakespeare: Othello
Von Anke Weber
147 S. Best.-Nr. **978-3-14-040069-5**
Lehrerheft. Best.-Nr. **978-3-14-040102-9**

William Shakespeare: Romeo and Juliet
Von Norbert Timm
143 S. Best.-Nr. **978-3-14-040056-5**
Lehrerheft. Best.-Nr. **978-3-14-040081-7**

William Shakespeare: The Sonnets
Von Anke Weber
48 S. Best.-Nr. **978-3-14-040114-2**
Lehrerheft. Best.-Nr. **978-3-14-040115-9**

William Shakespeare: Bits From The Bard
Nach Themenschwerpunkten zusammengestellt
Von Norbert Timm
48 S. Best.-Nr. **978-3-14-040057-2**
Lehrerheft. Best.-Nr. **978-3-14-040097-8**

Weitere Titel sind in Vorbereitung.

Schöningh Verlag
Postfach 2540
33055 Paderborn

Schöningh

Fordern Sie unseren Prospekt zur kompletten Reihe an:
Informationen 0800 / 18 18 787 (freecall)
info@schoeningh-schulbuch.de / www.schoeningh-schulbuch.de